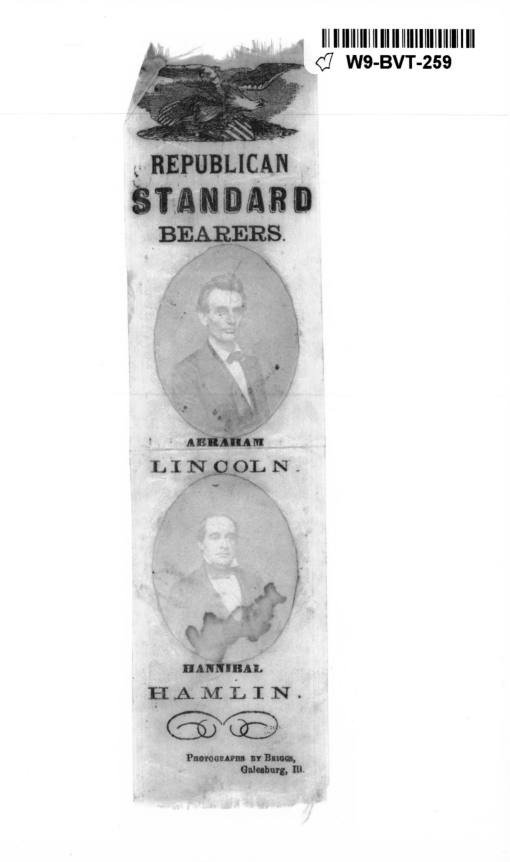

REPUBLICAN
STANDARD
BEARERS.

ABRAHAM
LINCOLN.

HANNIBAL
HAMLIN.

PHOTOGRAPHS BY BRIGGS,
Galesburg, Ill.

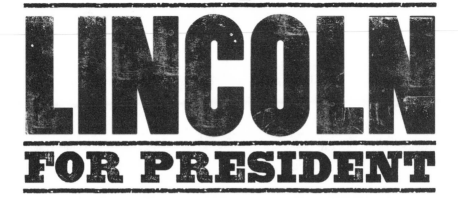

LINCOLN
FOR PRESIDENT

AN UNLIKELY CANDIDATE, AN AUDACIOUS STRATEGY, AND THE VICTORY NO ONE SAW COMING

BRUCE CHADWICK

SOURCEBOOKS, INC.®
NAPERVILLE, ILLINOIS

Copyright © 2009 by Bruce Chadwick
Cover and internal design © 2009 by Sourcebooks, Inc.
Cover design by Bruce Gore/Gore Studios, Inc.
Cover images courtesy of the Library of Congress; © hidesy/iStockphoto,
Bridgeman Art Library
Internal images © Corbis, Bridgeman Art Library
Sourcebooks and the colophon are registered trademarks of Sourcebooks, Inc.

This publication is designed to provide accurate and authoritative information
in regard to the subject matter covered. It is sold with the understanding that
the publisher is not engaged in rendering legal, accounting, or other professional
service. If legal advice or other expert assistance is required, the services of
a competent professional person should be sought.—*From a Declaration of
Principles Jointly Adopted by a Committee of the American Bar Association and a
Committee of Publishers and Associations*

Published by Sourcebooks, Inc.
P.O. Box 4410, Naperville, Illinois 60567-4410
(630) 961-3900
Fax: (630) 961-2168
www.sourcebooks.com

Library of Congress Cataloging-in-Publication Data
Chadwick, Bruce.
  Lincoln for president : an unlikely candidate, an audacious strategy, and the
victory no one saw coming / Bruce Chadwick.
     p. cm.
  Includes bibliographical references.
  1. Lincoln, Abraham, 1809-1865--Political career before 1861. 2. Lincoln,
Abraham, 1809-1865--Political and social views. 3. Presidential candidates-
-United States--Biography. 4. Presidents--United States--Election--1860. 5.
Political campaigns--United States--History--19th century. 6. Republican
Party (U.S. : 1854-) 7. United States--Politics and government--1857-1861.
I. Title.
  E457.C437 2009
  973.7092--dc22

2009023197

Printed and bound in the United States of America.
SB 10 9 8 7 6 5 4 3 2 1

For Marjorie and Rory

Contents

Acknowledgments

I have written several books that involved Abraham Lincoln and never quite understood the magic about him. *Lincoln for President* was a long and comprehensive study of his first election campaign and, after all of that work and all of that time, I still do not understand all of his magic. Perhaps we never will.

I now grasp part of it, though, discovered in writing this book. I found out exactly how he was elected president and why he was one of the best pure politicians in the nation's history. To do that, I had to wade through rolls and rolls of microfilm, read over one hundred books and sift through boxes full of notes. I had to find and read the letters and journals of hundreds of people who knew the sixteenth president or worked with him. I read more nineteenth-century newspapers than I knew were published.

To accomplish that task, and to finish the work, I had much help. I want to thank the staff at the Guarini Library, at New Jersey City University, especially Fred Smith. Additional thanks go to the staff of the Firestone Library at Princeton University and the research staffs at the libraries of Harvard University, Rutgers University, the Morris County Free Library and Randolph libraries (N.J.), and the Abraham Lincoln Library in Springfield, Illinois.

I want to thank Dr. Matthew Pinsker, at Dickinson College, for reading the manuscript and making suggestions to improve it. He was most helpful. I want to thank all the professors at Rutgers and Princeton who read parts of it and also offered suggestions.

Thanks to Joanne Bruno, Vice President for Academic Affairs at New Jersey City University, and her committee, for granting me a sabbatical to research and write the book.

Thanks to Hillel Black, my editor at Sourcebooks, who helped turn this from a good idea into a solid historical work. Thanks, too, to the editorial staff at Sourcebooks, including Peter Lynch, Todd Stocke, Anne Hartman, and Kelly Bale.

I want to thank my agents at McIntosh and Otis, Elizabeth Winick and Rebecca Strauss, who helped to put this project together. Finally, thanks to my wife Marjorie, who assisted in the research and read through the manuscript several times in order to help me.

Prologue

The 1860 presidential election, one of the most critical in United States history, has often been presented as a rather staid four-man race in which Abraham Lincoln, through little effort of his own, was able to slip in the back door of the White House, even though he won only 39 percent of the popular vote. In many books, movies, plays, and stories he is wrongly depicted as a man far above politics whom the nation naturally turned to in its hour of need. His Republican Party won the 1860 election, of which the key issue was presented exclusively as slavery, most agreed, because the country had split into two camps—North and South. The slavery forces won in the Southern states, and the antislavery forces, the Republicans, took the Northern states and their huge electoral votes and won the election.

Lincoln won, historians seemed to suggest, because the Democratic Party was torn apart and its three different candidates—Stephen Douglas, John Breckinridge, and John Bell—split the opposition vote, giving Lincoln victory. Subsequently, the conventions and election were thought to have provided little drama. The major biographers of Lincoln paid little attention to them. One of his earliest biographers, Carl Sandburg, in his *Abraham*

Lincoln: The Prairie Years, devoted just 40 of 900 pages, or just 5 percent of the book, to the election. Later history works followed suit. David Herbert Donald's 1995 Pulitzer Prize–winning *Lincoln* devoted only 14 of its 600 pages to the 1860 race, or just 2 percent of the work. Richard Carwardine gave only 9 percent of his Lincoln Prize–winning book, *Lincoln: A Life of Purpose and Power,* to the campaign, and Doris Kearns Goodwin, in *Team of Rivals: The Political Genius of Abraham Lincoln,* only spent 38 of 754 pages on the campaigns.

A new look shows, however, that Abraham Lincoln did not back into the presidency but avidly chased and finally captured it after prodigious work in what was a dramatic and often gripping race filled with feuds, jealousies, secret agreements, lies, failed promises, and betrayals among both parties and all four candidates.

Lincoln's biggest strength was not simply that he was opposed to slavery. His greatest asset was that he was an outsider, from the distant reaches of Illinois, the western rim of America's population center at that time, far from the politicians in Washington who had maneuvered the nation into the mess it found itself in 1860.

Over the previous twelve years, Lincoln held no national office, did not vote for or against any of the laws that were causing such firestorms in the 1850s. Fed up with a divided country and sick of the politicians who divided it, people were looking for a fresh face. As an outsider, Lincoln had few real enemies in the political world, unlike the other men in the race, all longtime public officeholders. No one in the Republican Party had any reason to feud with Lincoln, but enemies collected by other candidates over long careers in the public spotlight hurt them.

Lincoln was popular in the northwestern states (today the Midwest), whose combined population had nearly doubled in the previous ten years.

They were key to any election and to each party's political future. Lincoln was a well-to-do, successful lawyer who ran as a blue collar "rail-splitter." He was nicknamed "Honest Abe," a scandal-free man of convictions riding the religious and moral wave against slavery in an era tinged with widespread political corruption. He was flexible, a man who could change as the nation and its people changed. He made it a point from an early age to know what was on the minds of the people as they tumbled through a generation of constant upheaval. He had beaten the powerful Stephen Douglas, the mainstream Democratic nominee, once in the popular vote in the 1858 U.S. Senate race and promised to do it again in the presidential contest.

Most important, though, Abraham Lincoln was a masterful politician who had spent nearly three decades building alliances with other politicians throughout his home and neighboring states. He had traded favors with dozens of party leaders. He rode his horse over the chilly back roads of many regions in the North, even strife-torn Kansas, in sunshine, rain, and snow, delivering speeches on behalf of candidates running for office. He was a superb strategist who knew how to target swing counties and towns, conduct efficient public opinion polls, and tailor campaigns in specific areas.

He was not merely the spokesperson for the Illinois Republican Party but one of its hardworking founders. He spent years courting, and winning, the support of Illinois' huge immigrant population, which by the late 1850s represented over 30 percent of the state's vote. He devoted as much time as he could with newspaper reporters and editors, even those from Democratic papers, in an effort to earn publicity for himself. Lincoln was careful, over years of political storms that saw many different groups ride the whirlwind of public opinion, never to champion or denounce any particular group and never to disclaim his long years in the defunct Whig Party. He developed a close-knit group of friends who became trusted political operatives, amateurs who would outsmart the best political bosses of the day and who would bring Lincoln the presidency.

He was, in short, a pragmatic politician, a man who knew the peoples' pulse, a man of great perseverance with an enormous capacity for work, who assiduously sought some kind of high office all of his life—history's man of opportunity—and finally succeeded in 1860.

The Republicans were never the happy beneficiaries of votes from the old Whigs, Free Soilers, German Americans, or Know-Nothings, as often reported, but the active pursuers of all groups that could bring victory in the most dramatic election in the nation's history. They were a party led by men in different states who, county by county, town by town, put together efficient machines that brought triumphs. The new party, formally organized in 1854, was fueled by crossover votes, particularly from disenchanted Democrats, and by record Republican registrations of new voters, mostly young, and high voter turnouts. They were able to place dozens of men on key congressional committees and help to turn the direction of the federal government. Then, as the White House finally seemed within reach on the hazy horizon in 1860, the Republicans, led by Lincoln, strategically zeroed in on the key states that could bring them victory.

The Republicans were a major party in 1860 because of their opposition to slavery. Throughout the 1840s and 1850s several new, small antislavery parties, such as the Liberty and Free Soil parties, had some success in elections. Slavery had haunted America since the first slaves arrived in 1619 in Virginia. Thomas Jefferson put it best. Slavery, he said, was like holding a wolf by the ears—you can't hold it in comfort and can't let go out of fear for your safety. The issue had no strong political traction until the controversial Kansas-Nebraska Act of 1854, which permitted the residents of territories to determine whether or not they wanted slavery.

Opposition to the spread of slavery in Kansas and Nebraska caused all the small antislavery parties to merge with disgruntled Democrats and new voters to form the Republican Party.

One of those new Republicans was Illinois' former congressman Abraham Lincoln, who was furious in his opposition to the Kansas-Nebraska Act. He said that by permitting the expansion of slavery, "we are proclaiming ourselves political hypocrites before the world…by thus fostering human slavery and proclaiming ourselves, at the same time, the sole friends of human freedom."[1]

The new party was also fueled by the hundreds of antislavery societies, the abolitionist movement, and the publication of numerous antislavery books, such as Harriet Beecher Stowe's *Uncle Tom's Cabin* and Hinton Rowan Helper's *The Impending Crisis: How to Meet It*, both highly critical of the South.

The antislavery movement grew, too, in response to the 1857 Supreme Court decision in the Dred Scott case. The high court ruled that slaves who fled their plantations had no rights and upheld the Fugitive Slave Law. If all of that was not enough to make the election of 1860 a powder keg, abolitionist fanatic John Brown and a small brigade of men seized Harpers Ferry, a federal ammunitions depot in Virginia in the fall of 1859, and were later captured and hanged.

The swirling political scene brought about the destruction of the Whig Party over slavery in 1852 and the creation of the Know-Nothing Party, an anti-Catholic, anti-immigrant group that gained surprising power in the early and mid-1850s. It also caused a deep divide among Democrats, North and South.

All of this combined to promise Americans that the 1860 presidential campaign would be one of the most important in history.

It was a remarkably modern campaign whose issues were similar to the issues of the twenty-first century. It was a campaign of "family," "values," and "character" in which the corruption of the ruling party and the personal integrity of the candidates became a key issue. It was a contest that hinged on the feelings of the voters on immigrants, whom they feared were sneaking into the United States and taking their jobs and being supported by their tax dollars. It was a campaign that inspired thousands of America's youth, who called themselves the Wide Awakes. And like so many modern campaigns, it promised "change" as a new party tried to sweep out the old. And it was a contest in which the race issue forever wove itself into the political psyche of the American people.

The Republicans and Lincoln benefited from an extraordinary series of blunders by Stephen Douglas, one of the Democratic nominees, blunders a raw political rookie would not make. The Republicans had the assistance, as well, of fierce Democratic infighting that stretched all the way from the White House to the smallest rural precinct. The Democratic nominees, Douglas in the North and John Bell and John Breckinridge in the South, constantly vied with each other for money, workers, and newspaper coverage, and the result was weakness for all. The three Democratic nominees made the mistake of running against each other and not against Lincoln.

The Republican nominee, usually portrayed as an old man in stovepipe hat and shawl, run as "Old Abe" by the party, was actually a buoyant, strong, and exceptionally healthy fifty-one years old (the second youngest man to be elected president up to that time). He was a young man leading young men who were challenging many of the political traditions of the nation.

Abe Lincoln was a vibrant public figure. He was a riveting orator who mesmerized audiences of 20,000. He was a hardscrabble politician who worked crowds from small picnics to huge outdoor throngs in an effort to win elections.

He was a man, too, who understood the deeper problem of 1860—the collision of North and South over very different economic systems and slavery. The South relied on slave labor to fuel its agrarian economy and for generations had controlled the federal government, which supported slavery to achieve that end. By 1860, Northerners were on the brink of the Industrial Revolution, which relied on paid labor by free men and was supported by millions of free labor workers who feared that the slave labor system, now threatening to spread into the territories, would cost them their livelihoods. They were men who believed that when some men were slaves, all men were slaves. They detested the Southern politicians who controlled the government that they felt was committed to ruining them.

In four short years, the Republicans managed to buy up or control hundreds of daily and weekly newspapers, almost as many as the Democrats, and used them in a saturation campaign about Abe Lincoln and their candidates. They even published their own campaign newspapers that were distributed throughout the country. This book will show that the public opinion polls that people rely on today are not new, that Abe Lincoln was running them as early as the 1840s and that in 1860 they played a critical role in the campaign.

This is a behind-the-scenes story, a backstage pass to a wild and colorful campaign filled with the marching Wide Awakes, torchlit parades, raucous rallies, colorful banners that crossed entire city streets, and bands of every shape and size. It was the first in which a Republican won the White House, the first in which a candidate, Douglas, personally campaigned for the presidency in a whistle-stop train tour that crisscrossed the land, North and South, and the first in which a political convention was unable to nominate a president and collapsed around itself.

It is a view of a roller-coaster election from a perch on the shoulder of Abe Lincoln. It will show that the Republicans were not the lucky winners of the 1850s political fallout but tenacious and focused politicians who seized the moment in every village and crossroads in America as they built a surprisingly contemporary political machine. They were a force that by 1860 had become unstoppable.

Mostly, though, it is the story of Abe Lincoln. It is a story never completely told because historians and political scientists, seeing a four-way race, never peeked behind the curtains of the 1860 election. Many saw Lincoln as a docile man in the 1860 campaign, despite the assertion of his law partner, Billy Herndon, that Lincoln was not "(sitting) still in his chair in Springfield" waiting for history's tide to bring him the nomination and election. "Lincoln was as vigilant as he was ambitious. There is no denying the fact that he understood the situation perfectly from the start," declared Herndon.[2]

Using Lincoln's own papers and the papers of others, plus many newspaper accounts, this book paints a picture of Lincoln as a master puppeteer, completely in charge of his own campaign from his home in Springfield. He made all the decisions, mapped strategy, patched up intraparty feuds, made promises, supported friends, cajoled enemies, and, on election day, wrought a miracle.

INVADING

★ ★ ★ ★ ★ ★ ★ ★ ★ ★ ★ *the* ★ ★ ★ ★ ★ ★ ★ ★ ★ ★ ★ ★

WIGWAM

Throngs of Abraham Lincoln admirers were everywhere in Chicago, Illinois, in May 1860 for the Republican National Convention. The rapidly growing city was full of snaking parades, speeches, demonstrations, and parties. Pro-Lincoln crowds surged around the entrances to the Wigwam, the 10,000-seat rectangular hall built just for the convention, every day, cheering for Illinois' native son Lincoln. The Lincoln supporters marched with wide banners proclaiming him as "Honest Abe" and "The Rail-Splitter" and tossed "Lincoln nails" out of wagons. They cheered their man on the main avenues of the city and in the tiny lanes, early in the morning and late at night.

The large and rambunctious crowds gave Lincoln's campaign manager, Judge David Davis, an idea. The tickets for the convention were apportioned out to each state so that no one candidate had more supporters than another. Davis managed to get Jesse Fell, a friend who was in charge of the tickets, to print thousands of duplicate tickets to the Wigwam. These were quietly distributed to thousands of Lincoln supporters who were told to arrive very early in the morning on the day of the balloting for president. The tickets, which were perfect counterfeits, got them past security guards. By the time the regular ticket holders arrived later, the Wigwam was jammed with 10,000 howling, screaming Lincoln supporters—with their "official" tickets. Guards turned away the actual ticket holders, who complained bitterly.[3]

Among these legitimate ticket holders were members of the huge crowds of supporters of the convention favorite, U.S. Senator William Seward of New York, who had arrived by train along with some of the "lower sort" of politicians Carl Schurz detested who worked with Thurlow Weed, Seward's hardworking campaign manager. They had spent the week in crowded Chicago holding their own Seward parades, complete with brass bands and enormous banners that stretched across entire city streets.[4] On their trains from New York, the Seward entourage had brought along their own large band that marched in special "Seward" uniforms.[5] They, along with supporters of the other presidential candidates, were all turned away because the Lincoln people had taken their seats with the counterfeit tickets.

The Republican Convention that would nominate Honest Abe for president was under way.

CHAPTER 1

Lincoln Enters the Ring

No former effort in the line of speech-making had cost Lincoln so much time and thought as this one...

—LINCOLN LAW PARTNER BILLY HERNDON

The great hall at Cooper Union in New York City was jammed with people on the winter night of February 27, 1860. Every seat in the 1,500-seat auditorium was taken, and hundreds of New Yorkers lined the aisles and leaned against each other, like salmon piled up tightly together in a fisherman's net, along the walls of the hall. A large throng of residents packed the corridors outside the great hall, standing on their toes, looking over the shoulders of others in front of them to see the brand-new political sensation from the West. The speaker was Abraham Lincoln, a former congressman and lawyer and antislavery Republican who had gone head to head with Senator Stephen Douglas in debates and had actually defeated the Little Giant in the 1858 Illinois Senate race in the popular vote, although he lost in the state legislature's ballot for the seat. He was a new figure on the political scene, brought into tens of thousands of homes in the East via the dozens of newspapers and a new wire service that covered his confrontations with Douglas in the 1858 race that made the country lawyer from far-off Illinois an emerging national figure.

So many people wanted to hear this outsider from the very rim of the established United States that the lecture had been moved from a smaller church run by Henry Ward Beecher across the East River in Brooklyn. Even Cooper Union, one of the largest halls in the biggest city in America, could not hold all of the people who wanted to get a look at the frontier orator. It was yet another chance for Lincoln, a man of opportunity, to once more plead his cause, to again keep himself in front of the public. He had been lecturing, politicking, and campaigning since he was twenty-three years old, with limited success, losing about as many elections as he won. But he went on giving long and fiery speeches, traveling great distances on horseback to support candidates, and writing party platforms in Illinois to keep himself open for whatever opportunities might present themselves to him on the distant horizon.

Lincoln rose to his full height of six feet, four inches and strode to the narrow, waist-high podium, low for a man of his gargantuan size in an era when the average man was nearly a foot shorter then he, and began to speak, his gray eyes referring occasionally to notes on blue sheets of paper. He looked awkward to the crowd of well-dressed New Yorkers. He was so eager to make a good impression on the Cooper Union audience that he bought a new black frock coat just for the speech, but he did not want anyone to know that. So he told the man who invited him to speak that he could only appear if he was advanced a speaker's fee of $200 because he had no money and the $200 would cover his expenses to visit his son Robert in prep school in New Hampshire after he delivered the speech.

The trip to see his son then became the reason why he gave the much-hailed speech; the $200 actually paid for the coat.[6] Most suits did not fit him very well. His pants were too short, and his enormous size-fourteen feet stuck out from under them like two Mississippi River flatboats. His coat sleeves were short and could not cover his oversized, bony hands and wrists. This suit fit better than most. The Mathew Brady photograph of him in it, taken while he was in New York for the Cooper Union speech, later became one of Lincoln's favorite portraits.

His tall, angular body was always bent forward a bit so that he would not tower over people he spoke to. He was reed thin, and his rather homely face, with its prominent wart, shallow cheeks, and dark eye sockets, was a little pale. His hair was badly combed. People who knew him said that when he was not speaking in public he always wore an aura of sadness about him. Others said he had a rather comical look with his large body, badly cut clothes, and oversized head. When he spoke, though, he rarely referred to scribbled notes on the papers he held in his large hands, particularly about slavery. His friends said there was nothing awkward about him at all and that "he appeared like a prophet of old."[7]

That is how he struck the crowd at Cooper Union. One man there, Noah Brooks, wrote:

When Lincoln rose to speak, I was greatly disappointed. He was tall—oh, how tall! And so angular and awkward that I had, for an instant, a feeling of pity for so ungainly a man. His clothes were black and ill fitting, badly wrinkled—as if they had been jammed carelessly into a small trunk. His bushy head, with the stiff black hair thrown back, was balanced on a long and lean head stalk, and when he raised his hands in an opening gesture, I noticed that they were very large.[8]

Another onlooker, George Putnam, agreed. He wrote, "Lincoln made a picture which did not fit in with New York's conception of a finished statesman."[9]

This would be a different speech for Lincoln. He had gained fame as a serious speaker, but one who added humorous stories to his talks. There would be none of that tonight; this was his most serious speech. His law partner, William Herndon, said that "no former effort in the line of speech making had cost Lincoln so much time and thought as this one."[10]

As soon as Lincoln began to speak, he enchanted the crowd with his torrent of words. His speech soared and tumbled, climbing up long hills of rhetoric. He built up the Republicans and tore down the Democrats in a speech that kept his listeners enthralled. It was clearly the speech of a man who wanted to be president but did not say so. He was careful never to mention New York Senator William Seward, the party's front-runner for the presidential nomination in 1860, or Salmon Chase, the powerful Republican governor of Ohio, but let the spotlight shine only on himself. He stressed his fiscal conservatism, his support of the working man, outlined his frontier background, and described the long history of slavery in America. Lincoln set moderate guidelines for the Republicans on slavery in 1860—keeping it out of the territories but letting it remain where it was in the Southern states. Finally, though, at the end, as his speech reached its apogee, he launched into a brilliant denunciation of slavery, the scathing denunciation they all had come through the cold and the chill of a February evening to hear.

Joseph Choate, in the audience, was transfixed by Lincoln, observing, "His eye kindled, his voice rang, his face shone and seemed to light up the whole assembly."[11]

Lincoln said:

If slavery is right, all words, acts, laws, and constitutions against it are themselves wrong, and should be silenced and swept away. If it is right, we cannot justly object to its nationality, its universality. If it is wrong, they cannot justly insist upon its extension—its enlargement.... Their thinking it right, and our thinking it wrong, is the precise fact upon which depends the whole controversy. Thinking it right, as they do, they are not to blame for desiring its full recognition as being right; but, thinking it wrong, as we do, can we yield to them?... Neither let us be slandered from our duty by false accusations against us, nor frightened from it by menaces of destruction to the government nor of dungeons to ourselves," he declared as his thin voice sailed out high and loud, full of thunder, over the mesmerized crowd. "Let us have faith that right makes might, and in that faith let us, to the end, dare to do out duty as we understand it.[12]

He turned and began to walk back to his chair as a long and loud thunderclap of applause poured over his tall and bony body, a floodtide of approval. One man in the crowd said, "I forgot his clothes, his personal appearance, and his individual peculiarities.... I was on my feet with the rest, yelling like a wild Indian, cheering this wonderful man."[13]

The people in the audience rose to their feet, cheering and shouting madly. Women hauled out handkerchiefs and waved them through the air, and men stomped on the floor with their boots, banged canes against the sides of wooden chairs, and tossed their hats into the night air.[14]

The presidential election of 1860 had begun.

★ CHAPTER 2 ★

A Politician of Unwavering Ambition

I will be entirely frank. The taste is in my mouth a little...

—FROM A LETTER ABOUT THE PRESIDENCY ABRAHAM

LINCOLN WROTE TO A FRIEND TWO WEEKS

BEFORE THE REPUBLICAN CONVENTION

In the late fall of 1859, journalist Henry Villard rode down a bumpy dirt road in Missouri in a creaky two-horse carriage with others on his way to Ohio after spending several weeks at Pikes Peak, in Colorado, on assignment for the *Cincinnati Commercial*. It was a bitterly cold November morning. They soon spotted a small, black, one-horse buggy riding slowly along the road, its two passengers shivering against the biting winds of the early hours of the day. The driver wore a short jacket, no overcoat, gloves, or blankets, and his long, thin legs were cramped up against him as his reddened hands grasped the thin leather reins. The horses' breath nearly froze in the prairie air. The sky was a brilliant cobalt blue. The hunched-over driver was freezing. It was Abraham Lincoln. Villard, who had met Lincoln by chance a year before at a railroad station, stopped and greeted him and, seeing how cold he was, loaned him a buffalo robe to keep warm. Lincoln, grateful, told him he was on his way back from Kansas, where he had been speaking on behalf of Republican candidates for local office.[15]

Abraham Lincoln was a professional politician. He first ran for office when he was just twenty-three years old, lost, and had been running for office ever since. The tall lawyer from Sangamon County, Illinois, did win his second election, in 1834, to the Illinois state legislature, and was reelected three more times. He tried unsuccessfully to secure his Whig Party's nomination for Congress in 1844 but was elected in 1846. His political career went into decline at the elective level in 1849, when he left Congress (the Illinois Whigs rotated their congressmen), but he continued at the political level as he campaigned for Whig candidates in the 1848 presidential election and solidified his position as one of the leaders of the party in Illinois.

That was the year Lincoln mapped out a political career leading to high office of some kind. Many historians have written that Lincoln's career did not resume again until after the Kansas-Nebraska controversy of 1854, which ignited Lincoln's long-term opposition to government slavery policies, and that before then he was in "retirement." A closer look shows that Lincoln decided as early as 1848 that if he could not remain in office he would conduct letter-writing campaigns for elected and unelected political figures in Illinois and around the country. He constantly campaigned for others and gave lectures to maintain close ties to politicians and civic leaders who might later help him in some future campaigns. He also tried to maintain good relations with the press and to always keep himself in front of the public.

He was a politician with incredible perseverance and resiliency and a man with an unusually calm attitude about victory and defeat, which enabled him to absorb setbacks that might have crushed others. Losses merely sidetracked Lincoln and strengthened his resolve to run again. He worked hard to get himself elected to the U.S. Senate by the state legislature in 1855 but failed when his opponents conspired to deny him the nod. He wound up backing Lyman Trumbull, a compromise candidate, in order to block someone else. Instead of being bitter about an election that was practically stolen from him, Lincoln wholeheartedly supported Trumbull.[16] Instead of being demoralized by the U.S. Senate race he should have won in 1858 against Stephen Douglas the following year he stumped throughout the Midwest for Republican candidates.

He worked hard as a politician. When at home, Lincoln conducted intense letter-writing crusades. Those followed three paths: 1) to get others to help him win election to some office, 2) to state his policy on issues to people who might help him get elected to some office, and 3) to help others network in the system so they might one day help him do the same and win an election. He always set himself up as someone who, one day, could help others if they helped him. He kept up correspondence with hundreds of people and, through their letters, was able to assess the political situation in their states and counties.

Lincoln always knew what the people were thinking. He had made it his business, from chats with customers in his general store in the 1830s to the last critical days of the Civil War, to talk to everyone about what they thought of politics and events. Via his polls in different states, endless letters, and visits from people ranging from the local blacksmiths to U.S. senators, Lincoln kept his finger on the pulse of America.

He worked hard to be liked by people. He believed that people will help, and not hurt, someone they like. He did this through extensive personal charm and a keen sense of humor.

Lincoln was an ambitious man. When he first ran for the state legislature, a raw and bony candidate at age twenty-three, he let everyone know in a column he wrote for the *Sangamon Journal*:

> *Every man is said to have his peculiar ambition. Whether it is true or not, I can say for one that I have no other so great as that of being truly esteemed of my fellow men by rendering myself worthy of their esteem. How far I shall succeed in gratifying this ambition is yet to be developed.*[17]

He told the voters of his district quite frankly that if he lost the election, he would run five or six times again until he was victorious. Unlike many politicians, the prospect of defeat did not bother him. He was always convinced that somehow, some way, he would convince people that he should hold public office. And he wanted public office, writing to one man of a prospective race for Congress in 1843, "I would like to go very much."[18]

That ambition was always in him. It was the feeling, admired by all in the nation at that time, that anyone, regardless of birth or station in life, had the right to advance as far as he could in his chosen field—that was the promise of America.[19] He told Lynn Greene, a New Salem resident who helped him understand English grammar books, that he believed there were many good people who did not achieve greatness. He believed "it was for him to become so," she noted.[20] He told a local schoolteacher that he would become an elected official one day.[21] Later, his law partner, Billy Herndon, said that Lincoln was the most ambitious man he ever met, that "he was always calculating, and always planning ahead. His ambition was a little engine that knew no rest."[22]

Herndon later told friends that Lincoln's yearning for high office of some kind began to form in his mind in 1840, when he was thirty-one, the first year he went out on the national stump. Herndon said, "He was flattered in 1833, '34, and '35 by (merchant Denton) Offutt and others in New Salem…and made to believe that he would be a great man and he dreamed of it then as he told me—always delicately and indirectly."[23] He knew better than to accept high office that meant little, though, later turning down the chance to be the governor of sparsely populated Oregon in 1848 because it was too remote and would be a political graveyard for him.

Lincoln's early desire for success grew and was fueled by his accomplishments. The Whig Party made him one of its stump speakers for the national election in 1840, encouraging him to talk about national issues and slavery.

Ambition realized is glorious, but ambition thwarted can be demoralizing. Lincoln's dreams of greatness were often dashed. He was disappointed when men he considered inferior to him were elected or appointed to office. Lincoln always felt frustrated by the triumphs of Stephen Douglas, his longtime rival and fellow Springfield resident and friend. Lincoln always seemed to miss the prizes in politics after great struggles, but they always seemed to fall gracefully into Douglas' back pocket.

His defeats made Lincoln jealous. He said in 1856:

> *Twenty years ago, Judge Douglas and I first became acquainted. We were both young then; he a trifle younger than I. Even then, we were both ambitious; I, perhaps, quite as much so as he. With me, the race of ambition has been a failure—a flat failure; with him it has been one of splendid success. His name fills the nation; and is not unknown, even, in foreign lands. I affect no contempt for the high eminence he has reached.*[24]

He hid his ambition, always acting humbly, underlining his belief that he was eager to eliminate slavery eventually and to hold the Union together, telling many audiences that "I have never failed, do not now fail, to remember that in the Republican cause there is a higher aim than that of mere office."

He felt, too, that as an unknown man there was little he could do to push himself, relying on history to provide opportunities. He later commented, "I have not controlled events, but events have controlled me."[25]

In the 1858 race against Douglas, an emotional Lincoln told his huge audiences that his goals meant more to him than ambition. He said:

> *I claim no insensibility to political honors. But today could the Missouri restriction (on slavery expansion) be restored, and the whole slavery question replaced on the old ground of "toleration," be necessity where it exists, with unyielding hostility to the spread of it, on principle, I would...gladly agree, that Judge Douglas should never be out, and I never in, an office, so long as we both, or either, live.*[26]

When the Whig Party began to disintegrate in the early 1850s, its Northern and Southern factions ripped apart by the slavery issue, Lincoln did not immediately jump into the arms of the newly formed Republicans when they began to organize in 1854. He slowly moved away from the Whigs during the latter half of 1854 and through much of 1855 and 1856 and told people he was simply an "anti-Nebraska" man, uncertain which direction to take as new parties sprung up in Illinois and the nation. He was also in no hurry to join the Republicans at first because many anti-immigrant, anti-Catholic Know-Nothings had become members.[27] Later, convinced that the Republican Party was the best bet among them to become a major organization, Lincoln went to its first state convention in Bloomington, Illinois, in 1856 with his friend David Davis, a judge. He gave a ringing speech against slavery (some said it was the best speech he ever delivered) that brought the overcrowded hall of people to their feet. From that moment on, he was not merely a Republican but a founder and leader of the party.[28]

Lincoln knew before he even arrived that the Republican Party had some old Whigs, but that it was mostly made up of new men reeled into politics by the uproar over slavery in the territories (30 percent of all Republicans or "anti-Nebraska" candidates elected in 1854 in Illinois had never been in politics before). He knew that slavery had been growing as a salient issue in campaign politics. It had surfaced as an important issue in the 1853 elections and then increased in importance in 1856, 1858, and 1859.[29]

Lincoln understood that in him people saw a lifelong opponent of slavery. He best expressed his hatred for it in an 1855 letter to his friend Joshua Speed, discussing one of their steamboat trips in the 1830s. Lincoln wrote:

> *You may remember, as I well do, that from Louisville to the south of the Ohio there were, on board, ten or a dozen slaves, shackled together with irons. That sight was a continual torment to me, and I see something like it every time I touch the Ohio, or any other slave border. It is…a thing which has, and continually exercises, the power of making me miserable.*[30]

Lincoln was also a former congressman, a veteran leader of the Whig Party, a good speaker, and a man with considerable connections, a man whom the Republicans could utilize as a leader. Lincoln turned the Republicans from yet another small political organization into a party powerful enough to gain a majority in the Illinois statehouse in just four years, and elect four of nine congressmen and a mayor of Chicago by 1860. He did it with shrewd political maneuvering, running the party in a way that offered opportunity to many office seekers but did not eliminate any through underhandedness or trickery.

Lincoln was a careful politician. One of his most delicate tasks as party leader was to smooth over disputes between feuding members of his party, a chore that required the wisdom of Solomon, the patience of Job, and much luck. He did so with great skill but always bemoaned the complexities of the problems his friends got themselves into. Many involved pitting two men against each other for nominations for the state legislature. In one feud the man who lost the nomination, after agreeing to abide by the party's decisions, was irate. He was one of the most popular men in the county. Party organizer Ward Hill Lamon, thirty-three, Lincoln's former law partner and then attorney general for Illinois' eighth district, wrote him in the middle of August 1860: "Our friends say there is danger of our losing the county unless a different state of things exists. F. is headstrong and revengeful…. What is the remedy?"[31] Lincoln then solved the squabble.

Lincoln sometimes veiled his moves by telling others to tell people they were acting without his knowledge when they were doing just that, such as an incredibly complex political mess he straightened out between warring Republicans in Freeport, Illinois, in the spring of 1860. At first, he wanted to be subtle. He wrote party organizer Leonard Swett, "I see no objection to the letter you have written to (John) Shaffer. Send it to him, but do not let him know I have seen it."

Unhappy with the secretive method, Lincoln then changed his mind and concluded, "Tell him to come down and see me."[32]

In another delicate move, he had to head off a feud that threatened to turn into a legal nightmare between his own trusted political aide, Norman Judd, and John Wentworth, the mayor of Chicago, both of whom wanted to run for governor of Illinois. Their relationship rapidly deteriorated into libel threats. Lincoln, who needed Judd as campaign worker and Wentworth as his man in Chicago and Cook County, both keys to victory in Illinois, managed to talk both men out of the legal suit and convinced each to back a third man for governor.

Running the Illinois Republican Party was an enjoyable and rewarding experience for him. It gave him the chance to meet and befriend hundreds of party workers and voters, to develop the future of the party, and to put his personal imprint on life in the state. He did not complain about the hard work and travel it entailed; he loved it. "Never in the presidency did he surpass the political skill with which he shaped the Republican Party of Illinois, held it together, and made himself its leader. In his relations with other Illinoisans, one finds the same patience and respect for human dignity that characterized the wartime president," wrote political scientist Don Fehrenbacher.[33]

As a politician, he became the master of the intrigue that occurred behind the scenes. He frantically wrote a party worker that opponents were trying to develop a new plan to select candidates in Lincoln's assembly district that would hurt him. He needed his help. He wrote the man, "I want nothing to prevent your getting an article in your paper of this week, taking strong ground for the old system under which Hardin and Baker were nominated, without seeming to know or suspect that any one desires to change it.… Don't fail on any account to get it in this week."[34]

And, best of all, he was a shrewd political analyst who was easily able to determine why his party won and lost elections. He did that after the Republicans' first national election, in 1856, telling party leaders that presidential candidate John Frémont lost Illinois and Pennsylvania because he was unable to win the votes of the former Whigs that the Republicans had been courting.[35]

The results of Lincoln's alliance with the Republicans were plentiful. Just a few months later, in 1856, at their Philadelphia national convention, the new Republican Party almost nominated a startled Lincoln for vice president (he received 110 votes, losing to New Jersey's William Dayton). Lincoln knew he had found a new home.[36]

Lincoln was a man who did all of this through great personal pain and emotional difficulty. He was a melancholy man who might have been a manic depressive. He was buoyant at times, but he was also quiet and distant at others. These "black" periods in his life—that could be triggered by any number of different events—consumed long periods of time, said those who knew him.[37] His restlessness and depression carried over into his sleeping habits. He could barely sleep on some nights and on others woke up from frightening nightmares. Sometimes he dreamed that he died. In one nightmare, he was a witness to his own wake.[38] On other nights, he dreamed that the country was involved in a war of some kind and he had to help run the nation. During the day, as others turned to the lighthearted novels serialized in newspapers, he became morose reading and rereading depressing sections from Shakespeare's *Richard III* and *Macbeth*.

He had suffered great personal loss in his life. Lincoln's mother died when she was a young woman, when Lincoln was just nine, and then his sister died young. His fiancée, Anne Rutledge, died at twenty-two, and he was so heartbroken over her passing that he grieved for months. He and Mary's first son, Edward, died in 1850 when he was just four years old. The tenth anniversary of his death was in 1860. One of Lincoln's other sons, Tad, suffered from what specialists today would label attention deficit disorder. Tad also had a pronounced speech problem and was emotionally dysfunctional for years. He was a hyperactive, difficult child who brought Lincoln great problems in his family's relations with others. All of his life, Lincoln struggled in his marriage with his wife, Mary, whom friends said advocated for him too hard socially and politically and treated him badly inside and outside the home. A consummate politician who knew he could lose elections as often as he won, Lincoln had difficulty abiding with her disappointment at his defeats. After his loss to Trumbull in his bid for a Senate seat in 1855, Mary refused to speak to Trumbull's wife, a longtime friend; her husband always had to add Mary's fictional regards to Mrs. Trumbull whenever he wrote Trumbull a letter.[39]

Mary was often unstable, shouting at house guests, fighting with neighbors, and endlessly gossiping in hurtful ways. She was very moody, often adopted different personalities, and would sometimes begin raving that wild cats were out to get her. She frequently fought with her husband, and he spent many nights sleeping on his back porch or at his office. She made relations with friends difficult in social settings, and he had few friendships with any women, no matter how harmless, because of Mary's inordinate jealousy. The pain inside Lincoln, the feelings of inadequacy as a husband, and his wife's temper and attitude were troubles that beset him as soon as he woke each day.[40] These drove him to seek satisfaction through politics to somehow fill the emotional gaps inside him, to make up for his personal problems by basking in the cheers of the crowd. Like so many people who find work a tonic for grief or depression, Lincoln worked hard all his life. Work and success helped him to overcome his personal troubles.[41] That combination, too, molded him into the good and decent man who was tough enough to later lead the United States through a great war and vulnerable enough to do it with compassion, all fused with a love of people and country.

Abraham Lincoln was a man, too, who fully understood that his country and his people were changing, that a new nation was being forged by political, intellectual, and religious forces. He emerged as a public figure at a time when the Second Great Awakening was sweeping the country. The second awakening pulled people away from traditional churches and moved them to start new churches. It was fueled by a new breed of fire-and-brimstone evangelical preacher—and targeted slavery as one of its major issues. The movement had caused great change in Illinois and elsewhere (in 1860, nearly 400,000 people in Illinois, one-fourth of the population, belonged to the evangelical churches).

Lincoln was not a regular member of any church (he was a nominal Presbyterian), but he was a deeply moral man. He understood that his own hatred of slavery evolved from not only political thinking but a rooted moralistic feeling about peoples' freedom. He was not overly religious, but he understood that many in America were. That religious, or moral, feeling that he had was shared by millions during the Second Great Awakening.[42]

The antislavery societies, spawned by the Awakening, were large organizations opposed to slavery, along with many church groups, and they, like the churches, framed all of their arguments in religion. Theodore Weld, head of one antislavery society, said, "God has committed to every moral agent the privilege, the right, and the responsibility of personal ownership. This is God's plan. Slaveholders annihilate it. (Slavery) crushes the body, tramples into the dust the upward tendencies of the intellect, breaks the heart, and kills the soul."[43]

Those Southerners who claimed that they were good to their slaves were lashed by religious groups for their hypocrisy. "The daily practice of forcibly robbing others and habitually living on the plunder cannot but beget in the mind the habit of regarding the interest and happiness of those whom it robs, as of no sort of consequence in comparison with its own," said one minister.[44]

The Democrats were aware of religion's power but ignored it. George Woodward wrote President James Buchanan's attorney general, Jeremiah Black, in 1860:

> *We are a churchgoing people, and antislavery has become the cherished dogma of Northern theology. Not only so, but personal religion has come to be measured by the zeal of slavery agitation. In almost all the churches, above mentioned abolitionism has become, practically, a test of good standing, if not church membership.... We are an educating people—abolitionists born in hell and nursed by the new Episcopal Churches have entered into our schools, school books, and school literatures. Now it is to be supposed that abolitionism so incorporated with our thrift, our religion, our education, is going to die out just as it is about to clothe itself with the patronage and power of the government? I look for no such improbable event. On the contrary, I expect it to wax more aggressive, more destructive.*[45]

Lincoln craftily framed all of his antislavery arguments—over a twenty-year period—within the framework of morals and religion. Democrats like Stephen Douglas, John Breckinridge, and President James Buchanan discussed slavery as a political issue—states' rights—but Lincoln discussed it as a moral issue, enabling him to marshal all voters with evolving religious feelings behind him and turn politics into a religious crusade.[46]

Lincoln also realized very early that America was developing a growing middle class that was increasingly politically oriented. He saw that all around him as the state of Illinois changed. Now, in 1860, Illinois had almost two million residents. Chicago, a tiny crossroads the year Lincoln first ran for office, had 112,000 residents by 1860. Men who used to live along rivers now lived in city enclaves, and men who used to till farms now worked for factories and corporations. People in that middle-class world, in Illinois and America, had been imbued with religion and, as the 1860s approached, realized that politics was a natural outlet for religious fervor. More and more people voted and became involved in politics in some way in order to turn their strong feelings about religious issues, particularly slavery, into law.[47] This growing tide of involved middle-class people was turning away from traditional political parties and politicians and searching for new ones, such as the brand-new Republican Party and Abraham Lincoln.

Since 1840, Lincoln had been active in the Whig Party. That year he helped organize a drive to get as many people as possible to the polls to vote for Whig presidential candidate William Henry Harrison. Those who watched him said he showed the skills of older and far more experienced men in the party.[48]

The year before that election, 1839, was the first year that Lincoln took on Stephen Douglas in public debates. They met head to head as part of a four-against-four party policy debate in November 1839 and again a month later. The following year Lincoln accepted several invitations to speak alongside Douglas in the presidential campaign, constantly holding his own against a man who was fast becoming one of the best public speakers in the United States.

One of the steps in his campaign for a national office of some kind began later, in 1848, when he campaigned throughout Illinois for Whig candidates and presidential hopeful Gen. Zachary Taylor, running against Lewis Cass. He arrived in the state from Congress in Washington DC in October and immediately went to Chicago to begin a month-long stump tour that took him through a number of counties and wound up with him giving nine speeches in his own Seventh Congressional District. Taylor lost Illinois in the election, but local politicians pointed with envy to Lincoln's record—Taylor won in all but one of the nine counties where Lincoln stumped for him.[49] It was another sign of the growing personal popularity of Lincoln throughout the state. His sustained success as a local political leader moved him to joke in Congress that year that if men like Lewis Cass could run for president, so could he.[50]

He also accepted offers to speak in seven different cities for Taylor in Massachusetts that year, giving him eastern exposure. His speaking tour began in Worcester on September 12, and from there he went on to Boston, New Bedford, Lowell, and Dedham. He told listeners in each town the same thing: he and the Illinois Whigs were just as opposed to slavery as the people of Massachusetts. They did not want it to spread to the territories but would permit it, unhappily, in the Southern states where it currently existed. He appealed to them to ignore the new Free Soil Party because a vote for them was not only wasted but would hurt Taylor.

His speeches drew excellent notices from Whig newspapers and were deplored by Democratic papers. The *Boston Atlas* called it "one of the best" speeches ever heard in the areas, but the *Norfolk Democrat* found it "nauseous." The Free Soil papers found him "witty."[51]

In 1858, he had defeated Stephen Douglas in the popular vote for the U.S. Senate and gained national press attention. By the spring of 1860, as the political conventions began, Abraham Lincoln, a political veteran, had grown into a likable and respected man, an astute politician who dreamed, somehow, of winning the Republican nomination for president.

CHAPTER 3

The Relentless
Little Giant

There are great portly fellows (at the Democratic Convention) with protuberant
stomachs and puffy cheeks, red foreheads, thin and grizzly hair, dressed in glossy
black and fine linen, with the latest style of stove pipe hats and ponderous gold
headed canes—perspiring and smoking and engaged in mysterious conversations
concerning caucus strategems of intense interest to themselves.

—REPORTER MURAT HALSTEAD

Stephen Douglas was only five feet tall and overweight. Supporters said he had a bold, leonine appearance. Critics were harsh. One journalist wrote that he was "a queer little man, canine head and duck legs."[52] His bombastic voice and political clout more than made up for his size, and both combined to win him the nickname "the Little Giant." By the time the Democratic convention opened on April 23, 1860, he had become one of the most important political figures in America, a man who had held office of some kind since he was twenty-three years old. Douglas had served in the Illinois state legislature, worked as Illinois' secretary of state, and had spent time on the state supreme court (the youngest justice in its history), in the House of Representatives, and in the U.S. Senate.

He was also one of the architects of the Compromise of 1850 that brought California into the Union as a free state, abolished the slave trade in the District of Columbia, established the Fugitive Slave Act, and admitted New Mexico and Utah into the Union with the slavery issue unresolved there. He also sponsored the infamous Kansas-Nebraska bill, which permitted residents of new states to decide whether they would become slave states or would be slave free. He was also a well-read statesman and intellectual as well as an astute politician who almost won his party's nomination for president in 1856 and had been talked about as a certain future president since he was thirty-seven years old. And, like Lincoln, he had borne great personal tragedy, the death of both his wife and daughter in childbirth in 1853, and still managed to be productive as a public official.

Douglas was a natural politician. He was born in Vermont in 1813 and never knew his father, who died when he was two years old (like Douglas, Lincoln lost a parent at an early age; his mother died when he was nine). Douglas apprenticed as a cabinetmaker in Vermont before moving to Illinois as a young adult to practice law. Friends in Vermont reported that Douglas was an energetic teenager and that reading consumed him. At sixteen, he was as forceful and persuasive as he would be at forty-six. He was glib and talkative in and out of school and could hold his own as a teenager, engaging adults in discussions about politics. Debating came naturally to him. His great flaw was a stubbornness and a quick temper, which often landed him in shouting matches. Fellow politicians and voters did not see his temper as a drawback, but rather as the strong backbone of a man ready to "mix it up" with friend and foe alike.

Like Lincoln, Douglas accepted defeat with resigned acceptance. He never held grudges against the few men who defeated him and often kept them as social friends, especially Lincoln. He saw himself as a professional politician and understood that he would win some fights and lose others. He also realized that as the titular leader of the Democratic Party in Illinois he had responsibilities to work with party leaders and to campaign for men seeking other offices. He never shirked those responsibilities and, like Lincoln, had fond memories of stump tours in the wind and rain. He did everything he could to hold his party together.

He had few equals as an orator. Douglas was the finest public speaker in Illinois when he was still in his twenties, and his stature grew over the years. He used his short, five-foot frame to great advantage, standing up ramrod straight and then tilting back a bit to symbolically take on all challengers despite his size. He was able to deliver speeches designed to fit time periods, whether ten-minute homilies, one-hour lectures, or three-hour stump speeches, and he was often invited to speak throughout Illinois, Washington DC, and, later, the nation. He had a deep voice that could linger on words and phrases to create humor or, in other instances, deliver biting criticism. He could be authoritarian, especially in attacks against foes who opposed his policies, and he could be funny.

Douglas had come very close to becoming president at the age of forty-three in 1856, had a very good chance at the age of forty-seven in 1860, and if he didn't make it then, still had another three or four elections in front of him. He looked like a president, with his finely cut clothes, unlike his friend Lincoln, who no one ever accused of looking distinguished. Douglas behaved like a president, had the necessary legislative connections a president needed, and he thirsted after the job.[53]

As the Democrats gathered in Charleston (they were supposed to gather in Columbia, South Carolina, but moved to Charleston following a medical epidemic in Columbia), and Lincoln followed his movements in the newspapers, Douglas, recently remarried, should have been about to experience his greatest achievement: nomination for the presidency of the United States. Instead, he was on the eve of one of the greatest political catastrophes in American history.

Douglas had championed the rights of slavery in Southern states where it had always existed and had even married the daughter of a slave owner. He believed new territories and states should have slavery if they so desired—"popular sovereignty." In 1858, in his debates with Lincoln, and in subsequent speeches, though, he had changed his mind, supporting the rights of territories to vote down slavery if they wanted in the same breath that he said they could approve it. Then, just a year after the debates with Lincoln, he became the leader against the slaveholder-dominated Kansas legislature—one of two contending legislatures in that strife-torn territory—defeating its proposed proslavery constitution, passed in the town of Lecompton, and earning the hatred of President Buchanan, who had supported it. One Democrat said of the Southern delegates "that they hate Douglas with a perfect hatred is very clear. They will never forgive him for defeating the Lecompton Swindle."[54] The Southern Democrats in his party denounced him for his muddled views and for playing politics with slavery just to win reelection to the Senate in his race against Lincoln and, in so doing, betraying them. He did not understand that the traditional American love of popular sovereignty, primarily on the frontier, had died with the success of slavery.[55] Virginia planter Edmund Ruffin called Douglas "a great political scoundrel."[56]

Buchanan, still smarting from Douglas' attempts to defeat him at the 1856 Democratic convention and annoyed at what he perceived as Douglas' haughty attitude toward him, continued to spend as much time as he could weakening his power. As president, Buchanan had worked against Douglas, a senator from his own party, during Douglas' race against Lincoln in 1858. Douglas raged that "the time has now arrived when the democracy of the whole country should hold meetings in the cities, towns, and counties, and proclaim in tones that will command respect their devotion to and determination to sustain and carry out in good faith the great principles of self government" and argued that Kansas' Lecompton Constitution was "a scheme so monstrous as to force a constitution at the point of the bayonet down the throats of an unwilling people."[57] Douglas wrote a friend that "we are sure to triumph. Keep the ball rolling and the party united. It will be all right in the end."[58] Friends had warned Buchanan that the bombastic Douglas would "run amok" against Buchanan in the Senate, and they were right.[59]

The president did everything he could to hurt Douglas. He fired some of Douglas' appointed federal workers from their jobs in Illinois and talked to the editors of numerous Democratic-controlled newspapers to denounce Douglas. He even convinced another Democrat to run against Douglas and Lincoln as a third-party man to drain votes away from the Little Giant and let a man from the opposition party win the election. His vicious campaign against Douglas had quickly passed the bounds of professional ethics. Douglas' friend John Heiss, of the *Washington Star*, told him that the president "hates you in the most bitter and unrelenting manner," and an editor of the *Illinois State Journal* told him that "it is wholly a personal matter" with Buchanan.[60]

Worst of all, Southern democrats began to refer to the hated Douglas as a "Republican."[61]

Southerners were angry over Douglas' turncoat slavery policy. They made fun of his noble insinuations that Northerners and Southerners would become friends and intermarry on the plains of the territories. No member of any party was vilified like Douglas was by the Democrats.[62] Their feelings were best expressed later in the U.S. Senate by Senator Judah Benjamin of Louisiana.

> *Having said that (no slavery in the territories) to us here in the Senate, he went home and, under the stress of a local election, his knees gave way; his whole person trembled. His adversary stood on principle and was beaten and lo!, he is the candidate of a mighty party for the presidency of the United States. The senator from Illinois faltered. He got the prize for which he faltered. But lo! The prize of his ambition slips from his grasp because of the faltering.*[63]

The Northern Democrats applauded Douglas for all the reasons the Southerners deplored him. Douglas found himself stuck in the middle between the two groups.

Neither Douglas or the Northern Democrats wanted to meet in Charleston, South Carolina, a gorgeous, old, wealthy city of columned mansions, cobblestone streets, and lovely gardens, but a hotbed of secessionist talk. South Carolina, however, was chosen as the convention site for 1860 at the end of the 1856 Cincinnati convention as an olive branch to the Southerners.[64]

The trains into Charleston that arrived from all over the country were crowded. Arguments between Northern and Southern delegates on the trains were heated. Local hotels overcharged delegates, who were paying $11 to $14 a day for room and meals (the top hotels in Chicago would only charge $2.50 a day during the Republican convention there [65]).

Wherever Northern Democrats walked, they witnessed slave auctions or had to listen to slave owners denounce Douglas.[66] On the Friday before the convention opened, ominous broadsides invited all to join the Southern Rights Caucus. Its members unanimously voted to leave the convention if Douglas was nominated.[67]

The convention was held in the two-story South Carolina Institute, an old building in the heart of the Charleston business district. The hall seated 3,000 people on wooden chairs that were screwed together for the gathering. A gallery that held several thousand spectators, which would be filled with secessionist South Carolinians daily, overhung the main floor. Hundreds of women dressed in long gowns, wide-brimmed hats, and elaborate makeup sat in the galleries. It rained one morning, and the women, most of whom did not bring umbrellas, remained in the lobby of the building instead of going out in the rain for lunch at local restaurants. Dozens of men stayed behind, too, to socialize with them.

There were rumors everywhere. The gentlest suggested that Douglas was about to leave the Democratic Party and become a Republican. The harshest declared that all of the Southern states would secede from the Union and form a Southern empire. The most prevalent was that the Douglas delegates were all drunks and had been on a nonstop drinking binge for the last few days. One rumor that everyone seemed to believe was that Alabama's U.S. senator and silver-tongued orator, William Yancey, had prepared a speech that would run eight hours a day for three entire days.[68] The Democrats were a colorful group. Reporter Murat Halstead wrote:

They are great portly fellows with protuberant stomachs and puffy cheeks, red foreheads, thin and grizzly hair, dressed in glossy black and fine linen, with the latest style of stove pipe hats and ponderous gold headed canes—perspiring and smoking, and engaged in mysterious conversations concerning caucus stratagems of intense interest to themselves.[69]

The days just before the first gavel banged down to open the convention proved tedious for those who arrived early, such as New York financier, millionaire, and Democratic powerbroker August Belmont. A bored Belmont wrote his wife from Charleston:

> *We do not make much progress. An immense deal of time is lost by talk. Though I am glad that I came in order to partake in the interesting work before us, I am passing a most stupid time. Everybody is so taken up with politics that you cannot hear another word spoken. Last evening, I went to a party given to some of the delegates. It was the most stupid of all stupid gatherings I have ever been at. There were about twelve ugly women with about sixty ugly men.*[70]

Outside the convention, slaveholders and powerful Southern politicians denounced the Northern Democrats as traitors. The threats to end slavery were embodied in Douglas' candidacy. Halstead wrote that "Douglas was the pivotal individual of the Charleston convention. Every delegate was for or against him; every motion meant to nominate or not nominate him; every parliamentary war was pro or con Douglas."[71]

Halstead saw the convention fight as a cultural as well as political battle. He wrote:

> *However great may be the weight of the Douglas men in the convention, he will be assailed most bitterly. The fight against him involves, for a very large class of Southern politicians...the issues of life; and those Southern men have a great advantage over Douglas men in that they are sincere. They have principles. They stand upon convictions, and will fight from their bones until the flesh be hacked.*[72]

The Democratic Party was a mess. Amid the swirl of controversy over states' rights hovered the administration of James Buchanan, who decided not to run for reelection, along with his views, which threatened to divide the Democrats. Buchanan's policies over the last four years were that of a middle-of-the-road politician, a president determined to hold the Union together in spite of support for measures that threatened to tear it apart, such as the Kansas-Nebraska Act, the Dred Scott decision, and the thorny Lecompton proslavery constitution in Kansas.

He agreed that slavery should remain where it was and be permitted in the territories, but he did not want the issue to split the nation apart. He wrote, "Our Union rests upon public opinion, and can never be cemented by the blood of its citizens in a civil war. If it cannot live on the affections of the people, it must one day perish. Congress possesses many means of preserving it by conciliation; but the sword was not placed in their hand to preserve it by force."[73]

Douglas' position at the convention started badly and became worse. Dissension ruled. The Little Giant knew as soon as the first gavel banged down to bring the gathering to order that there would be problems between North and South.

The largest rift was in the New York group. Its Democratic Party was controlled by the Tammany Hall political machine. In the mid-1850s, Fernando Wood, the young, ambitious mayor of New York, angered Tammany Hall by filling thousands of city jobs instead of putting Tammany retainers in them. Tammany boss Dean Richmond, a close friend of President Buchanan and many Southern leaders, was outraged. Tammany promptly kicked Wood out of the organization and worked to defeat him in the next mayoral election. Undaunted, Wood, who had a huge following in New York, a staunch Democratic city, formed Mozart

Hall, his own political machine, staged a comeback and got himself elected mayor for a third term in 1859. Now, as the convention was about to open, two separate delegations, one from Tammany Hall and one from Mozart Hall, arrived from New York and demanded to be seated. Wood, who had political ties all over the country, had been convinced by leading Southerners that they would name him vice president on the ticket, with a Southerner as president, if he would help them defeat Douglas. Wood, extraordinarily ambitious, felt that in four years he could be president. He had enemies in Tammany, however, and they had strong friends in Charleston too.

The convention leadership finally seated the Tammany people. Wood and his friends remained in Charleston, though, because Wood was now free to politick for the vice presidency.

The Southern Rights Caucus, led by Alabama's Yancey, demanded that the party's platform be voted upon before the presidential ballot, which was out of order, because they were convinced that if a Southerner was nominated for president, the platform, which they wanted to support slavery, would be important. There was no basis for the Southerners to truly believe that a Southerner would be nominated for president. Douglas was well ahead in all ballot counts. The only other possible candidates were Kentucky's James Guthrie and Virginia's R. M. T. Hunter, and nobody gave either a real chance. There was also John Breckinridge, the vice president of the United States. Breckinridge was from Kentucky, though, and had pledged to support Guthrie.

Surprisingly, the Douglas men agreed. They felt that if they forced a fight on the platform, few Southerners would leave. Besides, Douglas was so far ahead of everyone else that the loss of a few delegates would not change the outcome.[74]

It would also enable the Douglas men to hammer out the platform they wanted, making it easier for the Little Giant to win the election. To back up his men on the floor of Institute Hall, Douglas let it be known that he would not accept the nomination if the slavery platform was approved. This denouncement of the proslavery Southerners was a huge blunder, one of many that would plague the Douglas campaign.

Senator Robert Toombs of Georgia said: "Douglas men made a great mistake in voting to go to the platform before nominating (a president). A rupture then became inevitable, but he and his friends expected to profit by the secession of two or three states."[75]

Reporter Murat Halstead wrote that "their game then was to have three or four states, at most go out. They wanted a little eruption, not a big one."[76]

They got a big one.

The convention was immediately torn by the inability of the platform committee to agree on slavery. The Southerners insisted that the party had to take an all-or-nothing position on slavery or the Southerners would not accept it. Edward Barksdale of Mississippi added that the Fugitive Slave Law had to be upheld. He wrote, "Adopt that platform (without the law) and the result will be the election of a Black Republican… William Seward."[77]

Halstead wrote in his different newspaper columns, "It is perfectly clear, glaringly apparent here, seen in every face, heard in every voice, and pervades the city like an atmosphere, that the doctrine of the Democratic Party must be that of exerting all powers of the federal government for the extension of slavery."

Ironically, the arguments over slavery at the Democratic conventions, like those at the Republican gathering, were only about the extension of slavery and not slavery itself. And the extension discussed so heatedly was in the plains of the West where there were only a few hundred slaves and no anticipation that more would be needed.[78]

Thomas Pugh of Ohio answered at once that the Douglas Democrats would not back down. The Northerners, who were more numerous, stuck together on a compromise, pro-Douglas plank. Southerners protested. Confusion reined. What followed was much loud shouting, roars from those in the gallery, and threats on the floor from men on both sides. Delegates threw their hands in the air, and some jumped on top of chairs to bellow out their protest.

The convention was adjourned for the day after the delegation from Alabama announced that they might leave and go home. Dozens of Southerners raced to the telegraph office to wire their parties and friends back home to ask what they should do if Alabama walked out.

On April 30, the seventh day of the convention, the platform fight reached its crescendo. The Alabama delegation head, L. P. Walker, announced that Alabama was leaving the convention. A moment later, Mississippi announced they would follow. D. C. Glenn, a Mississippi delegate, jumped on top of his chair and turned to face the Ohio delegation, seated directly behind Mississippi on the convention floor. He delivered a riveting twenty-minute speech that ended with Glenn telling the Ohioans, the convention, the gallery, and the American people that within sixty days there would be a new country: the United South. A roar of approval thundered down on him from the South Carolinians who packed the gallery.

The stampede was on. As the Mississippians and Alabamians made their way through the cluttered aisles, delegates from Louisiana and South Carolina rose and followed them out of the hall. Next to flee were the men from Florida and Arkansas. They were later joined by the delegates from Georgia and Texas. The departure of most of the South, which even included one-third of the tiny Delaware delegation, left the convention in tatters.[79]

South Carolinians applauded the walkout. Halstead wrote that "there was a Fourth of July feeling in Charleston last night, a jubilee…. In all her history, Charleston had never enjoyed herself so hugely."[80]

By the early hours of the morning, the convention was in ruin and so was Stephen Douglas.

President Buchanan's men, determined to slaughter Douglas, insisted that the two-thirds vote needed to nominate still be enforced even though the Southern states had walked out, knowing this would make it impossible for Douglas to win. The vote for the two-thirds rule passed, 141–112, driven by New York's 35–0 vote on the question. The two-thirds requirement slipped the rope around the neck of Douglas, who was being hanged by both the Southerners and Northerners.

Douglas was finished. He received 145½ votes on the first ballot, as he expected, well ahead of Virginia's Hunter (41) and Kentucky's Guthrie (35½). Douglas moved to 147 on the second ballot and to 150 on the ninth. Then he stalled. Neither the Southerners supporting Hunter or Guthrie would budge to give Douglas the nomination. The highest Douglas moved was to 152½ on the twenty-third ballot. The voting went on and on, for a draining fifty-seven ballots, without a winner.

At the White House, President Buchanan smugly told a crowd later that he supported the two-thirds rule. And, he said, after it caused the convention to collapse, it meant that "no Democrat was bound to give the nominee (Douglas) his support."[81]

Convention leaders, seeing that the gathering was hopelessly deadlocked, decided to suspend the voting and start over again in Baltimore on June 18. The cooling-off period might offer everyone a chance for a fresh start. Or it might not. Journalist Halstead warned that "the scenes around me are those of dissolution in the Democratic organization."[82]

A gloomy Georgia senator, Alexander Stephens, said, "Men will be cutting one another's throats in a little while. In less than twelve months, we shall be in a war, perhaps the bloodiest in history."[83]

One delegate smirked, "Stephen A. Douglas was a greater man than Abraham Lincoln, for while Lincoln split rails, Douglas split the Democratic Party."[84]

Lincoln was more perplexed than anything else about the meltdown of the Democratic Party; he called their convention a "fandango."[85]

Douglas was so exasperated by the experience in Charleston that he offered to withdraw as a candidate. [86] His offer, tendered half in seriousness and half in challenge, was rejected. Douglas was assured by all that he would be nominated at last in Baltimore, but the convention leaders had completely misgauged the depth of the delegate's anger in Charleston. Baltimore would not be their political heaven but their hell.[87]

CHAPTER 4

The Democrats Split in Two

The best days of America are once more dawning...

—CONSTITUTIONAL UNION PARTY LITERATURE

The bolters from the Democratic convention in Charleston came to their hall in Baltimore like cherished celebrities from days gone by at a contemporary old-timers baseball game. Like the great players who were always seen by the crowd as superior to the current stars, the veterans of the Democratic Party wars strode onto the floor to thunderous applause from the crowd. People in the audience would spot the old warhorses as they arrived and point them out to others around them, citing their states, their positions, and all the years they served in Congress. There was John Bell, the senator from Tennessee. There, elegantly dressed, was John Crittenden, the senator from Kentucky. Smiling at old friends from old campaigns was Washington Hunt, the former governor of New York. There was Erastus Brooks, the editor of the *New York Express*, Mayor Thomas Swann of Baltimore, Joe Ingersoll of Pennsylvania, Austin Baldwin of Connecticut, and Alexander

Stuart of the prominent Stuart family of Virginia. They were the old-timer all-star team, the men the people had loved and who in turn would prevent the chaos they feared from the younger politicians who had taken over the Democratic and Republican parties.

This Constitutional Union Party, a formidably named political organization, met on May 9. The men in it saw nothing unusual in a presidential race with at least three parties. The United States in 1860 was full of political parties. In the thirty-one states, there were sixteen that had fully operational third parties and some that had four and five. Presidential hopefuls had to win the support of a major party and then the support of the smaller parties. So a three-party race in 1860 was not extraordinary; there had been a three-party race in the last election, in 1856.[88] Third parties were not new in American politics. The Anti-Mason Party was started in 1826 and was followed by the Locofocos in the 1830s, the Liberty Party in the 1840s, the Free Soil Party in the 1840s, and the Know-Nothings (later American Party) in the 1850s. Millard Fillmore was the presidential candidate of the American Party in 1856.[89]

The Constitutional Union Party was made up of disgruntled Southern Democrats, old-line Whigs, transformed Know-Nothings, and hundreds of former public officials and political figures. They were returning to the fray at an advanced age in what each saw as a final chance to save the nation from Seward, Douglas, and whatever wild-eyed extremists they were certain the Southern fire-eaters would run as an independent if they were unable to stop Douglas in this same city when the mainstream Democrat convention reorganized there at the end of June. Highly respected, most of them were over the age of fifty, with long records as public officials, and were certain that their cooler heads would convince everyone that the solution to America's woes was to return to the simpler times of George

Washington and Thomas Jefferson. A reporter for the *Selma Reporter* wrote of the delegates at that state's convention that they were "the right sort of men…gray haired patriots who love their country more than party…a fine, intelligent looking assembly."[90]

The silver-haired delegates, in fact, even shouted out that the only platform they needed was the Constitution.

The delegates to the Constitutional Union convention had three goals: 1) defeat William Seward, who would be the Republican nominee for president, 2) prevent secession by electing their men, probably a Southerner at the top of the ticket and perhaps a Northerner for vice president, and 3) put off all argument on the slavery question and hope that the issue goes away. They all wanted, as one speaker said, "to let bygones be bygones" and to have North and South patch up their differences.[91]

They also urged the disgusted Democrats and the faltering Republicans to adopt the Constitutional Unionists as a compromise party that could, at least for four years, maintain peace in the United States.[92]

They were certain that a large number of Southern Democrats would not support Douglas but would certainly not turn to the Black Republican Seward. If the Constitutional Unionists could offer a respected, capable candidate, he could sweep all of the Southern states. If that same candidate was a political moderate who was palatable to some Northerners, he might just triumph in enough states in the North to win the presidency.

The dreams of the delegates were not far-fetched. There was every chance that large numbers of Democrats would indeed abandon Douglas and almost no chance that Seward could win a single county in the South. Those disgruntled voters had nowhere to go.

Most of all, the delegates of the brand-new party wanted to stop the division in the nation over slavery. It might rage in the House and Senate if the Republicans gained control of both, but if the Constitutional Unionists could win the White House, they could squelch the fires and, by executive action, prevent much more movement on the issue. A well-known public figure, a governor or senator, would also have friendships in the House and Senate to succeed at that. They could put the slavery issue on a back burner until calmer heads could reconsider it and reach a compromise, just as their generation had reached the Missouri Compromise in 1820 and the Compromise of 1850. Politics was the art of compromise, and they were veterans, skilled politicians and compromisers. They had saved the nation twice with such agreements, and they would do it again.

They met in an old church, and the press was surprised at the sizable turnout. Some reporters counting heads claimed there were more Democrats at this convention than in Charleston. It also contained several extremely important national leaders and, if rumor and gossip were true, was rather well connected to the middle and lower levels of campaign operatives in counties, cities, and towns who could win the election for them. It was clearly a group with which the regular Democrats and Republicans had to contend.

The number of states represented of the forty-one in the Union grew from a handful to a dozen and then to nearly twenty. The men on the floor told each other they had a real national party. Then a deep voice suddenly announced that the delegation from Texas had arrived. The Texans, dressed in buckskin and some with long, flowing beards—there to make their hero Sam Houston president—received a thunderous roar of approval as they marched in to take charge as they must have marched when they met Santa Anna at the battle of San Jacinto.

The delegates, on a patriotic mission, did not feud with each other and immediately began the task of picking presidential and vice presidential nominees.

The presidential nominee was John Bell, sixty-four, a former Speaker of the House, secretary of war, and former U.S. senator who was seen as a moderate. One of the founders of the Whig Party, Bell voted against the Kansas-Nebraska Act, which gave him support in the North, but he was a longtime slaveholder (he owned 166 slaves) who could win in the South. He was a balding man who sported large sideburns; his face featured a small mouth. He was cold and aloof with a dry and rather calculated way of speaking. Bell then chose Edward Everett of Massachusetts, the famed orator and former U.S. senator, as his vice president in order to show the North that Bell was not a secessionist.[93]

The delegates were delighted with their choices. In Bell and Everett they saw a team of dependable public men who could guarantee the nation at least four more years of peace and could work with Northerners and Southerners to bring about an acceptable solution to the slavery issue.[94]

They even had the added fortune to have the best speech of the convention delivered by none other than the grandson of Patrick Henry, Army Maj. G. A. Henry of Tennessee, who told the cheering crowd:

> *We are Union people. With what face could we meet the wondering nations, if by strife and hate and blinded councils, and the blasted sway of demagogues accursed, we throw away the richest heritage that God ever gave to man, blot out our fair escutcheon to all coming time, deliver down our names to be accursed, teach despots that freedom is but a dream, quench its fair light wherever it may dawn, and bid the lovers of mankind despair?*[95]

The party stressed its devotion to the Founding Fathers and added that it was an umbrella for all. In one of its first statements sent to newspapers, party officials proclaimed that "our ticket gives no offense, it contains no offense." They vowed that Bell and Everett were middle-of-the-roaders, a "household ticket," and that "the best days of America are once more dawning."[96]

Party speakers all over America reminded voters that Bell and Everett could pull together again the warring factions of party and nation, split between "the dizzy heights of antislavery fanaticism on one hand and the deep sea of (the Democrats) on the other."[97]

Bell reminded all that "this must be the party of the country, of the Union, of the Constitution."[98]

There was also much praise for the popular Everett. When he died several years later, he would become one of the few non-presidents whose passing was honored by flags flown at half-staff across the nation and the complete shutdown of all government offices.

"Edward Everett is at this moment better known throughout the length and breadth of this land than any other living being at this good hour," said delegate John Watson of Mississippi.[99]

Party workers organized their ratification meeting outdoors, in Baltimore's Monument Square. Within hours, they managed to build a large stage anchored with four high towers from which draped likenesses of John Bell, Edward Everett, George Washington, and Henry Clay. American flags hung everywhere. A nighttime rally featured a long series of speeches interrupted by patriotic songs by an orchestra put together in just a single day. Pamphlets were printed and distributed, donations begged, and thousands of hands shaken by the candidates. Hundreds of lamps and torches, strung from the sides of buildings and lampposts, illuminated the square. It proved that these men not only could give memorable speeches, but that they were effective politicians who could get things done. This was no patriotic picnic they planned for John Bell. This was a full-scale national campaign that would be just as effective as those mounted by the Democrats and the Republicans. They meant business.[100]

They had one large advantage that the Democrats and Republicans did not. As a newly created third party, they did not have to win the election outright. All they had to do was get Bell enough states to prevent Seward or Douglas from winning the presidency in the electoral college and throw the contest into the House of Representatives, where anything could happen.

★ CHAPTER 5 ★

A Great Speaker
Is Born

There is not much of me...

—ABRAHAM LINCOLN ON WHY HIS BIOGRAPHY

WAS SO SHORT

Abraham Lincoln, whose first efforts at public speaking in 1832 were awkward, had become a much better orator over the years. Lincoln usually started off poorly. His prodigious height and reedy voice often surprised crowds that gathered to listen, as did his ungainly physical appearance and badly tailored suits. The Republican had a normal-sized trunk but exceptionally long legs and arms and huge feet. He had high cheekbones that accentuated his ordinary face and hair that was never properly combed. Law partner William Herndon said he "was not a pretty man by any means."[101]

One man who met Lincoln said that "he was as rough a specimen of humanity as could be found."[102] Others were alarmed at his initial morose appearance. He had, one woman said, "the saddest face you ever saw." One man said, "His body seemed a huge skeleton in clothes."[103]

Even his friends did not think him much of a politician in those early years. Law partner Ward Hill Lamon said of him, "He looked about as unpromising a candidate as I could well imagine the American people were ever likely to put forward."[104]

He tended to stretch his body and move his arms about at the start of many speeches. He began his speeches with a distinct midwestern twang, using the words "meester" for "mister, "waal" for "well," and "git" for "get." A reporter for the *New York Tribune* was amused when he first covered one of Lincoln's speeches and wrote that "the tones, the gestures, the kindling eye, and the mirth-provoking look defy the reporter's skill."[105] Another reporter wrote of "a shrug of the shoulder, an elevation of his eyebrows, a depression of his mouth, and a general malformation of countenance so comically awkward that it never fails to bring down the house."[106] Another writer said that his walk was a cross between a derrick and a windmill.

But within ten minutes, the logic and power of what he was saying took peoples' attention away from his appearance.[107] An audience that listens to a speaker for any length of time, especially for over an hour, adjusts itself to the tone of his voice so that after a while it seems familiar. Even people who started by laughing at him finished admiring him.

One man at a rally wrote:

Lincoln is the leanest, lankest, most ungainly mass of legs and arms and hatchet face ever strung on a single frame...ugly. And when he unfolds his everlasting legs and arms and rises to speak, his unique countenance, expressive of the most complete equanimity, the auditor will feel inclined to beat a most precipitate retreat. But a few moments dispel the illusion and he finds himself listening early to a most profound and concise reasoner...(with) flashes of genuine wit.[108]

Lincoln spoke as often as he could and by 1840 was delivering dozens of speeches each year. Politics in the nineteenth century was entertainment. Political campaigns were eagerly anticipated as a diversion. Thousands of people would turn out to listen to different candidates—local, state, and congressional—when they arrived in town to "stump," or campaign, for office. Several local speakers appeared first and then the candidate would talk for between one and three hours. Speeches were preceded or followed by marches and picnics. Evening speeches were accompanied by torchlight parades. Huge bonfires would light the meadows or town squares where speakers addressed crowds. Each party had a campaign theme song, such as the Republicans' ditty, "Ain't You Glad You Joined the Republicans," which was sung as thousands of people marched in political processions. Huge banners and posters with illustrations of the candidates' likenesses dotted towns and cities. A rally was an all-night event, designed to be as amusing for the masses as it was intended to be an educational forum about the issues of the day.[109] Given that spectacle context and the need for speakers who would please the crowds with different kinds of speeches, orators like Lincoln offered folksy narratives and humor as well as fire-and-brimstone politics and were very popular.

Lincoln was much in demand on the stump, where he gave speeches for other Whigs and, later, Republicans. He drew large audiences. Lincoln had improved as a speaker, and all recognized it. A reporter who heard him in 1856 wrote:

> *For an hour he held the assemblage spellbound by the power of his argument, the intense eloquence. When he concluded, the audience sprang to their feet and cheer after cheer told how deeply their hearts had been touched, and their souls warmed up to a generous enthusiasm.*

Stephen Douglas called him the best stump speaker the Republicans had. Another reporter wrote of a Lincoln speech that "all the strings that play upon the human heart and understanding were touched with masterly skill and force, while beyond and above all skill was the overwhelming conviction pressed upon the audience that the speaker himself was charged with an irresistible and inspirational duty to his fellow man."[110]

Later, William Jennings Bryan said that "Lincoln's power as a public speaker was the foundation of his success."[111] Longtime friend Elihu Washburne, now a Republican congressman from Illinois and chairman of the Republicans' 1860 Congressional Campaign Committee but earlier a man who served in Congress with Lincoln as a Whig, said he was "the most effective stump speaker I ever listened to."[112]

John Nicolay, one of his secretaries after the election, said that photographers never captured the magic that he displayed at rallies. He wrote that Lincoln had a face "that moved through a thousand delicate gradations of line and contour, light and shade, sparkle of the eyes, and curve of the lip, in the long gamut of expression from grave to gay and back again, from the rollicking jollity of laughter to that serious, far away look."[113] He was not ungainly for his height, according to Nicolay. He wrote that Lincoln's walk was "vigorous, elastic, easy rather quick, firm, dignified, no shuffling or hesitating."[114]

A woman wrote that he had "patient, loving eyes…(they) lay in deep caverns, waiting to spring out at an instant call," and a man added that when Lincoln was talking to people, his "melancholy shadows disappeared in a twinkling."[115]

Lincoln spoke with great fervor against slavery and laced his talks with humorous stories to denigrate the opposing candidates. He said of Douglas that, as a young man, he often sold whiskey to Douglas, who drank it happily. Now, though, he did not sell whiskey any more, but Douglas still drank it happily. At other times, he drew laughs with stories with himself as the butt of the punch line.[116]

His funny stories served two purposes. First, they put his audiences at ease. He made them feel comfortable as they laughed. They were then ready for the message he wanted to deliver. Second, the stories put him at ease too. One reporter who covered him said that when he started his string of tall tales, his entire manner of speaking changed. He wrote, "His body straightened up, his countenance brightened, his language became free and animated."[117]

Many of Lincoln's tales had phrases that became part of the national language, such as "Don't swap horses in the middle of a stream," and, about defeat, "I'm too young to admit that it doesn't hurt and too old to cry." And of course, there was "You can fool all of the people some of the time and some of the people all of the time, but you can't fool all of the people all of the time."

He did not develop his own stories but wrote down ones he heard. He changed the characters or dialogue and presented them as his own version. He was also a voracious reader of newspapers and magazines and clipped out jokes and funny stories and kept them in his files. He was as organized about his humorous stories as he was about his politics.[118]

He used them primarily to make political points, but he also employed them to connect himself to the people in his audiences. He had the ability to not only tell a funny story but to reach all of the people listening, chuckling with them, making them equal to him and him equal to them. The stories helped sew together the idea of Abraham Lincoln as a man of the people, not just another politician looking for a vote.

There was gentle humor in some of his descriptions of political opponents too. Of nonstop talkers he said, "A longwinded man could compress the most words into the smallest ideas of any man he knew."[119]

There was always the touch of the "old prophet" in him, though, and on occasion it carried him to political heights. One of his best speeches, in 1838, mesmerized listeners with its imagery when he talked of the power of Americans to stand their ground. He said, "All the armies of Europe, Asia, and Africa combined, with all the treasure of the earth…in their military chest, with a Bonaparte for a commander, could not by force, take a drink from the Ohio, or make a track on the Blue Ridge mountains, in a trial of a thousand years."[120]

His enemies feared him. When he and Douglas agreed to their debates in 1858, a friend of the Little Giant told him that he would win easily. Douglas nodded negatively and told him he was wrong, that "Abe Lincoln is the most dangerous man in America to debate."

His oratory helped bring many into the Republican ranks. James Putnam, of Buffalo, New York, was one. He was a leader of the American Party in the late 1850s but switched to the Republicans because of Lincoln. He wrote to Leonard Swett, "Do you know, Swett, I think him (Lincoln) one of the most remarkable speakers of English living. In all that constitutes logical eloquence, straightforwardness, clearness of statement, sincerity that commands your admiration…strength of argument…he is infinitely superior to Douglas."[121]

Other politicians soon realized that the prairie lawyer made a favorable impression on crowds and that their candidates won when Abe Lincoln spoke for them. Local newspapers enjoyed his mix of humor and politics and enjoyed his speaking style.

And people liked him. One reporter from Ohio toured different towns in Illinois and wrote, "I find that there is not a man in the region who says a word against the honesty of Abraham Lincoln. They like his sociability and his familiarity. He is so universally regarded as a plain, unassuming man, possessing strong common sense, wedded to a quickness of perception that detects the right from the wrong."[122]

Another reporter wrote in 1848, "He spoke in a clear and cool, and very eloquent manner, for an hour and a half, carrying the audience with him in his able arguments and brilliant illustrations, interrupted by warm and frequent applause."[123]

Lincoln was invited to hundreds of towns and cities to give speeches from 1840 to 1860. In 1840, when he was campaigning for reelection to the state legislature and also as a presidential elector, he took on Douglas in speeches all over the state.[124]

Lincoln enjoyed the stump and gave as many speeches in as many places as he could in an effort to make himself better known, chalk up debts from different politicians, and to show everyone that he was a staunch party man. He made over sixty speeches in 1854, most denouncing the Kansas-Nebraska bill. In 1856, when the Republicans asked him to campaign for presidential nominee John Frémont, Lincoln made over fifty speeches, mostly in central and southern Illinois, where locals introduced him, ironically, as a Southerner because he had been born in nearby Kentucky.[125]

Throughout his campaign swings in 1856, he appealed to independent voters to attach themselves to the Republicans and not to waste their vote for a third-party candidate (the American Party's Fillmore), who could not win. He tested his policies on the stump, too, fine-tuning his approach to issues such as slavery, high tariffs to protect American workers, which he promoted as early as 1844, and better conditions for laborers of any kind, which he was espousing in the early 1840s.

And he made certain that he remembered the names of just about everybody he met in every town where he spoke. He not only recalled names but also people's jobs, political offices, philosophical leanings, and sometimes, even which seat they occupied at a dinner he attended. As president, he once named all of the guests at a dinner party he attended in

Worcester, Massachusetts, fourteen years earlier. This incredible memory enabled him to make fast friends all over the country, friends who would work for him and his causes later.

The year 1858 was his busiest as a campaign speaker. He won his party's nomination for the U.S. Senate and gave dozens of speeches throughout the state, highlighted by his seven famous debates with Douglas. The debates drew an average of close to 10,000 people, with a low of 1,000 and a high of 20,000. He used those debates, like he used all of his public appearances, to build himself up and force his political opponents to confront the issues he raised.

He started that 1858 Senate campaign with his historic House Divided speech, delivered when he accepted the party nomination. In it, he told the men in the hall, and newspaper readers all over America, that a house divided against itself could not stand. "I believe this government cannot endure, permanently half slave and half free. I do not expect the Union to be dissolved—I do not expect the house to fall—but I do expect it will cease to be divided," he told the crowd. "It will become all one thing or all the other."

He was a shrewd politician who was always working on strategy. He planned to ambush Douglas in their debate at Freeport by getting him to acknowledge, as he did, that although he was for slavery if the residents of Kansas and Nebraska voted for it, he was also against it if they voted it down. Lincoln's aides argued that it set up Douglas to denounce slavery and win the Senate race in predominantly antislavery Illinois. "True," Lincoln answered, "but I am killing larger game. If Douglas answers, he can never be president, and the battle of 1860 is worth a hundred of this."[126]

Lincoln did lose the Senate seat to Douglas in the vote of the state legislature, but his defeat of Douglas in the popular vote by 4,500 votes convinced him that events were moving rapidly and that Douglas, whom he always thought invincible, could be beaten in a presidential race. Lincoln had always seen himself as the caboose to Douglas' mighty train, from his first days in the state legislature to his years in Congress to his chilly days on the campaign trail. Douglas was a man from his own town who constantly dwarfed him in stature and success. Life had been glorious for Douglas and difficult for him, Lincoln believed.

He wrote of peoples' view of Douglas:

> *They have seen in his round, jolly, fruitful face in post offices, land offices, marshalships, cabinet appointments, and foreign missions, bursting and sprouting out, in wonderful luxuriance, ready to be laid hold of by their greedy hands. And as they have been gazing upon this attractive picture so long, they cannot, in the little distraction that has taken place in the party, bring themselves to live up to the charming hope; but with greedier anxiety they rush about him, sustain him, and give him marches, triumphal entries, and receptions, beyond what, even in the days of his highest prosperity, they could have brought about in his favor. On the contrary, nobody has ever expected me to be the president. In my poor, lean, lank face nobody has ever seen that any cabbages were sprouting out.*[127]

When he beat Douglas in the popular vote in the 1858 Senate race, Abraham Lincoln was finally free to fulfill his ambitions. The chains fell to the ground. He no longer had a deep, inner foreboding that Stephen Douglas would always somehow stop him.[128]

Lincoln's defeat in the race against Douglas disappointed him because he was still without public office, but it did not slow him down. The Douglas debates, which had extensive press coverage, had made him a minor national figure, and requests for him to campaign for candidates around the nation poured in.

The most appealing invitation came from the Ohio Republican Party, which wanted him to counter speeches Douglas planned to make in that state. It was a chance to gain exposure in another state where Republicans were doing very well, to go head to head with Douglas once more (although he spoke a day or two after Douglas had been to each town), and as always, to meet people who might help him later.[129]

James Blaine of Maine attended one of the Lincoln-Douglas debates in 1858. Blaine, a congressman, was very impressed by Lincoln, and two years later, as a delegate to the Republican convention, he talked Maine Governor Lot Morrill, a Lincoln supporter, into delivering the entire Maine vote to Lincoln.[130]

During his September 1859 trip to Dayton, Ohio, Lincoln met a number of local politicians after his effective speech, which, as usual, drew a large crowd. More than eighteen months later, he received a letter from Edwin Parrott, one of the state legislators he helped elect on that trip, urging him to run for president.

The Ohio Republicans were so impressed by Lincoln's speeches for the party and his character that after he left, they published his orations in newspapers throughout the state.[131]

After that campaign swing, he accepted four invitations to speak in Wisconsin and then a half dozen to talk in Illinois. In December 1859 he was off to Kansas to campaign for Republican candidates running in territorial contests. Lincoln had barely unpacked his bags when the invitation to speak in New York, at Cooper Union, arrived in the mail. Following Cooper Union, he made twelve more speeches in a thirteen-day trip through New England.

Reporters present at his speeches said his themes were uniform. He wanted to hold the Union together no matter how much pressure was brought to bear on its sturdiness by the secessionists. He held that line from the first days that he began speaking in public. He never let questions about secessionists deflect him from that core belief in his speeches; he ignored the Southern sympathizers.[132]

He was famous for speaking out against slavery with a rare combination of eloquence and ferocity. He saw slavery expanding to all of the United States if not stopped right away. He said in 1859:

> *When this is done (slavery in the territories), the miners and sappers will have formed public opinion for the slave trade. They will be ready for Jeff Davis and (Alexander) Stephens and other leaders of that company, to sound the bugle for the revival of the slave trade, for the second Dred Scott decision, for the flood of slavery to be poured over the free states, while we shall be here tied down and helpless and run over like sheep.*[133]

He despised slavery. Lincoln said:

> *I hate it because of the monstrous injustice of slavery itself. I hate it because it deprives our republican example of its just influence in the world—enables the enemies of free institutions, with plausibility, to taunt us as hypocrites—causes the real friends of freedom to doubt our sincerity, and especially because it forces so many really good men amongst ourselves into an open war with the very fundamental principles of civil liberty—criticizing the Declaration of Independence, and insisting that there is no right principle of action but self-interest.*[134]

He was always careful to remind audiences that he did not think blacks better than whites, and he always noted that he believed the two races could not live together, side by side, because of physical differences. But he insisted that they had the same rights. Lincoln said, "He (Negro) is not my equal in many respects.... But in the right to eat the bread, without the leave of anybody else, which his own hand earns, he is my equal, and the equal of Judge Douglas and every living man."[135]

Again and again, he reminded audiences wherever he found them that while he was for equality for slaves someday, he was also a champion of the white workers. In 1836, when he was just twenty-seven years old, he ran for reelection to the state assembly and wrote a newspaper that "I go for admitting all whites to the right of suffrage who pay taxes or bear arms." He said in 1859, when he was fifty, "It is well known that I deplore the oppressed condition of the blacks; and it would, therefore, be very inconsistent for me to look with approval upon any measures that infringe upon the inalienable rights of white men."[136]

Lincoln courted the press and was fond of journalists, such as Henry Villard, who found him driving a buggy across a cold Missouri plain. He was just one of hundreds of editors and reporters who got to know Abe Lincoln during his life. Lincoln was a journalist himself, in the 1830s, when, to save money, the *Sangamon Journal* hired its state representative, Lincoln, to cover the legislature. He owned a newspaper, too, in Springfield, a German journal, during the year before his election. His two personal secretaries, the men who ran the White House for him, John Nicolay and John Hay, were both former reporters. So were Charles Ray and Joe Medill, of the *Chicago Press and Tribune*, who became operatives for him at the Republican convention in 1860. His secretary of the navy was Gideon Welles, editor of the *Hartford Press*.

Lincoln openly promoted himself to newspapers, frequently sending them articles about current issues and urging them to publish them.[137] He coaxed friends who were friendly with newspaper editors to use their influence to get the papers to write favorable stories about him. He stopped to talk to reporters and editors wherever he went, always looking for favorable coverage or, at least, some mention of his views. Whenever he was in a city to speak, he would stop off at the local newspaper office to say hello. He took newsmen into his confidence, showing them advance copies of speeches and asking their advice. He often finished a speech and then, a few hours later, walked over to the local newspaper office and asked the reporter covering it for his opinion.[138] In New York, he went to the offices of the *New York Herald* the night of his Cooper Union speech and was given a tour of the newsroom. He made sure he shook hands with everyone. Many people who passed through Chicago later remember meeting him relaxing at one of the desks in the main newsroom of the *Chicago Press and Tribune*, where he had many friends among the reporters and editors. He kept in touch with reporters and editors he met via letters.

The newspapers of the 1850s and 1860s were owned and run by opposing political parties, and Lincoln made every effort, in person or by letter, to get his views and political endorsements out to their editors. Newspapers were important. The creation of the Associated Press and completion of many telegraph lines by the mid-1850s meant that stories from Illinois that formerly took a week to reach New York now made it in minutes. New technology and the increase in railroad lines enabled large New York newspapers, such as Horace Greeley's *New York Tribune*, to reach a national readership, selling thousands of copies in various states beyond New York (the *Tribune* published a New York City edition and a thinner national edition. The national edition's circulation in Illinois alone in 1860 was nearly 10,000. It was 5,000 in nearby Wisconsin.[139]) The more editors and reporters Lincoln met and befriended on his various speaking tours meant the chance for increased coverage of his work.

It was through the press that he advanced his views to the public. He was certainly not as well known as William Seward, Stephen Douglas, or a dozen other men in 1860, but his activities did gain him notoriety in the spring of 1860 when the Republican convention convened in Chicago and the Democrats met in Charleston. He had worked hard at press relations and struggled mightily to become the best known has-been in politics.

CHAPTER 6

The Underdog Rail-Splitter Versus the Firebrand Senator

I think slavery is wrong, morally and politically. I desire that it should be no further spread in these United States and I should not object if it should gradually terminate in the whole Union.

—ABRAHAM LINCOLN

Chicago was the fastest growing city in the United States on May 16, 1860, the first day of the Republican convention. The skies had cleared after a rainstorm soaked the town the night before. The city was the perfect symbol of the burgeoning northwest region of Illinois, Indiana, Michigan, Wisconsin, Minnesota, and Iowa, where populations had doubled, tripled, and quadrupled since 1850. A small lakeside community as late as 1832 with a population of 150 people and an annual tax rate of $48, Chicago had exploded in size over the past thirty years. Sitting snugly on the southern shore of vast Lake Michigan, Chicago was the heart of the enormously profitable and ever-growing Great Lakes shipping industry. It was the hub of the expanding railroad systems that were beginning to crisscross

America. Its railroad men and politicians were campaigning hard for a transcontinental railroad, out of Chicago, which would connect California and the West Coast states and territories to the rest of the country.

Chicago's population had increased to nearly 112,000 by 1860, making it one of the largest cities in America.[140] Its several newspapers battled each other for circulation. The city had a busy theater district, over a dozen amateur baseball teams whose games drew good crowds, thriving factories, attractive parks, long sandy beaches on the shore of Lake Michigan, and more than forty large, luxurious hotels. And everyone, it seemed, was eager for the Republican National Convention. The city's hotels ($2.50 a day for the opulent ones) were jammed, and political rallies were held every day and every night. There were ceremonies of some kind everywhere that delegates roamed. The city sponsored parades for the Republicans, bars offered cut-rate drinks, and hundreds of people milled about the city's train stations to greet the arriving delegates. Red, white, and blue bunting seemed to hang off every building on the wide vistas of Michigan Avenue, which ran parallel to Lake Michigan. Chicago had turned itself into a carnival for the Republican Party. Huge banners were strung over the busiest streets, flags hung from the fronts of stores and homes, transportation omnibuses were covered with bunting, dozens of small cannons fired throughout the day from different locations, and large crowds of colorfully dressed residents staged parades down different avenues.[141]

The overwhelming favorite for the Republican presidential nomination in 1860 was New York Senator William Seward, a firebrand antislavery radical who had inflamed the nation with his "Higher Law" and "Irrepressible Conflict" speeches, which argued that the laws of God overrode any decision of the U.S. Supreme Court or Congress on slavery. A newspaper straw poll of all the delegates arriving in Chicago showed him to be the clear choice.[142]

Seward was one of the nation's most experienced and respected public officials. His stellar career began when, just twenty-nine years old, he was elected to the state senate in New York on the Anti-Mason Party ticket. He became a Whig in 1834 and ran for governor of New York and lost. Then, in 1839, at the age of thirty-eight, he was elected governor and served two terms. As governor, he thwarted several Southern states trying to recover runaway slaves and passed stringent antislavery laws for New York. By 1840, he had become one of the earliest, and most influential, opponents of slavery in the North. He retired in 1843 and became wealthy practicing law. The Whigs persuaded him to run for the U.S. Senate in 1849. He was elected and, a year later, delivered his famous "Higher Law" speech in the Senate, which made him the darling of the abolitionists all over the North.[143] He made his dramatic "Irrepressible Conflict" speech while campaigning to elect Edwin Morgan as New York's governor in 1858.[144]

That speech ended dramatically. He told the huge crowd that overflowed an indoor arena in Rochester, New York:

> *A revolution has begun. I know, and all the world knows, that revolutions never go backward.... While the government of the United States, under the conduct of the Democratic Party, has been all that time surrendering one plain and castle after another to slavery, the people of the United States have been no less steadily and perseveringly gathering together the forces with which to recover back again all the fields and all the castles which have been lost, and to confound and overthrow, by one decisive blow, the betrayers of the Constitution and freedom forever.[145]*

The speech encouraged antislavery crowds but inflamed Southerners against him. Newspapers all over the nation carried copies of it in their pages, and people debated it for months.

Seward switched to the Republicans in 1855 as the Whig Party decayed in New York. He became more famous as a Republican than he had been as a Whig, quickly assumed party leadership roles, and was considered the leading contender for the presidency in 1856. The party sought a compromise candidate, one who could win votes in the West, though, and nominated John C. Frémont.

Seward did not protest. His close friend and longtime campaign manager, Thurlow Weed, warned him that the Republican Party was not strong enough to carry a national election yet and that their nominee would lose. Weed told Seward that he would be better off waiting four more years. Frémont lost.

Weed had never been wrong. He and Seward met when Seward entered the state legislature and they became close friends. No one admired Seward more than Weed. He said the senator had "unmistakable evidences of stern integrity, earnest patriotism, and unswerving fidelity. I saw also in him a rare capacity for intellectual labor, with an industry which never tired and required no relaxation, to which was added a purity and delicacy of habit."[146]

George Baker, an adviser of Seward's, said Weed was "the greatest politician this country ever knew." This was high praise for the monarchial Weed, whose friends, in deference, called him "Lord Thurlow."[147]

Seward continued to gather support for national office and by 1860 was the front-runner. He was a radical on slavery; had thousands of political connections; was a veteran lawmaker, a brilliant speaker, experienced campaigner; and was known everywhere. He also had Weed, the brilliant political boss of New York State, as his mentor. The pair had virtually unlimited access to campaign funds. Seward also controlled New York, the biggest state in both convention and electoral college votes. As a New Yorker, he could easily carry the delegations from the nearby New England and mid-Atlantic states.

His supporters were legion. Marcus Ward, a New Jersey political boss, distributed hundreds of copies of Seward's famed "Higher Law" and "Irrepressible Conflict" speeches to delegates at the convention. Ward wrote Seward, "The ('Higher Law') speech has done a world of good, not only to you, but to the country."[148]

The speech reminded everyone that the Republicans were unified in their opposition to slavery. It gave the new party a signature issue and a moral mandate that made it unique. Carl Schurz said, "There has never been in the history of this republic a political movement (Republicans) in which the moral motive was so strong." A twentieth-century political scientist agreed. "The party is like a band of brothers, crusading together for righteousness and against evil," wrote James Sundquist.[149]

Horace Greeley and his powerful *New York Tribune* newspaper were longtime enemies of Seward, and the senator feared Greeley would turn delegates against him. His political aides, who despised Greeley, told him not to worry. Weed wrote him on the eve of the convention, "The sentiment of the people is right, and reliable" and reminded the senator that he was bringing thirteen railroad cars full of supporters to Chicago with him. They brought their own band, whose musicians played the Seward theme song, "Oh, Isn't He a Darling" wherever it found a crowd to listen to them.[150]

Seward received letters of unflagging support from every state. M. L. Hull, an Indiana politician, who slid in a plug for Lincoln as his running mate, wrote Seward, "You will carry the state (Indiana). I have stumped portions of the state several times and most of it twice as an elector.... If (you) can burst the hands of the conservatives we should have a glorious triumph for you and Lincoln."[151]

Others told Seward that his radical views were no longer a liability because of the Democratic Party collapse that had started at their Charleston convention. Henry Brewster Stanton wrote him that "the only check was the fear in some quarters that Seward could not be elected. But Charleston has cleared the track and now we want to get William H. Seward on and put him through."[152]

The Republicans had told Americans for six years that they wanted to stop any movement of slavery into the new territories and were unhappy with it in the Southern states, although they saw no reason to eliminate it there. No one had espoused that limited-slavery view more than the New York senator.

Seward looked presidential. He was a handsome man with refined manners, about five feet eight inches tall, thin, with narrow shoulders. There was a gracefulness to his physical movement; everything seemed easy for him. Seward had bushy eyebrows over blue-gray eyes. His pronounced, hawklike nose anchored his face. Seward was one of the best-dressed public officials in the country, favoring the latest expensive suits from New York City stores. In the spring of 1860, Seward was poised to accept the Republican nomination for president.[153] In fact, reporters covering the convention were so sure of his selection that one wrote, "Seward feeling tonight runs like a spring flood."[154]

Salmon Chase, the governor of Ohio, was another contender. The tall, bearded, barrel-chested Chase, who had graduated from Dartmouth College at the age of eighteen, had become a lawyer and staunch abolitionist by 1836. As an attorney, he represented numerous runaway slaves who had fled to Ohio. He was one of the founders of the Liberty Party and, later, a founder of the Free Soil Party. He was elected to the U.S. Senate as a Free Soiler–Independent Democrat in 1849 and served there until 1855, when he switched parties and was elected the first Republican governor of Ohio. An efficient and intelligent administrator and fiscal wunderkind, he had support from virtually every county in Ohio and had a broad-based organization. Only Seward had more governmental experience than Chase and enjoyed as great an antislavery reputation.[155] Politically, Chase controlled Ohio, one of the Big Three (New York and Pennsylvania were the others) in the electoral college, and he could count on support from all the antislavery delegates in the country. He was certain he could win the nomination, even though all of the delegates in his own state were not behind him, and he did not relinquish that dream until the balloting was under way.[156]

Edward Bates, an antislavery moderate, was a congressman from Missouri, a border state. He was a former Whig and American Party leader. Many saw him as a candidate from the border states who could win in Missouri, Maryland, and Kentucky, as well as in the North. His supporters also saw him as a moderate president who could keep the country together. Bates was extremely popular among the delegates opposed to Seward.

Simon Cameron, the U.S. senator from Pennsylvania from 1845 to 1849 was a Democrat–Whig, and from 1857 to 1860 he was a Republican (his election brought on charges of bribery). Cameron was a wealthy industrialist and former newspaper editor who served as an all-powerful political boss in his state, capable of delivering votes and money at will. He was hopeful that Seward could be stopped and that the party would nominate him. He could bring a huge war chest, whose funds would be divided among numerous congressional candidates. He had friends in the media, and he was as equally well connected as Seward to voters up and down the Atlantic Coast.

There were a dozen other candidates with smaller chances, including Illinois' Abraham Lincoln. He was so obscure when the convention began, despite the notoriety he had achieved in his debates with Douglas in the 1858 Senate race and his many speaking tours in different states, that many newspapers printed his name as "Abram" Lincoln. One newspaper poll rating the chances of the top twenty-one candidates did not even include him.[157] Lincoln's detractors gave him little chance. He had not held an important public office in over eleven years and had lost two Senate races in that time. He had no national campaign experience, no contacts in the important eastern seaboard states, and no financial war chest. Unlike Seward, who had the nationally famous political leader Weed as his campaign manager, Lincoln was represented by a small group of unknown judges, lawyers, and newspapermen—Judge David Davis, Leonard Swett, Norman Judd, Jesse Dubois, Charles Ray, and Joe Medill—who had twice failed to elect him to the U.S. Senate and had no political connections outside of Illinois.[158]

They represented a candidate whom many believed could not win any delegations except his own state of Illinois (twenty-two votes) and perhaps pick up a few votes in Indiana. Even delegates who voted for him had their doubts that he could win the election. They worried about putting their faith in the hands of "the Illinois lawyer."[159]

Lincoln's campaign team arrived nearly a week before the convention began and registered at the completely sold-out Tremont House Hotel, one of the biggest and best in Chicago. They were led by the portly, bearded Judge Davis, a friend of Lincoln's for more than twenty years. The team also included Richard Yates, Republican candidate for governor of Illinois, Stephen Logan, Ozias Hatch, Orville Browning, state senator John Palmer, state treasurer William Butler, Jackson Grimshaw, Burt Cook, and German American political leader Gustave Koerner, a lawyer from Belleville, Illinois.

They were an untested team of country amateurs prepared to battle the legendary political team of Weed and Seward.[160]

They began to manipulate the convention before the delegates even arrived. The decision to hold the convention in Chicago instead of another city was reached by a single vote on the national committee—the vote of Norman Judd. He argued that if the convention was held in New York, the nation would think it would nominate Seward and that if it was held in Philadelphia, Cleveland, or St. Louis, it would select Cameron, Chase, or Bates. After all, Judd sheepishly pointed out, there was no possible candidate from Illinois who could be nominated. Chicago, in the middle of the country, he argued, would be a neutral ground for the party and would show the nation that it represented all the people.[161] It was his idea to have the party build the Wigwam, the enormous, rectangular, two-story-high, 10,000-seat wooden structure at the corner of Lake and Market streets, the largest indoor arena in the nation, just for the convention (and smaller wigwams for other state conventions). Judd had moved to Illinois from the East, served as a state senator, and was considered "the shrewdest politician…in the state" by Lincoln's friend Lyman Trumbull.[162]

Lincoln's men were convinced that their man's best chance—his only chance—was in his home territory. It was the first move in one of the most masterfully run nomination drives in the history of American politics, a campaign that showed the shrewdness of Lincoln and the hard work and political savvy of his aides, who worked hard for everything and were not the recipients of anything.

Lincoln, like the other candidates, observed the protocol of the time and did not attend the convention, leaving his nomination in the capable hands of Judge Davis, who saw this as his final chance to let the world know of the humanity and decency of his best friend, Abe Lincoln. Davis was a circuit court judge in the northwest area of Illinois when he first met Lincoln. They had become close companions, dining at each other's home and corresponding regularly. Politically, they were twins, favoring antislavery laws, the admission of Kansas as a free state, and homestead acts (often defeated by the Democrats in Congress). Davis even had Lincoln substitute for him on the bench when illness or weather prevented him from putting on his judicial robes.

Judge Davis, a calculating deal maker, labored mightily to get Lincoln elected to the Senate in 1855 but had to leave during the final day of balloting in the state legislature. Without Davis to cut deals with the lawmakers, Lincoln lost. Davis was extremely upset and blamed himself. Three years later, he helped organize Lincoln's brilliant Senate campaign against Douglas, but again was away on the judicial circuit during the critical last days of the campaign. Lincoln lost and again Davis blamed himself. This time, in the summer of 1860, Judge Davis vowed that Lincoln would not lose again. He would toil tirelessly, day and night, to make Abe Lincoln the president of the United States, despite the forces arrayed against him. His friend Jesse Dubois wrote Lincoln from the hotel: "Judge Davis is furious. Never saw him work so hard and so quiet in all my life."[163]

Davis, Swett, Judd, Dubois, Medill, and the others began their crusade on the first day of the convention, carefully working with the seating committee to separate the pro-Seward New York and pro-Cameron Pennsylvania delegations by a crowd of pro-Lincoln delegates. This would enable Davis to make certain the pro-Lincoln people flooded the aisles on cue to prevent the Seward people from running to the Cameron people for help when the balloting began. Davis also knew that the delegates from those two states had been feuding with each other ever since their arrival in Chicago.[164]

Judd, chairman of the Illinois State Republican Committee, was a short, balding, heavyset, bearded man. He had great influence with the *Chicago Press and Tribune*, lobbied with editors there to run pro-Lincoln editorials every day the convention was in session and to have newspapers delivered to every delegate hotel.[165] Each morning the newspaper they would read at breakfast would shout the name of Abraham Lincoln at them. Judd also used his contacts as the official attorney for a railroad to have the railroad transport thousands of Lincoln supporters to Chicago from all over the Midwest—free of charge.[166] Copies of both Lincoln's Cooper Union speech, reprinted in numerous newspapers and in a widely circulated pamphlet, and the complete transcription of his debates with Stephen Douglas in the 1858 Senate race, in book form, were distributed to delegates throughout Chicago.[167] The offices of the pro-Lincoln *Chicago Press and Tribune* were decorated with hundreds of fence rails to underscore Lincoln's nickname, "the Rail-Splitter."[168]

At night, the campaign team went to work. They realized Lincoln was an underdog—so did he—and knew they needed a cleverly designed marketing campaign to win the nomination for him.[169] Their pitch to the delegates was simple: Seward, Bates, Chase, and Cameron have many strengths, but they have many weaknesses too. Lincoln has strengths that you are unaware of. Let us tell you about them.

They outlined the presidential campaign in stark terms: The nation has been divided into North and South by slavery. The Republicans will never win in the South. They could win in the North, which has far more electoral votes than the South, but to do so they had to win close contests in every state. The key states were New York, Pennsylvania, Indiana, and Illinois, all of which Frémont failed to capture in 1856 (Illinois party leader Lincoln chose all the at-large delegates to the 1860 convention from his state, making certain that all of the Illinois vote went to him).[170] The Republicans needed 152 of the nation's 303 electoral votes to win the presidency. Frémont won 114 in the last election. If the party could hold those 114, all in the North, and add just New York, Pennsylvania, Illinois, and Indiana, it could reach 165 and win.

Davis told each delegation he spoke to the same thing: Seward is too radical on slavery and cannot win the moderate votes of Republicans or Democrats or the supporters of the barely alive American Party that ran Millard Fillmore in 1856. He will never capture the agrarian southern counties of Pennsylvania, Indiana, or Illinois, all adjacent to slave states where residents had relatives and business partners and where Democrat James Buchanan ran strong in 1856. He argued, effectively, that although most Northerners were adamantly opposed to slavery, many were opposed to complete equality for blacks. Most Northern states had laws that forbade black freedmen from living in certain sections of cities, shopping in particular stores, and attending white-only theaters. Freedom might be all right, but black-white equality was not. A radical such as Seward would be too unsettling for most moderate voters, the majority, even if they were against slavery.[171]

Seward was so hated in the South that after John Brown's attack on Harpers Ferry the previous year, a group of states' rights men offered a $50,000 reward "for the head of William Seward," whom they blamed the attack.[172]

Seward had no chance of winning any Southern state, they insisted, reminding the delegates how often Seward had criticized Southern states and how his acerbic tongue stung Southerners. In one jab, the New York senator said that the state of Virginia, the state all Southerners loved, "(had) exhausted soil, old and decaying towns, wretchedly neglected roads, and in every respect an absence of enterprise and improvement."[173]

Seward will lose the election, they insisted.[174]

They did not need to present much evidence. Most of the South had turned on Seward already, and congressional candidates from the 1859 elections reported much voter resistance to him. He had pleased the abolitionists by infuriating the slaveholders and moderates with his "Higher Law" speech in the Senate in 1850.[175] He did it again in 1858 in his Rochester "Irrepressible Conflict" speech when he was campaigning for the Republican nominee for governor.[176] Earlier, he said that "slavery must be abolished and you and I must do it."

Seward's long public career, which should have been a strength for him, turned out to be his greatest weakness. Thurlow Weed had also been accused of corruption in the 1859 legislative races in New York, and that hurt Seward because the Republicans had decided to make the corruption of the Buchanan administration a major issue in the 1860 presidential campaign. Despite virulent protests by Weed that he was innocent, many believed he had spread money around to ensure the election of Republicans. Seward was closely allied to Weed in New York. The charges hurt him.[177]

Seward would also have problems with the American Party supporters who had crossed over to march under the Republican banner in the late 1850s, particularly those in the lower counties of Pennsylvania. As a senator, he favored federal and state aid to Roman Catholic schools, an inflammatory issue with the anti-Catholic, anti-immigrant American Party members.

Seward also had problems getting along with anyone who disagreed with him. He saw criticism as "the malice of a thousand political assassins who undertake that job."[178]

He had division in his own state. Seward and Weed controlled the mainstream Republican Party, but newspaper editor Horace Greeley was a considerable foe of both. They split up in 1854 after Greeley wrote Seward a scathing letter in which he denounced and accused him of refusing to dispense patronage throughout the party, keeping it for his personal friends, and constantly lying to Greeley and others. He charged that Seward would declare his support for someone and then withdraw it. He did that to Greeley, the editor said, when Greeley wanted to run for governor. Greeley wrote, "Your consent was given, but instead of supporting me, you and your friends nominated that trimmer and little villain Henry Raymond (the editor of the *New York Times*), who is of no advantage to our party and a man whom to know is to detest."[179]

Greeley's letter angered many in the party and called into question once again the veracity of both Seward and Weed. If Seward had such enemies in his own state, what would happen if he was the nominee? If he won the election, would he renege on patronage promises once again, as he apparently did in 1854? The New York senator was well known all right...too well known.[180]

Lincoln's team found that many delegates they encountered had arrived in Chicago thinking the same thing about Seward. One, Richard Corwine of Ohio, told them that "we can not elect extreme men."[181] Greeley was dead set against any radical, telling delegates, "It is not yet time to nominate an abolitionist."[182] Just six months earlier, John Brown and his fanatical abolitionist followers had attacked the federal arsenal at Harpers Ferry, Virginia, earning the hatred of most Americans. This made it very difficult for many delegates to back the radical Seward.[183] Some did not care who was nominated, as long as he won. Fitz-Henry Warren said, "I am for the man who can carry Pennsylvania, New Jersey, and Indiana, with the observation that I will not go into cemetery or catacomb; the candidate must be alive, and able to walk, at least from parlor to dining room."[184]

Lurking in the back of their minds was the fear that Seward would lead the entire ticket to defeat. Lincoln man Swett said that "everybody who knows politicians knows that what they worship is the God of success."[185]

Chase had little support outside Ohio, the Lincoln people argued, and, like Seward, he was too close to the abolitionists. Cameron, they said, like Chase, was isolated in Pennsylvania. No one else wanted him (Cameron, though, from the first day of the convention, thought he could be a king-maker).[186] Bates, thought by so many to be the strongest candidate other than Seward, was painted as the weakest. After all, Davis told delegate after delegate, Bates was a former slave owner. He was a former American Party member who would never get the immigrant vote. He was a member of three different political parties in ten years and was politically unstable. Perhaps he could win the border states because he used to be a slaveholder, but he would lose every Northern state for that reason.

And finally, Judge Davis and his colleagues told the delegates that they lobbied, the best thing about all of the other candidates was the worst thing about all of them: they were longtime politicians and officeholders, pillars of the government. The American people in 1860 were sick and tired of politicians and were frustrated by the way the government handled the slavery crisis and by the corruption of the Buchanan administration. They were disgusted with years of politics-as-usual and the inability of career politicians, who cared about nothing except reelection, to address the changing needs of the people as the country rapidly expanded. The American people needed an outsider, someone fresh who could go to Washington and straighten things out with a new approach, an honest and decent man who could represent the growing middle class and the average American, a workingman, someone who had struggled and suffered like the average voter.

Lincoln's role as an outsider was one he himself had cultivated for years. In one letter he wrote that the country saw him as one side of the "ins and outs." As an outsider, he could attack the Democratic Party, the Buchanan administration, and any national issue because he had nothing to do with them. Other politicians, in office for years, could not denounce the government they helped run. Lincoln could attack whomever and whatever he wanted with no backlash. As an outsider who had not held national office for twelve years, he had no record that others could savage.

Finally, and most important as an outsider, Lincoln's strident antislavery speeches were not reported as widely as any of the key public officials of the day. He was far more radical on slavery than Seward in most of his speeches,[187] and in others he agreed with Seward's "irrepressible conflict" stand that his aides insisted had branded Seward as an unelectable radical.[188] In an 1859 speech in Chicago, Lincoln thrilled audiences when he said: "I think slavery is wrong, morally and politically. I desire that it should be no further spread in these United States, and I should not object if it should gradually terminate in the whole Union." How much more radical could a politician get on slavery?[189] More than any other factor, then, Lincoln's carefully designed position as an outsider—and as a workingman far removed from the genteel white-wine parties of the Washington crowd— made him a strong candidate.

Lincoln's strengths, they said, were considerable. Most important, he had beaten Douglas before, in the 1858 Illinois Senate race (in the popular vote), and Douglas would be the regular Democratic Party candidate in 1860. Lincoln could beat him again. Many Lincoln supporters argued, too, that Douglas was an overrated speaker and campaigner. Charles Ray, the editor of the *Chicago Press and Tribune*, argued that "the fact is Douglas has been grossly overestimated as a debater, both by himself and the public. An uncommon fertility of quibbles, an opulence of sophistry, and a faculty of obscuring the issue from the people...constitutes his entire capital."[190]

They argued, too, that Douglas' constant flip-flops on slavery would hurt him. Lincoln wrote that he was "the best instrument to put down and to uphold the slave power; but no ingenuity can long keep these antagonisms in harmony."[191]

Although Lincoln had always been opposed to slavery, he was seen by all as a moderate who only wanted to keep it out of the territories and not as a radical like Seward. That moderate stance could win in the southern counties of Illinois, Indiana, and Pennsylvania. His moderate stance was sufficiently antislavery to win in the abolitionist states of New England and was mainstream enough to carry the large states of Ohio, New York, and Michigan. He might even win some of the border states, such as Maryland and Kentucky (Lincoln's ringing denunciations of slavery from 1840 to 1860 were very conveniently swept under the rug by Davis and his men and astonishingly forgotten by delegates who must have heard him on his various speaking tours).

Lincoln was also a man of great personal integrity and had never been touched by scandal in over twenty-seven years of political life. No one in his family had ever been accused of wrongdoing. None of his political associates or friends had ever been involved in a scandal, either. Even his political enemies acknowledged his honesty, and people referred to him as "Honest Abe." The nation was riddled with political scandal, public office abuse, and big-city machine patronage in the 1850s, and most people considered politics corrupt.[192] Billy Herndon, Lincoln's law partner, often wondered why his best friend Lincoln was a politician. He called politicians "corrupt fish—dollar power seekers, mudhunters, scoundrels."[193] The country was reeling from corruption scandals in the Buchanan administration and was looking for an honest man such as Lincoln. The *New Hampshire Statesman* wrote of him, "Abraham never wronged anyone out of one cent, or spent a dollar that he had not honestly earned."[194]

Later, Herndon wrote that "he is an honest man. It gave him a firm hold on the masses…the trust and worship by the people of Lincoln were the result of his simple character."[195]

Lincoln was a man of his convictions. As far back as 1844, he spoke out against slavery and supported high tariffs to protect American businesses and stridently championed the workingman. He believed in those same principals in 1860. Between 1844 and 1860, many political parties had come and gone and politicians had changed their views many times as the political winds blew, but Abraham Lincoln, his advisers assured the delegates, had not. He knew what he wanted for the country and so did everybody else.

Lincoln was a former Whig and could win over the old Whigs, no matter what party they had scattered to. He had never said anything publicly against the American Party and could count on its support. They shrugged off reminders that Lincoln hated the American Party so much that when there was talk of a Republican Party in 1854, he refused to join it if the American Party people were in it. He wrote Owen Lovejoy of the immigrant-hating American Party then that "I do not perceive how anyone professing to be sensitive to the wrongs of the Negroes can join in a league to degrade a class of white men."[196]

He had the support of the large German population of Illinois and could carry immigrant groups in every state. The leaders of each state where Lincoln had taken to the stump to speak during the past year—New York, Massachusetts, Connecticut, New Jersey, Ohio, Indiana, Michigan, Iowa— were reminded how much he had helped local candidates and the positive reception he received there.

Lincoln was also the man of the future, and that was the booming West. The United States was bursting with nowhere to explode but in the West.

The populations of the western states had exploded in the last ten years. Illinois' population had doubled. Indiana's more than doubled, while Iowa's had more than tripled. The population of Wisconsin went from 305,000 in 1850 to 776,000 in 1860. Missouri's shot from 682,000 to 1.18 million.[197] Lincoln could carry all of those western states, which bordered Illinois, his handlers said. Moreover, as a westerner, he would also build a western foundation for the Republican Party in all the territories that would become states some day. And the Republican Party, they insisted, was already the party of the West.

The most dramatic voter shift to Republicans was not in the abolitionist northeast but in the West. The combined states of Illinois, Indiana, Michigan, Ohio, and Wisconsin gave the Republicans 37 percent of the area's seats in the House of Representatives in the 1854 election. Those same states gave the party 85 percent of the area's House seats in the 1856 election, more than doubling their strength. In some areas of some states the percentage was even higher, and in Ohio, in 1856, every single congressional district went Republican.[198] Clearly, as Judge Davis reiterated to delegate after delegate, the Republican future was in the West, and the West was Lincoln.

But what made Lincoln electable to most, Davis stressed and the delegates quickly understood, was the image he brought to the party, an image cultivated by Lincoln and by Davis at every turn. That was the image of Honest Abe, the rail-splitter, the man who worked with his hands all of his life, the workingman, the common man who understood the common man.

That image was created at the Illinois State Convention in 1858, which nominated Lincoln for the Senate. In the middle of the proceedings, John Hanks—the cousin of Lincoln's mother Nancy Hanks—and a friend marched through the middle of the hall carrying actual rails that Hanks and Lincoln had split together to build fences decades before. It had been years since Lincoln, a very successful lawyer, had split rails, but Davis saw the image as the perfect public perception of the Lincoln that he wanted to sell to the public. Here was a man actually born in a log cabin who taught himself to read, a man who had gone through business failures and lost loves like so many others, who worked with his hands to build his home and nurture his family. He was the American workingman, the free labor, hardworking, blue collar, middle-class workingman.

Politicians across the country thought "the rail-splitter" was the perfect symbol for the party of the "workingman." New York's William Bourne wrote Lincoln, "Let the working men of the west be well informed of the platform (and) movement of working men."[199]

It was a working-class perception that Lincoln knew would attract the masses. He wrote: "Public sentiment is everything. With public sentiment, nothing can fail; without it nothing can succeed."[200]

Davis blanketed Lincoln's 1858 and 1860 campaign paraphernalia with images of the rail-splitter. It was on broadsides, letterheads, newspaper ads, and lampposts. A massive torchlight parade for Lincoln on the first night of the 1860 Republican convention in Chicago featured hundreds of young men carrying split rails and banners with Lincoln's picture underneath fiery letters that spelled out RAIL-SPLITTER. Rail-splitter floats appeared in all Republican parades. The party referred to Lincoln as "the Rail-Splitter" and to his son Robert as "the Prince of Rails." It was as solid an image as the log cabin of William Henry Harrison in the 1840 election. Lincoln was no millionaire like Cameron, no patrician like Seward, no high-powered lawyer like Douglas, no European ambassador like President Buchanan, no Southern aristocrat like Breckinridge. He was the rail-splitter, a man of the people.[201]

Davis was careful never to criticize any of the candidates or their supporters because he would need them later, but he made it clear to many that they needed someone who could get elected president if Seward could not get the nomination on the first ballot, as Seward anticipated. That candidate was Abe Lincoln.

CHAPTER 7

One Last Night to Steal the Nomination

(The noise at Lincoln's nomination) was a concentrated shriek that was positively awful.

—REPUBLICAN DELEGATE AT THE CONVENTION

The crusade to win Abe Lincoln the presidential nomination was highly organized. His campaign leaders—Judge David Davis, Norman Judd, Leonard Swett, and the others—met with each delegation from the swing states separately and then formed a committee of twelve delegates representing the different states as an umbrella group. That committee visited delegates of each of the doubtful states and asked them who they would back if Seward did not claim victory on the first ballot. Davis tried to convince them to endorse Lincoln as their second choice. Davis then let everyone in Chicago know that the leaning states were now going to back Lincoln after the first ballot. Judge Davis wrote Lincoln in Springfield: "We are quiet but moving heaven and earth. Nothing will beat us but old fogy politicians. The hearts of the delegates are with us."[202]

Charles Ray, a reporter for the *Chicago Press and Tribune* who also worked for the Republicans, wrote Lincoln, too, and told him to trust Davis: "Don't be too sanguine. Matters look well as things stand today. I would rather have your chances than any other man."[203]

Davis and his team next met with individual candidates to convince them to switch their state delegation votes on the second ballot. The meetings often lasted long into the night. His strategy was simple: try to get one hundred votes for Lincoln on the first ballot, more on the second, third, fourth, and subsequent rounds so that delegates could sense a growing swell of support. Never push Lincoln as the primary candidate—keep him in the wings.[204]

Davis' most powerful ploy was to dangle important cabinet posts before state party leaders. Lincoln had told him to "make no contracts that bind me."[205] Davis casually ignored the admonitions, telling friends that "Lincoln ain't here, and don't know what we have to meet. So we will go ahead as if we hadn't heard from him and he must ratify it."[206]

The protectors of Lincoln lore have long used this admonition to suggest that he was only concerned with the great issues and problems that befell the nation and that he advised his supporters to do the same. Even so, he was unable to stop them from politicking. Another view might suggest that the cabinet post promises and the general maneuvering at the convention belonged to a three-step process on Lincoln's part.

Step One: by staying home, he would not be involved in deal making. *Step Two:* he then sent a single note to the convention team asking them not to make any deals "that bind me." His letter said nothing about deals that would bind Judge Davis, Joe Medill, or anyone else on the team. They made the deals and they were binding on them, not Lincoln. If Lincoln was so determined not to make any deals, why did he say nothing about them to his advisers before they left Springfield? The message about arrangements was a single line Lincoln penciled onto the margin of the front page of the *Missouri Democrat* newspaper that he handed to Ed Baker, a local journalist who was on his way to Chicago to see Davis. The line repeated the letter's instructions. How meaningful was a newspaper margin note?[207] *Step Three:* Lincoln in the end, when selecting his cabinet, approved all of the deals that were made by his team, denying that he made any.

Rumors began to fly around Chicago, many of them apparently planted by the Lincoln team and all designed to weaken support for the opposition. Gustave Koerner started one by telling a crowd that he heard that if Bates was nominated, not only would all German Americans refuse to vote for him, but they would cross over and vote for Douglas.[208]

The team's first target was the bombastic Simon Cameron, whose 54 Pennsylvania delegates were crucial to win the necessary 233 for nomination. It was reported Cameron's representatives insisted on a cabinet post to swing Pennsylvania's votes on the second ballot.[209] Davis reportedly then promised that Cameron would become a member of Lincoln's cabinet. Joe Casey, who helped to arrange the deal, wrote Cameron that "Seward could not carry the state…. It (the switch to Lincoln) was only done after everything was arranged carefully and unconditionally to reference to yourself—to our satisfaction—and we drove the anti-Cameron men from this state into it."[210]

Cameron had also made gestures to Seward about a cabinet post through Weed as early as March 15. The two men had apparently agreed on a cabinet post at a Philadelphia meeting.[211]

Davis and his team next convinced Chase's people that he could not be nominated himself and should switch to Lincoln. Bates' people followed. Talks were then held with Caleb Smith, a friend of Davis' from Indiana and a political leader there. Initially, Smith supported Seward, but he was asked by Davis to deliver Indiana to Lincoln on the first ballot to give him the magic number of 100 in order to make him a viable contender. He was also asked to second Lincoln's nomination to gain strength from the western states and to get his friend Columbus Delano of Ohio to work for Lincoln in that delegation.[212] Discussions were then held with the politically powerful Marylanders, Francis and Montgomery Blair, to swing their votes to Lincoln on ballots two or three. None of Lincoln's team ever admitted they actually offered cabinet posts to any of the state leaders or, later, to William Seward in the middle of the campaign. But when Lincoln was inaugurated on March 4, 1861, Simon Cameron became secretary of war, Seward was named secretary of state, Chase secretary of the treasury, Smith secretary of the interior, Bates attorney general, and Montgomery Blair postmaster general [213] (Seward's men made similar offers, including a pledge of $100,000 for Indiana's congressional campaigns).[214]

Lincoln reportedly decried their actions. He is said to have told friends that "they have gambled me all around, bought and sold me a hundred times."[215]

What Judge Davis and his men also did, shrewdly, was convince all of the delegates at the Republican convention that this race for the presidential nomination was just between number-one candidate Seward and number-two candidate Lincoln. All believed that, forgetting Lincoln had been a little-known candidate before the convention. His team soon convinced everyone Lincoln was a prime contender for the presidential nomination.

Davis' final assault took place at the convention itself.

Members of the huge crowds of Seward supporters had arrived by train, along with some of the "lower sort" of politicians Carl Schurz detested who worked with Thurlow Weed, Seward's hardworking campaign manager. They had spent the week in crowded Chicago holding their own Seward parades, complete with brass bands and enormous banners that stretched across entire city streets.[216] On their trains from New York, the Seward entourage had brought along their own large band that marched in special Seward uniforms.[217] They, along with supporters of the other presidential candidates, were all turned away from the Wigwam because the Lincoln people had taken their seats with the counterfeit tickets.

The powerful Thurlow Weed was working just as hard as Davis. Weed, who moved from his role as political boss of the New York Whig Party to the state's Republican Party, applied pressure throughout the East Coast to get Seward the nomination. He wined and dined delegates from every single state at his palatial New York mansion and convinced them that Seward in the White House would be as gracious as Weed. He charmed them all. Sam Bowles of Massachusetts wrote Weed after a visit to his home, "There are few men I care to know well, but my faith in human nature and in you were warmed and cheered (by the visit)."[218] Weed personally talked Seward out of pursuing the presidency in 1856 but was determined to win it for him now in 1860.[219]

To do that, Weed set up headquarters at the elegant Richmond House Hotel and invited hundreds of delegates to meet him there. Most were charmed, but Carl Schurz, a German American leader who was a Lincoln man, was appalled by Weed's slick approach to the delegates. Schurz called Weed in his expensive lair "Faust."[220]

There were rumors that Seward, through Weed, was promising "oceans of money" in campaign funds to the states they needed to win the nomination.[221]

During the second day, the convention adopted a modified antislavery plank satisfactorily hammered out mostly by the Seward men. The gathering was now ready to ballot for their presidential candidate. There didn't seem to be much doubt who the winner would be. Thurlow Weed had swept through Chicago like a hurricane, lining up votes for Seward in the different states. All of Weed's men thought Seward would be nominated on the first ballot. So did most Republican governors, senators, and congressmen. Most reporters felt so too. Even Horace Greeley, Seward's archenemy, was convinced Seward would be nominated.

Davis had only one more night to steal the nomination from Seward's backers, but it was all the time he needed. That evening, Davis and his men worked the rooms of all the delegate hotels in Chicago one last time trying to get every vote they could for the first ballot and, more important, pledges for switches on the second, third, and subsequent ballots. The floor team of Carl Schurz and Austin Blair (of the Maryland Blairs) knocked on the doors of the designated state leaders in Wisconsin and Michigan. Another team targeted Pennsylvania, Indiana, and New Jersey. Orville Browning, another team member, went from one state caucus to another, hotel to hotel, room to room, emphasizing Lincoln's support of foreign-born citizens, particularly those in the Midwest.[222] Davis also put to work Henry Lane, candidate for governor of Indiana, and Andrew Curtin, candidate for governor of Pennsylvania, convincing them that if they had to run with Seward, they would lose their races. Journalist Murat Halstead, who covered the convention, reported that he saw Lane scurrying from hotel room to hotel room at Tremont House, his cane in his hand, at 1:00 a.m. the night before the balloting.[223]

The Wigwam was mobbed with people inside and outside, on the sidewalks and in the streets. Thousands congregated on the following morning (some said the total of people inside the hall and on the surrounding streets topped 25,000 people [224]). The arena was made of pine wood. There was room inside the open two-story building, its ceiling held up with numerous wooden pillars, for 460 delegates, 60 reporters, and 10,000 spectators, half standing and half sitting. Although barely finished in time for the convention, the Wigwam was handsomely decorated by dozens of volunteer women whose husbands or boyfriends were staunch Chicago Republicans. They filled the convention hall with evergreens, artificial flowers, state coats of arms, banners, bunting, and streamers. There were dozens of oversized American flags and enormous portraits of the first fifteen presidents. Large murals, all with some theme that tied the Republicans to the Bible, hung on the walls.

The Republicans stood, cheered, and stomped their feet at every spoken word. One gushed that it was "a glorious omen of the future—a prophetic sign, large with golden promise of a glorious harvest of truth and right next fall."

The Democrats hated it. A reporter for the Democratic *Daily Chicago Herald* wrote that "it…looks like a man who has got up in a terrible hurry to take an early train and in his haste has overlooked some portion of his attire. It is an odd jumble."[225]

Working diligently all day, Davis and his men managed to halt the anticipated Seward avalanche on the first ballot. Seward received 173½ votes, Lincoln 102 (as projected by Davis and including 26 from Caleb Smith and Indiana), Bates 48, Cameron 50½, Judge John McLean 12, and Chase 49. There were a few scattered votes for several others. Davis' stacking of the Wigwam with thousands of loud Lincoln supporters paid off. Whenever Lincoln's name was mentioned, the crowd roared its approval and delegates uncertain of their allegiance looked up.

Lincoln handler Leonard Swett, a bearded lawyer who had traveled the legal circuit with Lincoln for eleven years, wrote that the cheering at Lincoln's nomination was so loud that "a thousand steam whistles, ten acres of hotel gongs, and a tribe of Comanches might have mingled in the scene unnoticed."[226]

Seward's supporters, so certain of victory on the first ballot, were shocked. Delegate Elbridge Spaulding, a congressman from upstate New York, wrote, "There is more opposition by the friends of others than was anticipated."[227]

Davis' efforts at increasing support for Lincoln on the second ballot worked. Seward edged up a little, but only to 184½. Lincoln leaped to 181 when Cameron delivered 48 of his votes from Pennsylvania and Chase gave him 14 more. His supporters cheered the switches. Bates dropped to 35, Chase to 42½.

Lincoln's man Swett wrote, "Our program was to give Lincoln 100 votes on the first ballot, with a certain increase afterwards, so that in the convention our fortunes might seem to be rising and thus catch the doubtful. Vermont had agreed to give us her second vote, so had Delaware, New Hampshire, an increase. It all worked to a charm."[228]

On the third ballot, Lincoln almost went over the top, pulling 231½ to Seward's 180.[229] The Blairs came through on that ballot, with 9 Maryland votes. Cameron gave almost every Pennsylvania vote to Lincoln, and Chase of Ohio delivered 29 more. When the balloting ended with Lincoln just 2½ votes short, Ohio delegate David Cartter, unable to hear anything in the din of the noise in the hall, was nudged by the man sitting next to him on the convention floor. A young Lincoln worker, Joe Medill, who, like all journalists, knew how to make his presence felt, put his mouth close to Cartter's ear and, above the shouting and gavel banging and roar of the crowd, whispered to Cartter, a strong supporter of Chase, that "Chase could have anything he wants" if Ohio now put Lincoln over the top. Cartter, a big man with a shock of thick black hair and a face that still carried pock marks from a bout with smallpox, rose, caught the eye of the convention chairman and announced with a slight stutter that four Ohio votes were going to switch to Lincoln, giving him the nomination.[230] As his voice faded, all ten thousand people in the Wigwam leaped to their feet and began to cheer. Ladies waved their handkerchiefs, and men threw their hats into the air.[231]

A reporter wrote that "the audience, like a wild colt with a bit between its teeth, rose above all cry of order, and again and again the irrepressible applause broke forth and resounded far and wide."[232] Another observed that "the Democratic Jericho shook at the shouts and blowing of trumpets and holding of torches in the left hands of Republican Gideons." A Lincoln supporter declared, "There was such an outburst of cheering as made the vast edifice actually tremble. It seemed as though it would never end." Another reported the noise was like "a concentrated shriek that was positively awful."[233]

A clerk tallied up the vote for the official count, stood, waved the sheet toward the skylight of the oversized arena, and at the top of his lungs shouted, "LINCOLN!" At the announcement, a cannon positioned on the roof for the occasion boomed over the city, and over 100,000 people who had known Abe Lincoln in some fashion for most of their lives cheered and yelled and hugged each other on the streets below. All the church bells in the city began to toll, and whistles on steamboats and locomotives blew.[234]

Across Illinois that night, bonfires blazed, cannons were fired, drums were beaten loudly, and roving gangs of teenaged boys cheered. Citizens in towns from one end of the state to another celebrated the nomination of their native son, "Honest Abe," the rail-splitter.[235]

The men on his convention team were jubilant. Swett wrote, "(Lincoln) is a pure-minded, honest man, whose ability is second to no one in the nation. In twenty years, he has raised himself from the captaincy of a flatboat on the Mississippi to the captaincy of a great party in this nation."[236]

Years of stump speeches, letter writing, friendships with newspapermen, politicking, lobbying, arm-twisting, traveling, and hard work by himself and his friends had finally paid off for Abraham Lincoln, the rail-splitter from Sangamon County. The tall, thin man who had failed so often in search of some kind of political opportunity had finally found one in his nomination for the highest office in the land.

The Republican platform, as expected, criticized Buchanan (on top of everything else, they painted him as a doddering old man, out of touch with the people)[237] and called for the elimination of any slave trading from Africa, the prohibition of slavery in any new territories, denounced the Dred Scott decision, and pledged the party once more to the intent of the Declaration of Independence that all men are created equal. The antislavery planks in it were substantially toned down from the 1856 platform, however, as the Republicans carefully targeted moderate voters. The platform was a craftily executed declaration of governmental principles written to please millions of voters who might not vote Republican on the slavery issue alone.

One of the most persuasive planks called for higher tariffs to protect American businesses, particularly the iron and coal industries in Pennsylvania and New Jersey. Voters in these states and some others were still angry at the 1856 Democratic platform that spurned tariffs and advocated free trade between countries, putting many American corporations in jeopardy. Another plank called for the completion of a transcontinental railroad as a way to bring development into California and other western territories and cut down on foreign imports and costs of transportation. The Republican platform also sought an end to the vigilante warfare in Kansas and the admission of Kansas as a free state, sounder federal fiscal policies, higher wages for blue-collar workers, higher profits for farmers, and an end to governmental corruption.

It called for immediate passage of the Homestead Act, which would open up the settlement of the West by guaranteeing pioneers free land. The Homestead Act would give them 160 acres of free land if they worked it for two years, thus providing opportunity for a better lease on life. President Buchanan had vetoed the act earlier in the year, driving thousands of farmers out of the Democratic Party and into the arms of the Republicans.

It called for a new and extensive federal program to develop the country's rivers and harbors for commerce and shipping. Finally, in a carefully worded paragraph, the Republicans stood opposed to any change in current naturalization laws and pledged the protection of newly arrived immigrants, a distinct blow to the American Party.

These platform planks were important to many Northerners, especially residents of the northwestern states who saw tariff protection, the Homestead Act, and the building of a transcontinental railroad as helpful to their growing businesses. They had lobbied for these bills, and yet the Democrats constantly voted them down.[238]

The Republican Party, in short, gave the nation a campaign platform with something for everybody and its own vision of a booming country that would increase trade, make lives better for workers, and expand westward while quietly assimilating the millions of newly arrived immigrants. The passage protecting immigrants actually received a louder and longer burst of applause from the crowd than the slavery planks.[239]

The delegates' passage of the platform did not cause disputes in Chicago, as the platform did in Charleston. It was a platform, too, that did not hurt the party's chances for victory in one region of the United States in order to promote something important to another region. Lincoln had been warning Republicans against that danger for nearly a year. He wrote Schuyler Colfax in July 1859 that "the point of danger is the temptation of different localities to campaign for something which will be popular just there but which, nevertheless, will be a firebrand elsewhere, and especially in a national convention. As an instance, the movement against foreigners in Massachusetts; in New Hampshire, to make obedience to the Fugitive Slave Law punishable as a crime; in Ohio to repeal the Fugitive Slave Law. In these things there is explosive matter enough to blow up half a dozen national conventions…a point should be made to avoid everything which will disturb Republicans elsewhere." He bluntly told Colfax that "in every locality, we should look beyond our noses."[240]

And they had nominated a humble and grateful man. When he read the telegram informing him of his nomination at the offices of the *State Journal* in Springfield, Lincoln was quiet. Then he rose and told those around him that he had to go home to deliver the news to his wife. Following a tumultuous reception a few days later in Springfield that included bonfires, rockets shot into the air, and a night of fireworks, Lincoln thanked the convention committee for the nomination. He added humbly that it was "a responsibility which I could almost wish had fallen upon some one of the far more eminent men and experienced statesmen whose distinguished names were before the convention."[241]

The results of the convention balloting stunned the townspeople of Auburn, the tiny village in upstate New York where Senator Seward lived, as much as they astonished the Seward team in Chicago.[242] They were so certain he would be nominated that they dragged one of the old Revolutionary war cannons from the armory to his front lawn to fire as soon as their neighbor's nomination for president was secure. The largest hotel in town prepared a huge dinner to celebrate Seward's selection, and the manager bought baskets filled with bottles of champagne, which were stationed at various places in the hotel. Hundreds of Seward supporters thronged around the senator and his family at his house. When news of Lincoln's victory came via messenger, all were crushed. Partygoers left Seward's home after offering condolences and accompanied others who dragged the unfired cannon slowly back to the armory in a sad procession. The hotel manager put away his champagne. A devastating silence fell over the tree-lined streets of the community.

Throughout the nation, intrepid Seward supporters were astonished at the outcome of the Chicago convention. Men and women in numerous cities had made huge SEWARD FOR PRESIDENT banners that now could not be used. A publishing house in Boston had printed thousands of copies of Seward's presidential campaign biography, now useless.[243]

"The 'Defender of the Rights of Man' was sacrificed on the altar of expediency—sacrificed for Abraham Lincoln, a bar room politician," wrote the editor of the *Auburn Democrat.*[244]

The Seward forces were bitter. They were not angry at Lincoln or his operatives, who were no different than Thurlow Weed in their tactics and efforts to get their candidate nominated. Their anger was directed at the people they felt betrayed them in just about every single state that supported Lincoln, particularly Simon Cameron and Horace Greeley.

Weed apparently thought he had a deal with Cameron to swing Pennsylvania to Seward on the first or second ballot. He wrote Seward, "Not a word from Cameron…his three men…not looking UNDER ANY CIRCUMSTANCES to your nomination…. Cameron would be in the field until I could see them (his men) again." Weed cabled Seward from a railroad station in Chicago as he was about to depart for Springfield to meet with Lincoln and try to cut a deal with the new nominee to have Seward join the cabinet as secretary of state, if Lincoln was elected. It would give Seward a chance to help run the country, because Weed and Seward believed Lincoln, a novice, was incapable of doing so. The position of secretary of state would also give Seward exposure in foreign affairs, build new alliances, and then, as everyone expected, would enable him to win the White House in 1864.[245]

The other enemy was Greeley, whom both Weed and Seward were convinced had swayed delegates away from Seward to Lincoln. Weed was livid. He wrote, "Greeley is malignant" adding that the Blairs, whom he also believed betrayed him, were "perfidious."[246]

James Gordon Bennett, the editor of the *New York Herald*, and a close confidant of Seward's, was even angrier at newspaper rival Greeley. He wrote, "Horace Greeley I dismiss in two words…a snake."[247]

Republicans across New York State felt alienated from the party, which they were convinced had been seized by frontiersmen. "I wash my hands of the (election)…no funds…no speeches. Greeley and company may run their own machine," wrote A. Oakley Hall, New York City's former district attorney.[248] Their alienation and refusal to work for the ticket would cast ominous shadows over the Lincoln campaign when it plunged into the last stretch in late October.

It annoyed many in New York that someone with no national connections could defeat the most connected politician in the country; George Grier wired Seward, "They commenced by voting for an outsider!"[249]

It also amazed New Yorkers that Lincoln had outmaneuvered Seward and Weed, the two best politicians in the country. That must have brought a smile to the face of Leonard Swett. He wrote later of Lincoln the politician, "He managed his politics upon a plan entirely different from any other man the country has ever produced."[250]

Seward himself maintained a dignified public face, nodding graciously to those who visited him at Auburn. During the week following the convention, he spent much of his time quietly tending to his garden. His composure surely was not helped when he received a letter from Cameron on May 20 that began, "I am mortified that my state contributed to your (defeat)."[251]

Seward soon let it be known that he was thinking about resigning from the Senate and ending his public career. This announcement, of course, engendered a wave of letters from people all over America begging him to stay in politics. Many were convinced that Seward should be elected president in 1864. They were radical Republicans hoping Seward could somehow mentor Lincoln if he was elected, and many were simply Americans who, regardless of political feelings, admired Seward for his long career of public service.

"But to you what is the presidency?" wrote Massachusetts Senator Charles Sumner, a close friend of Seward's who tried to cheer him up. "It is not needed for your fame."[252]

Gratified by the outpouring of letters and cables, Seward was also assured by Weed on his return from Springfield after meeting the nominee that a deal could be worked out to put him in the cabinet. He finally decided to remain in public life.

The decision did not surprise Abraham Lincoln. He paid little attention to it. Unfortunately, he also paid little attention to a scathing editorial in the *Louisville Daily Courier* that said Lincoln and his Republicans:

> *Cater to the passions and to the prejudices of the ignorant, feeling the fires of fanaticism and madness, with the Constitution, fraternity, and equality on their lips, are pressing on to the extinguishment of slavery, though to reach this end it be necessary to trample under foot the Constitution, to invade the sovereignty of the states, to violate the rights of individuals, to dissolve the Union, to inaugurate strife, anarchy, and civil war.*[253]

CHAPTER 8

The Birth of the Seceders

We should not be surprised even at this. In fact, we should not be surprised at anything.

—EDITOR, *LOUISVILLE JOURNAL*

The mood at the Democratic convention when it reassembled in Baltimore in June was no better than on its final, chaotic day in Charleston. The Northern delegates were still firmly behind Stephen Douglas and the Southern delegates were still against him. The two-thirds-vote rule for a nomination was still in effect, even though it had caused fifty-seven fruitless ballots in Charleston. There was still no agreement on a slavery platform.

The debate over the seating was rancorous. Pennsylvania delegates were willing to seat the Charleston defectors only if they agreed with whatever the decisions of the convention were on the slavery planks in the platform.[254]

George Loring of Massachusetts, trying to heal rifts, backed the Southerners. "I beg this convention to impose no obstacle to the admission of these gentlemen. I beg this convention to invite and assist them to come back," he said, accompanied by great applause from Southerners.[255]

The next day, many state delegates split on the question of whether or not to let the bolters back, but New York voted, a huge thirty-five-vote block, to bar them, and New York's votes carried the motion against the Southerners. Chaos reigned. Virginians, counted on from the beginning to not only back Douglas but shore up the remaining Southern support for the party, announced that they might leave the convention. Southerners continued to insist that the New Yorkers had betrayed them.

Douglas was so upset that, again, he wanted to take his name out of nomination for president.

Moderate Caleb Cushing of Massachusetts, unable to take the bitter disputes any more, then quit as president of the gathering. As soon as he did, the majority of delegates from Massachusetts, led by Ben Butler, surrounded by his own bodyguard, stalked out of the hall.

Southerners fumed at that. Kentuckian James Leach wrote in a statement with others, "Discord and disintegration have prevailed."[256]

Ironically, though, it was not the Deep South states that led the second walkout of 105 men from twenty-two states; it was Virginia.

Virginia's departure startled Northerners and pleased the seceders, who saw in Virginia, the home of Washington, Jefferson, Madison, and Monroe, a cloak of patriotic respectability for the bolters. Virginia's men left, followed by just about every other Southern delegate. They were finished with the Democratic Party, driven out by Douglas (now being labeled "a corrupt fungus" by the *Charleston Mercury*)[257] and the New Yorkers.

The exodus had Republicans chortling. "(The two conventions) were the most brilliant fizzles of the age," wrote Lyman Samuel.[258]

The remaining delegates finally did nominate Stephen Douglas for president and Benjamin Fitzpatrick for vice president. The Douglas men were thrilled with Fitzpatrick, the U.S. senator and former governor of Alabama. Having Southerner Fitzpatrick on the ticket would help Douglas win in the Southern states.

John Dawson of Pennsylvania leaped to his feet to gush over the nomination of the Little Giant. He declared, "Douglas is a man of acknowledged talent, and everywhere regarded as the accomplished statesman, skilled in the art of ruling. Born under a New England sun, yet by adoption a citizen of the west, honored and cherished in the valley of the Ohio and on the slopes of the Atlantic, he should now be of the whole country."[259]

Stephen Douglas had finally won a nomination to be president, but it did not seem to be worth very much. He lamented, "The Democratic party will be demoralized, if not destroyed, by the breaking up of the convention…(it will) inevitably expose the country to the perils of sectional strife."[260]

Democrats feared their party had collapsed. Several Democratic and Republican newspapers ran the headline DEATH OF DEMOCRACY. One newspaper chronicled the glorious history of the party and then wrote that it had "died of Douglas." One editor wrote a clever obituary of the party that began, "Died—at Charleston, on the 23rd."[261]

After two months and three conventions, Democrats around the country were dazed. The editor of the *Louisville Journal*, shaking his head at the final mess in Baltimore, wrote, "We should not be surprised even at this. In fact, we should not be surprised at anything."[262]

The Seceders' Convention

The Democratic seceders entered the hall one by one; they were buoyant. The sourness of the Democratic conventions, both of them, was gone. They were happy men, delighted to be in a hall at the Maryland Institute in Baltimore, where they were convinced that they could nominate their own candidate for president, elect him, and make history.

They were there for the Southern Democratic Party convention. Just about all of the Southerners denied access to the mainstream Democratic convention attended and some Northerners too, such as Caleb Cushing from Massachusetts and V. L. Bradford of Pennsylvania. There were men from the border states, such as O. R. Funston of Virginia and W. P. Bowie of Texas and J. E. Dresbit of California. They had stormed out of the regular Democratic convention and washed their hands of the hated Douglas.

The platform passed quickly at the one-day gathering. It was a revised version of the slavery manifesto: the bolters insisted the federal government permit slavery in all the new territories, not challenge slavery where it existed, enforce the Fugitive Slave Law, permit territories to enter the Union as slave states, and annex Cuba, where slavery also existed (their only key non-slavery call was for a transcontinental railroad). The men had been urged in numerous Southern newspapers to forge a party that upheld the Southern view on slavery and other issues and ignored the views of the North, to "overthrow the fanatical and corrupt horde, who are striving to make the government and the Union a den of thieves."[263]

With the passage of the platform out of the way, they then quickly began balloting for president. The group considered several men, including John Dickinson of New York, Joseph Lane of Oregon, and Jefferson Davis of Mississippi (who turned them down) but finally picked Kentucky's John Breckinridge, the U.S. vice president. They selected Joe Lane of Oregon as the vice president.

Breckinridge, just thirty-nine years old, was a graduate of Kentucky's Centre College and the law school at Transylvania University. He fought for the United

States in the Mexican War. He had thick, wavy hair that he carefully combed; his eyes were wide and bright. A man with a sense of humor, he often posed in office portraits to look like Napoleon Bonaparte. When he learned that he was nominated, Breckinridge was troubled. He did not want to be president. He had urged supporters from Kentucky to keep his name off the ballot at both Democratic conventions and had stood behind fellow Kentuckian James Guthrie as he was nominated at both. Now, a presidential nomination in hand, the plum so many politicians strive for and never achieve, Breckinridge balked and at first turned it down. He did not want Abraham Lincoln or Stephen Douglas to be president, but he didn't want the job, either.

Neither the nomination of Breckinridge or Bell caused Douglas and his supporters any alarm. Leonard Swett wrote they were "basing their hopes on the supposed failure of the seceders to unite upon any line of action."[264]

Breckinridge, highly respected throughout the country, was the fourth prospective nominee, and that made many political leaders fearful that the Southern candidates would split the electoral college vote and throw the election into the House of Representatives, where a Northern-Southern battle would emerge.

That crisis brought about one of the strangest dinner parties in American history at the home of Mississippi Senator Jefferson Davis in Washington DC. The party, on the warm summer night of June 25, 1860, was a convention in its own right, the fifth Democratic convention of 1860.[265] There, with Breckinridge and several party leaders in attendance, Davis proposed that they all quit the race to avoid splitting the Democratic vote and unite behind one other, single candidate, Horatio Seymour, the former Democratic governor of New York.[266]

Seymour had made many friends in the South over the years, and he represented a huge class of New Yorkers who did profitable business in the

South. He lived in very pro-Southern New York City. As the democratic nominee, he could sweep the Southern states. He could definitely win. The men were pleased with their choice.[267]

All except Douglas. He refused to leave the race, and then an angry Bell and Breckinridge decided to stay in it.[268]

Davis, upset that his peacemaker efforts were unsuccessful, played a small role in the campaign, even though he did back Breckenridge.[269]

Vice presidential nominee Fitzpatrick resigned from the ticket. It was dismissed callously ("He saw that he would be simply a target at which the entire masses of his state would turn their weapons," speculated the *Charleston Mercury*).[270]

The meeting only remained a secret for about two weeks, when President Buchanan described it to friends in New York.[271]

The wild four-way race soon became a five-way race. Sam Houston had always been an independent. He had been a governor of Tennessee, president of the Republic of Texas, and later, a governor of Texas when it was a state (the only man in American history to be governor of two separate states). He was a Southerner and a westerner at the same time. He was a diplomat and administrator and yet head of a revolutionary army that defeated Mexico. He was a legendary and much-beloved figure in the West and Midwest. Houston was an eccentric; he once toured Washington DC, dressed in a leopard-skin vest and Mexican blanket.[272] In 1860, he decided he wanted to be president, and if the Constitutional Union Party would not nominate him, he would nominate himself. Friends soon nominated him as the "hero of San Jacinto" on the Texas Unionist ticket (abolitionist Gerrit Smith was his vice president). They did so on the twenty-fourth anniversary of the battle of San Jacinto in a meeting on the battlefield itself. Houston was convinced Southerners would see that their future was with him and the ever-growing West. He was presidential candidate number five.[273]

Most Southern newspapers cheered the various rump Democratic parties for bolting in order to honor the South, but a few saw the split as ominous. The editor of the *Richmond Enquirer* wrote that the numerous parties would divide the Southern vote and, worse, "encourage the fanaticism of the North."[274]

CHAPTER 9

Will the House of Representatives Elect the President?

Lincoln or Lane?

—REPUBLICAN CAMPAIGNERS ON HOUSE OF
REPRESENTATIVES ELECTION

No matter how hard the strategists of Breckinridge and Bell looked at the electoral college vote in 1860 (Houston, under pressure from Southern newspapers, dropped out of the race on August 18[275]), they saw defeat. Neither of the splinter political parties had the money or organization to win the election outright over the surging Republicans or regular Democrats. They did have a chance though—by forcing the election to be decided by the United States House of Representatives.[276]

They had to campaign to win enough states to prevent either Lincoln or Douglas from a direct victory. In the House of Representatives, the two men stood a better chance than at the public polls. There were 303 votes in the electoral college; a candidate needed 152 to become president. The fifteen slave states had 129 electoral votes and the eighteen free states had 183.

Neither of the presidential candidates from the Southern Democratic Party or Constitutional Union Party could possibly carry all of the slave states and pick up 32 more votes in the free states. However, there was a chance that one of them could pick up California and Oregon, with 7 votes between them, and a distinct chance that one could win in Missouri, a border state. There was a chance that Breckinridge could win in Pennsylvania because its southern counties went heavily for Buchanan, Pennsylvania's favorite son, when he carried the state in 1856 and because he controlled much patronage there. Douglas could win in Indiana, where the Democrats won in 1856, and in Illinois, his home state. There was a strong possibility that Douglas could claim New York, where the Republicans barely beat the Democrats in 1856 in a three-way election. Douglas was very strong in Missouri too.

Collectively, they could stop Lincoln and throw the contest into the House.[277] Before the raucous Democratic convention, Douglas' men talked about the possibility of Douglas winning New York, Illinois, Iowa, Indiana, and half the states in the South. That outcome would have pushed the election into the House too.[278] (Southerners debunked this. "Name the crazy calculator!" said one.)

If the election did go to the House, Lincoln would lose. The Constitution states that if the electoral college fails to elect a president, the House must do so. Votes are not apportioned, though; each state has just one. Tiny Oregon's vote, in 1860, was just as powerful as New York's. Whoever won a majority of the thirty-three states in the House would be president. There was no mechanism for the vote of each state. If a state had six Republican and four Democratic congressmen, the state would probably cast its one vote for a Republican. The vote was to be taken in December, during the current Congress, elected in 1858. Newly elected congressmen could not participate, so any Republican gains in 1860 would not count.

Congress had fourteen Democratic-controlled states, fifteen Republican, and one controlled by the American Party. Three states—Kentucky, Maryland, and North Carolina—had the same number of congressmen from each party. That meant Lincoln needed seventeen states to win but could only count on fifteen. He might have won crossover support from Illinois, which had five Democratic congressmen and four Republican, because one Democrat already announced he would vote for Lincoln. That gave Lincoln sixteen states, if every state held the Republican line. No one in the South believed that Lincoln would win a Southern state, even though some Republicans thought that was possible. But the Democrats controlled the legislatures of Oregon and California, and they would probably pressure their congressmen to vote for a Democrat. If Bell did not finish strongly and won just a handful of states, he would have thrown his support to Breckinridge. Douglas would have been the real loser. He could run second in the popular vote but, losing most Northern states by slender margins and not winning any in the South, he could wind up fourth in the electoral college and not eligible for the House vote (the Constitution limited the House race to the top three vote-getters in the electoral college, not the popular vote). Douglas' followers would have split their votes between Breckinridge and Bell. Bell's supporters certainly would have voted for Breckinridge so as to put a Southerner in the White House. Bell's states would have given Breckinridge fourteen, and he would have had the backing of the American Party state to reach fifteen. He would have won the three equally divided slave states—Kentucky (his home), Maryland, and North Carolina—because their politicians, and their colleagues in the House, would have put enormous pressure on their congressmen to vote for a Southerner. Breckinridge could be elected (Bell's men, of course, penciled in their man's name wherever it read BRECKINRIDGE in that scenario).[279]

There was no mechanism for the vote of the congressmen. They were not bound by the election returns; they could switch parties or vote for a third-party candidate such as Bell. The party makeup was very volatile in 1860, and Bell's supporters in a state that he won could have legitimately claimed that their state's vote had to go to him. Bell, who got into the race as a moderate alternative who favored slavery, would quickly see that in a standoff between Lincoln and Breckinridge, the House might turn to him and he could be president. If Bell held the three states he was projected to take at the beginning of the race, the final House tally would be Lincoln sixteen, Breckinridge fifteen, and Bell three. Breckinridge's vice presidential nominee, Joe Lane, scoffed at that scenario but had his own. He was convinced that Bell would merge with Breckinridge in the House to make his running mate, Breckinridge, the president. Breckinridge and Bell could then edge Douglas aside as head of the Democratic Party and take over, offering assurances on the continuation of slavery to the South and brokering a deal with the North to satisfy slavery opponents there. It would help that Breckinridge had owned slaves at one point, even though he had freed them all.

Here, the Constitution became tricky. It said that the House election had to be held by March 4 and that the incumbent president and his cabinet had to leave office by that date. The Breckinridge and Bell forces could merge to put Breckinridge in the White House after dozens of ballots delivered no winner. They could also hold their states interminably, hoping the exhausted congressmen would finally turn to one of them for expediency. In the winters of both 1854–1855 and 1859–1860, the exact same scenario took place when the House spent months trying to elect a new Speaker. In the 1854–1855 vote, that took two months and 133 ballots, Congress finally elected Massachusetts' Nathaniel Banks. In the latter election, just three months prior to the 1860 conventions, the House turned away from the front-runners after two long months of fierce politicking and chose an unknown, New Jersey's William Pennington, just to have someone in the chair.

There was yet another possibility. If the House was unable to choose a president, and they could have been hopelessly deadlocked right through midnight on March 3, the presidency would fall into the hands of the Senate. The Constitution's wording was that if the House could not pick a president, the Senate would elect the vice president, who would then become the acting president of the United States. It could only vote from among the top two vote-getters for vice president in the electoral college— probably Republican Hannibal Hamlin and Southern Democrat Joe Lane of Oregon, a native North Carolinian who had become a political figure in Indiana and then in Oregon and served as a major general in the Mexican War. Here, Bell's vice president was left out.

Bell's vice president, however, was Edward Everett, a former United States senator, one of the nation's greatest public speakers, and one of the most popular politicians in the country. If the people could have voted from among Lane, Hamlin, and Everett, they would have chosen Everett. Yet, under the Constitution, as the number-three vote-getter, he was barred from any Senate vote. Clearly, the Southern senators would have rallied around proslavery Joe Lane and so would have Bell's senators from their Southern slave states. Lane also would have obtained the support of his native Oregon, his former homes in North Carolina and Indiana, and perhaps next-door neighbor California. The Constitution, though, says nothing about what happens next. It merely states that the Senate's vice presidential choice shall be the acting president. It did not say for how long; it did not order the House to continue voting for the president. Theoretically, Joe Lane could have been the acting president for four years (no one suggested it at the time, but Lane would have had no vice president since he was the vice president elect. In theory, the Senate could have made Breckinridge the new vice president, and Lane could have then resigned, making Breckinridge the president after all).[280]

It was also a possibility that Lincoln and others would file suit to postpone the House or Senate elections, claiming that the newly elected Congress should vote, not the old 1858 Congress. If he could delay the vote until after March 4, the new Congress would have been sworn in. These lawsuits could have dragged on for months, and Buchanan would have been gone and there would be no government.[281]

Speeches during the campaign and newspaper stories and editorials indicate that a House election was not only a very real possibility but one that was feared by the Republicans and much sought by the Democrats. Journalist Halstead wrote, "This (House election) is beyond question the game of the southern men."[282]

The *New York Daily Times* commenced discussion of the idea as early as May 23, 1860.[283] It was discussed widely in the press. The *Washington Constitution* wrote in the middle of July that the Southern politicians would somehow get the election sent to the House for a decision. Both the *Richmond Enquirer* and *Charleston Mercury* predicted that in the end the House would be unable to pick a president and that Oregon's Joe Lane would be elected vice president and acting president by the Senate.[284]

The extremist *Memphis Avalanche* predicted that Southerners would not win in the polls but would win in the House.[285] The *New Orleans Delta* urged several candidates to win all the anti-Republican votes and urged New Yorkers to back Douglas, whom the paper hated but realized was the only Democrat who could win there.[286] The leading Bell newspaper, the *Louisville Journal*, believed a House vote was the only way Bell could triumph.[287]

The Republicans constantly countered that claim and debunked Lane.[288] Many Lincoln rallies ended with a familiar question shouted from the speaker's platform: "Lincoln or Lane?"

The three Democrats did agree on one thing—if Douglas could win in New York, which had the most electoral votes, thirty-five, he could stop Lincoln even if the Republicans took Indiana, Pennsylvania, and Illinois.[289]

Election in the House was not uncommon in 1860. Thomas Jefferson had been elected by the House in 1800, defeating Aaron Burr, and John Quincy Adams gained the presidency there in 1824, defeating Andrew Jackson and two others. A House vote in 1860 would make three in fifteen elections.

The House issue was such an important topic that it was being discussed in letters and in newspaper columns as late as October 20, when S. K. Stow told Amos Briggs in a published letter in the Troy, New York, *Weekly Times* that the House would be unable to select anyone and that the Senate would pick Joe Lane.[290]

Later, however, as the political calendar ran out of time, the squabbling Democrats realized that to stop Lincoln they had to mobilize behind Douglas in New York, since the other two candidates had no chance in that solid Northern state. If the three opposing candidates were to put their differences aside and unify anywhere, it had to be in New York.

Everything in the campaign pointed toward selection by the House of Representatives. With four candidates splitting the vote and two of them proslavery Southerners, it appeared that Lincoln did not have any chance to become president.

Or did he?

the
PRESIDENTIAL
CAMPAIGN
★★★★★★★★★★★ *of* ★★★★★★★★★★★
1860

Abraham Lincoln was unnerved by the collapse of the Democratic Convention in Charleston, the weakening of Stephen Douglas, and the appearance of two new presidential challengers, Breckinridge and Bell. The newspapers reminded him and everybody in America that there was now a very real chance that there would be no victor in the electoral college and that the contest would wind up in the House of Representatives and the Senate. This was not the scenario Lincoln had hoped for that summer. He thought Douglas would win the nomination or that another traditional Democrat would earn it if the Little Giant did not. He never anticipated the postponement of the nomination, a second Democratic convention, a second walkout, or four candidates on the final ballot. Despite their turmoil, the Democrats could still win the election. Lincoln told Anson Henry in July, "But great is (the Democratic Party) in resources; and it may yet give its fortunes a turn."[291]

In the early summer of 1860, no matter what scenario he envisioned or twisted as far as he could, Lincoln now saw himself losing the presidency.

That's when Lincoln, an innovative politician since his twenties, came up with an unprecedented plan to capture the presidency—an all-sectional election campaign that would target only the Northern states. If he captured all of the Northern states but one, such as Pennsylvania with twenty-seven electoral votes or Ohio with twenty-three, and ignored the Southern states altogether, he could win the election. Winning almost all of the Northern states would be a difficult task, but Lincoln thought he could do it.

Lincoln envisioned victory if he could now spend all of his campaign money in the Northern half of the nation, put all of his surrogate speakers on tours through Northern states, lobby Northern newspaper editors, and circulate his campaign literature only in the Northern section of the country. That total effort on just one-half of the country could bring him victory. That chancy strategy had never been attempted before and would never be attempted so boldly again. The reason: it presented what seemed like too many problems.

But Lincoln agreed to that strategy. He concentrated his campaign on the Northern states, especially those near the Great Lakes. These had grown rapidly since 1850 and now had far more electoral votes than in past elections. In addition, New York had gained nearly one million residents since 1850, and Pennsylvania's population had grown by six hundred thousand. The population spurt made his radical election plan possible.[292]

Lincoln decided not to send any speakers to the Southern states, to cancel any funds the party had scheduled to be spent there, to ignore the usual campaigns to win regional newspaper support, and to no longer count on the independent voters in the South that the Republicans had been successful in rounding up in the last election. He knew that he was seen as Lucifer in the Southern states and did not believe he could win any of them, no matter how hard he tried. Southern cartoonists were already filling their newspapers with savage drawings of him as a close friend of African Americans.[293]

Lincoln understood that the racial events of the 1850s had created two consecutive presidential races with three or more parties in them. This shift prevented traditional alliances between political groups and isolated all four candidates in 1860. Victory could not be in alliances; he had to go it alone. None of the other party leaders understood that phenomenon.[294]

First, the possibility of capturing all of the Northern states, without losing more than one, was small just because of the enormity of the task. Second, to win the Northern states, Lincoln had to beat Douglas, the favorite in that area, which would be difficult. Third, he had to carry the Northern states that bordered on the South. Those border states contained large heavily anti-Republican, antiblack populations in their lower counties, such as in Indiana, Illinois, and Pennsylvania. Fourth, he had to carry the entire northwestern block of states, a difficult task for anyone, especially for a controversial figure like Lincoln (the fact that they were all nominally antislavery and against the Kansas-Nebraska Act helped[295]). Fifth, and finally, no matter how he and his handlers calculated and recalculated the electoral vote to get their magic victory number of 152 out of the 303 total, he had to win New York, the biggest state in America. The task was difficult, but Abraham Lincoln saw it as his best chance, perhaps his only chance, for victory.

His opponents did not. The two Southern democrats, Breckinridge and Bell, were each certain they could carry one or two Northern states, and Douglas believed he could capture Illinois, Indiana, and New York (some Bell strategists told him he would take Kentucky, Missouri, Tennessee,

Louisiana, Arkansas, and Texas as well[296]). They did not think it was possible for Lincoln to win 152 votes by taking every Northern state except one. Besides, newspaper editors and political pundits speculated, the three Democrats would probably realize that they had to run together as a fusion ticket, and that unified ticket would win in several key Northern states, again blocking Lincoln.

Lincoln, they believed, could not win. Or could he?

CHAPTER 10

A Great Speaker
Is Quiet

Make no speeches, write no letters as a candidate, enter into no pledges, make no promises, nor even give any of those kind words which men are apt to interpret into promises.

—WILLIAM CULLEN BRYANT, EDITOR,

NEW YORK EVENING POST

Springfield, Illinois, turned into a carnival in the summer and fall of 1860. The colorful and boisterous local Republican campaign club, the Wide Awakes, held meetings just about every day and most nights and staged parades through the narrow dirt streets of the city at least twice a week. These marches featured thousands of Wide Awakes in their traditional dress of black oilcloth capes and glazed hats, carrying their red and blue lanterns, huge banners with the one eye symbol of "wide awake" in the center, and dozens of gaily decorated wagons. A Wide Awake club in tiny Edgar, Illinois, had its own thirteen-piece band and a traveling glee club. In New England, the Wide Awakes were sometimes joined by the Summer

Blues, black marchers from Maine, and a group of men, all six foot two or taller, carrying rails.[297]

Most of the townspeople lined the streets of Springfield for the events, generally followed by picnics. Large broadsides, with illustrations of Lincoln and running mate Hannibal Hamlin of Maine, were nailed to fences and trees. The locals, good hardworking midwesterners, did a booming business selling replica fence rails and rail maulers to visitors. One charming feature of many parades was the Lincoln "nail wagon." This was a long, bulky wooden wagon drawn by horses manned by Lincoln supporters who operated a nail-making machine on it. As the machine spit out nails designed with an *L* on the flat head, the workers would toss the nails into the crowd, where people, particularly children, would leap and dive for their very own "Lincoln nails." A large banner on the side of the wagon read: NAILS FOR THE AMERICAN PEOPLE, WHO CAN HIT THE NAIL ON THE HEAD AND ELECT LINCOLN.[298]

Sitting quietly in his two-story, white-clapboard home in the middle of the festivals was the Republican nominee for president, under orders not to make public pronouncements or take pen to paper as the nominee without someone else serving as an editor. Judge Davis and his campaign team were terrified that undecided voters would get to know Abe Lincoln just as he was. They might have been able to sell him as a country boy and slavery moderate at the convention to delegates who did not know better, but they did not want anyone to see the real Abe Lincoln. The real Lincoln was one of the most dynamic, forceful speakers in America, a man with a consuming hatred of slavery, and an equally deep hatred of the Know-Nothings they were trying to court. If Lincoln was allowed to make speeches, as he said he wanted to do, his managers knew another fire-eating "House Divided" speech was on its way, a speech that would wreck his chances for victory as a moderate on slavery.

"Write nothing for publication!" urged John Fry, a personal friend since 1848, when they met at a political rally. "(That) killed Clay. For God's sake, don't let it kill you!"[299]

William Cullen Bryant, the editor of the *New York Evening Post*, told Lincoln that he represented "the vast majority of your friends." He wrote him that "they want you to make no speeches, write no letters as a candidate, enter into no pledges, make no promises, nor even give any of those kind words which men are apt to interpret into promises."[300]

Lincoln turned down everyone. He even rejected an offer from a Wide Awake club in Buffalo, New York, in early October and another from one in Concord, New Hampshire, on October 26. Both asked him to speak in front of a huge crowd of Wide Awakes and local Republicans—where he was assured nothing could go wrong.[301]

This was probably more false bravado on Lincoln's part, a wrinkle in his "who me?" public attitude toward the presidency in 1858 and 1859. He was just as shrewd as his advisers (they never believed that and later expressed amazement that Lincoln was so smart[302]) and knew that speeches on slavery ran the risk of allying him with the abolitionist radicals who were so unpopular. He wrote the *Louisville Journal* of his silence, "There are bad men…who would seize upon almost any letter I could write, as being an 'awful coming down.'"[303]

He was also apprehensive about the way he looked in public. Friend William Herndon said he always worried that people would think badly of him because his clothes never fit.[304]

All Lincoln did publicly was greet visitors. Hundreds of well-wishers made the trek to Springfield to see the standard-bearer of the party, getting little out of him politically. Tourists on their way to Chicago often stopped at Springfield, if they knew someone there, and managed to arrange a five-minute visit with the candidate, who charmed one and all with his homespun humor and stories. With a smile, he dismissed the hundreds of people who descended upon Springfield seeking jobs in the new administration. While he greeted all these people, he kept an eye on his rambunctious young son, Tad, who played in the governor's office all day.[305] Lincoln only made one public appearance all summer, at a huge Springfield rally on a hot August day, where he was nearly crushed by the surge of people and had to be whisked away in a carriage. He toyed with the idea of a major campaign speech at that rally, which had substantial press coverage, but was talked out of it by his aides. "Can it help you or hurt you?" asked George Fogg, secretary of the Republican National Committee, which had opened offices at the Astor Hotel in New York City. "It can only hurt." [306]

Remaining quiet meant that he could not respond to attacks from Douglas newspapers, such as the *Philadelphia Evening Journal,* that constantly portrayed him as a frontiersman who had very little political experience beyond the state legislature, except for a single term in Congress. He had no administrative experience beyond running a general store as a young man. Who would make this man president, they asked?[307]

The Democratic newspapers pilloried him, calling him "Old Ape" instead of "Old Abe" and insisting, as one did, that he looked "like a monkey taking medicine." The *New York Leader* said he was "a horrid-looking wretch." The *New Albany (Indiana) Daily Ledger*, like many journals, said he was "ugly." The *Jonsesboro (Illinois) Gazette* wrote that the Republicans "select their leaders from the lowest haunts of vice and infamy." A writer in the *Boston Herald* declared the Republicans were "inhuman monsters, practicing all sorts of rascality, cheating and defrauding creditors and refusing to pay their debts." A Minnesota newspaper insisted that the Republicans take down their huge Lincoln banner in the middle of town because Lincoln's face was scaring away business. One boy selling reproductions of a photo of Lincoln on the streets shouted to passersby, "Here's your likeness of Abe Lincoln. Buy one. Price only two shillings. Will look a great deal better when he gets his hair combed."

Lincoln was well aware of his physical appearance. Later, he looked at an appealing painting of himself and told the artist that "you took your idea of me from my principles and not my person." As a young man, he told a rally of himself that "I was a poor boy" and that he worked as a lowly paid flatboatman and that his breeches were always too short and showed his bare legs. One newspaper cartoonist drew him as the devil, and another portrayed him as the emaciated man in a "before and after" medicine ad.[308]

The Republicans fired back, insinuating in newspaper stories that most of the Democrats' supporters, especially those behind Douglas, were common drunks and that Douglas campaign strategy meetings were held in local saloons. The name-calling had been continuous for years. Back in 1855, several Republicans in Congress said that their Democratic colleagues were "drunk as owls."[309]

Douglas, his mainstream party shattered in two, decided his only chance for victory was to turn the election into a vote on Stephen Douglas and his long career, not a vote for the Democratic Party. He cast tradition aside and announced he would personally campaign from one end of the nation to the other, North and South, to bring his message directly to the people. Douglas thus became the first presidential candidate in history to actively campaign (no presidential contender would tour again until 1896). He was certain that public appearances and his well-known oratorical skills could carry enough Southern states, stop the Republicans in the electoral college, and give him a chance to win.

Lincoln was not particularly alarmed that Douglas was going on a cross-country stump. Douglas matched Lincoln as a public speaker, but he had been painted into a corner on the slavery-territorial question and had shown throughout 1858, 1859, and 1860 that he could not escape from that dilemma. The more he talked, the more he would position himself as the man eternally caught in the middle between Democrats North and South on slavery. Lincoln was certain that each speech Douglas delivered would help to further split the Democratic Party. His campaign manager Davis said, "I consider Douglas the most arrogant demagogue that ever disgraced humanity." [310]

The Republican candidate knew, too, that no matter how scripted Douglas speeches could be, no matter how careful he was in what he said, there was always the chance that he would expose himself further by answering questions yelled from a crowd or in a discussion with an official that he met or some reporter from a local newspaper. Another candidate could goad him into saying something he did not want to say. Lincoln had managed to do just that to him in their 1858 Senate debates. Lincoln understood Douglas' position completely. Douglas did not.

Lincoln was given the use of a conference room in the Illinois governor's office in Springfield, and it was there that he met the public and held meetings with aides. He met frequently with Judge Davis, Leonard Swett, and Jesse Dubois to plan campaign strategy and with them individually when the others were on the campaign trail. Lincoln played a greater role in his own campaign than any candidate in history up to that time. A look at the letters to him (more than eight thousand arrived in Springfield from June through November[311]) and the letters he sent out, plus his direction of emissaries to different states, show that he was in complete control of his campaign—from strategy to execution to publicity.

It was a strikingly contemporary campaign and broke new ground in American politics. The campaign reinforced the idea of American business versus foreign business, which remains a powerful issue today, through arguments on high protective tariffs. Lincoln sought the immigrant vote, as modern politicians do, and targeted immigrant population areas for hard campaign pushes. Lincoln became the classic man with no ties to the political system—the "outsider" image later adapted by Franklin Roosevelt, Jimmy Carter, Bill Clinton, Barack Obama, and others. It was a new party with new votes, and it conducted effective voter registration drives to bring young voters into politics. The Lincoln Republican campaign used single-sheet circulars and pamphlets as modern politicians use television and orchestrated huge media blitzes. The Pennsylvania state committee mailed five thousand pamphlets and circulars every day. The Illinois committee sent out more than six thousand in three weeks just to one county there.[312] By mid-September, the national committee was daily mailing out seventy thousand circulars to every state.[313]

They made maximum use of the strong role religions and churches played in the country, tying the entire antislavery part of their campaign to religion and the idea that God would not enslave any man. A large percentage of the population attended church regularly, whether traditional or evangelical churches, and the Republicans, aware of these American convictions, turned their political crusade against slavery into a religious crusade.

Several Lincoln supporters wrote songs for the contest, such as "The Campaign Quick Step," "Lincoln and Liberty," "Old Abe," "Honest Old Abe of the West," and a multitude of "Rail-Splitter" tunes. Their best jingle was their campaign song, sung out strongly by gatherings of as many as forty thousand people—"Ain't You Glad You Joined the Republicans," accompanied by the melody of "The Old Gray Mare."[314]

Lincoln and his campaign sought the new young voters for a new party and a new president.

Republican supporter Charles Leib of Chicago suggested a campaign newspaper, a propaganda weekly, to publicize Lincoln's positions. The paper, *The Rail-Splitter*, began publication in August and was distributed weekly through the end of October. Two Cincinnati, Ohio, men also published another edition of *The Rail-Splitter* there (several state Democratic organizations published Douglas "campaign journals" also).[315]

The Republicans seized on the corruption of the Buchanan administration as their top issue. The issue also underlined the honesty of Lincoln. Corruption also gave the Republicans a viable issue other than slavery, and despite the pivotal force of slavery in the election, they needed to downplay that issue in many states and counties because there was only marginal support for an antislavery crusade at the time. Corruption (and issues like the protective tariff and the Homestead Act) affected everyone. By harping on it, the Republicans could easily paint the Democrats and Buchanan as villains. Corruption was so rampant in the Buchanan administration, and so frequently reported in the press, that it had an almost Watergate investigatory mood to it. Republicans mentioned corruption in nearly all of their speeches.[316] One Republican said, "The present administration has been woefully corrupt and black with crime, and it's most alarming feature is that they keep multiplying and becoming popular."[317]

The Republicans did not have to look far to find examples of Democratic corruption under President Buchanan and his administration. In 1857 a House committee with a Democratic majority, led by Pennsylvania Congressman John Covode, revealed that a U.S. military post, Fort Snelling, in Minnesota, had been sold privately to group of businessmen led by Secretary of War John Floyd's personal banker and the brother of the collector of customs of New York, a Buchanan appointee. They also revealed that Floyd himself bought land for the government from that same group for an "exorbitant" amount of money.[318]

A separate investigation, conducted by Representative John Sherman (R-Ohio) found that U.S. Navy yards in New York and Philadelphia were overloaded with patronage people personally appointed by Buchanan and his underlings in the party. They also discovered that Navy Secretary Isaac Toucey wrote government contracts in such a way as to ensure that a contract for shipments of wood for the navy could only be filled by W. C. N. Swift of New Bedford, Massachusetts, who had contributed $16,000 to Buchanan's 1856 presidential campaign.[319]

Someone else uncovered a letter from Democratic operative W. C. Patterson to Buchanan asking for a machine contract because it would help guarantee the election of Representative Thomas Florence, a personal friend of Buchanan. Cornelius Wendell, former publisher of one of Buchanan's newspapers, the *Union*, in Washington DC testified before Congress that he had been earning over $166,000 a year from government printing contracts awarded him by the administration and had then turned over $100,000 of that sum to subsidize two pro-Buchanan newspapers in Philadelphia.[320]

S. J. Magree, a paper contractor, testified that in 1856, he received money from Wendell to give to the American Party in New Jersey so that they could split the Republican vote and ensure Buchanan's election there. Another investigation indicated that Buchanan's men awarded Pennsylvania newspaper publisher John Forney a government contract to print post office literature in return for support in the 1856 election. In May 1860 the Democratic New York City postmaster, Isaac Fowler, appointed by Buchanan, fled the country after he was charged with embezzling $155,000 in government funds. One month later, it was revealed that Secretary

Toucey's nephew was co-owner of a company awarded a coal contract by the navy office in Philadelphia. Pockets of Democratic corruption were discovered in states too. The last Democratic governor of Illinois, Joel Matteson, had something to do with the embezzlement of $230,000 in state funds and in 1859 agreed to replace the money over five years. The Republicans promptly charged in the 1860 campaign that Matteson's support of Douglas was made in return for a secret pledge from Douglas to free him of his debt.[321]

Even the House of Representatives doorkeeper was corrupt. He was fired for falsifying his official account book.

President Buchanan acknowledged questionable behavior but declared himself innocent of any charge of corruption. He raged that his name had been unjustly sullied, asserting that Congress had treated him like "a common pickpocket." He wrote to a friendly newspaper editor: "I have endeavored to be not only pure, but unsuspected. I have never had any concern in awarding contracts, but have left them to be given by the heads of the appropriate departments. I have ever detested all jobs and no man at any period of my life has ever approached me on such a subject."[322]

The Republicans fired back.

"The administration party…(is) responsible for all the evils which the country has suffered in consequence of their laying ruthless hands upon that time-honored compact of the fathers of our country," declared Republican Amos Briggs of Schaghticoke, New York, in October, one of many Republicans who tied the president to all the corruption around him.[323]

The Republican Party constantly upbraided the Democrats. New Jersey Republicans declared that the administration was "corrupt beyond example and to a degree which no nation can long exist," and numerous newspapers backed up those charges. J. E. Folet of Indianapolis, head of one of the Lincoln Clubs, wrote that the Republicans had to show "inflexible determination to conquer corruption and do everything that could possibly be done (to end it)."[324]

Corruption worked as a double-edged sword against the Democrats and the administration. Corruption hurt them on a surface level, implying that everyone in the administration and the party was crooked. It also worked against them on another level, even more lethal. Many, particularly Northern newspaper editors, insinuated that the money plundered from the federal government was not only going into the pockets of some individuals but was sent to secessionists in the Southern states for political purposes. It was also implied, albeit in veiled language, that the plundered funds were spent secretly in the Southern states to arm militias for an insurrection against the government over the slavery issue.[325]

The Republicans were so sure they could profit from the corruption issue that they inserted an anticorruption plank in their platform. It read:

> *That the people justly view with alarm the reckless extravagance which pervades every department of the federal government... To arrest the systematic plunder of the treasury; while the recent startling developments of frauds and corruption at the federal metropolis show that an entire change of administration is imperatively demanded.*[326]

Throughout the campaign, Republicans told each other repeatedly that the corruption issue was wining votes for them and was important to their overall strategy. Congressman John Sherman of Ohio felt that the attack on corruption was "the chief virtue of the Republican success,"[327] and Representative William Stokes (R-Tennessee) said on the House floor that he feared "thousands of people in the country" would vote for Lincoln solely because of the corruption issue.[328] Senator James Grimes of Iowa even felt that the corruption issue, state by state, was an even more effective vote-getting issue than the antislavery campaign.[329] August Belmont, the National Democratic chairman and the party's chief fund-raiser, wrote a friend that the people of New York were "disgusted with the misrule of Mr. Buchanan and the corruption which disgraced his administration" and said that it was one of the reasons that the Democrats faced an uphill fight against Lincoln.[330]

The corruption issue was so solid that none of the Democrats, not even Vice President Breckinridge, defended the administration. Southern Democratic newspapers were just as critical of Buchanan and governmental corruption as the Republicans, and it undermined the strength of the administration and, secondly, the strength of all the Democrats running for president. Southern Democratic newspapers repeatedly criticized their own Democratic Party over corruption.

The *Louisville Journal* charged outright that the Lecompton Constitution in Kansas (proslavery) was bought by Buchanan. Its editor, George Prentice, wrote:

> *Men in high places were bought with money for that purpose. $30,000 at least were used by the great agent in the purchase and sale of votes under this administration, directly to influence a few men... the Chief Executive proved himself the more liberal handler of the money received from fat public contracts than any other man. Our government...is beyond all question the most corrupt, shameless and profligate on earth.*[331]

CHAPTER 11

Lincoln, the Letter Writer

The Democrats are going to give us a harder race than we anticipated a few weeks ago...

—REPUBLICAN ORGANIZER JOSEPH MEDILL

The Republicans, though staunchly antislavery, were so touchy about the slavery issue and ties to the abolitionists that Lincoln ordered one of his aides to contact John Wentworth, Chicago mayor and editor of the *Chicago Daily Democrat*, and asked him to tone down his rhetoric, in which he portrayed Lincoln as a radical on slavery. He included lines like "abolitionists throw their banner to the breeze, inscribed with Lincoln's glorious words, 'the states must be made all free.'" The newspaper stories were sent to Lincoln by Joe Medill of the *Chicago Press and Tribune*, who told the Republican nominee that he had it from an unimpeachable source that armed Bell and Breckinridge men were going to overthrow the House and Senate and would install Breckinridge as president.[332]

In fact, the slavery issue is rarely mentioned in any of the correspondence between Lincoln and various politicians and political bosses throughout the country. Their chief concern during the campaign was not slavery but getting elected (throughout the fall, various local workers told Lincoln that Wentworth was slowly moving to Douglas and was fabricating Lincoln quotes to help him).[333]

Lincoln had to fend off rumors from the other side of the slavery question too. One of his enemies began an effective chain-letter crusade, completely misrepresenting his votes on the issue of slavery in the District of Columbia while he was in Congress. The letters, spread far and wide, argued that Lincoln consistently voted for slavery in the district, when he did not. The Republican nominee wrote to John Hill, who told him of the letter-writing campaign "(In the debates with Douglas)...I said I should be exceedingly glad to see slavery abolished in the District of Columbia."[334]

Little is known about their private meetings from the letters of Lincoln's inner clique (the recipients of many letters from Lincoln in the campaign were told to burn them), but the letters of Lincoln and his aides to politicians around the country were voluminous and painted a detailed picture of the campaign. They mapped out the nation, state by state, county by county, city by city, town by town, just as Lincoln had painstakingly done in his own campaign in the Illinois Senate race two years earlier.

The correspondence between Lincoln and political leaders and candidates sometimes totaled eight to ten letters a day. Most were long, analytic letters assessing the campaign in various states and counties. Many from Lincoln moved people from one area to another to increase campaign efforts. Others included notes to and from political bosses, such as Thurlow Weed, seeking late analysis of how the vote looked. Lincoln wrote at least sixteen letters to Weed in addition to the thirty sent to Weed by David Davis, Norman

Judd, and others. They sent over forty more letters to Alexander McClure, the state chairman in Pennsylvania. Lincoln wrote more than forty letters to Judd when he was on the road, more than sixty to Judge Davis, fifteen to Lyman Trumbull, thirty-one to Mark Delahay, an attorney and former newspaper editor in Kansas, a dozen each to Leonard Swett and Joseph Medill, and fourteen to Elihu Washburne. He corresponded regularly with James Harvey, a Pennsylvanian, who sent him four-to-six-page political analyses on a regular basis. Lincoln personally wrote or received more than six hundred campaign letters (not counting the hundreds that were burned) from June 1 to November 6, an average of six to seven per business day (letters from Illinois reached other Northern cities within two days; telegrams arrived within minutes). In all of Lincoln's letters to local political operatives, he asked the same question: "How does it look?"[335]

Lincoln was also kept informed on political events in one state via letters from political leaders in another. He learned on June 25 that William Moorhead of Pittsburgh was certain that Allegheny County (Pennsylvania) would back Lincoln with about 8,500 votes, against 3,500 for Frémont in 1856, from a letter he received from Schuyler Colfax in Indiana, who met with Moorhead there.[336] Lincoln learned from Weed in New York that the Republicans were in trouble in Rhode Island in late summer because Douglas men were able to raise enormous amounts of money from local manufacturing executives. (Weed then went to Rhode Island to begin work to turn the state for Lincoln).[337] Weed's claim was bolstered a few days later by Simon Cameron of Pennsylvania, whose sources told him that Douglas had made some kind of political bargain with the governor of Rhode Island in order to capture the state.[338] He learned from Joe Medill, whose newspaper connections provided a granary of information, that in October,

Douglas planned to spend two weeks speaking in Indiana and then would give speeches in Michigan on various dates between September 10 and November 5, 1860.[339] Pennsylvanian John Harvey told him that several local Republican congressmen who pledged loyalty to him were actually campaigning against him privately.[340]

Lincoln even received anonymous letters from Democrats who kept him abreast of developments in their party. One letter arrived in early September that accurately informed him of a meeting between Pennsylvania U.S. Senator William Bigler and eighty wealthy New Yorkers to raise money for Douglas. The contributors told Bigler they were convinced Douglas could not win and would not fund his campaign.[341]

Amos Tuck wrote him from New Hampshire that the latest Republican rally there drew a substantial crowd of more than eight thousand people and that Salmon Chase, George Fogg, and New Hampshire Governor Ichabod Goodwin gave excellent speeches for Lincoln.[342] Upon a visit to friends in Pennsylvania, Tom Dudley, a New Jersey political leader, told Lincoln that the state seemed safe based on his conversations with people there.[343] From his nomination to his election, Lincoln received hundreds of letters full of news, information, and opinion from all over America.[344]

Lincoln received frequent letters from local politicians whom he met on the stump between 1840 and 1859 and who wished him well or wanted to campaign for him, all the result of Lincoln's helping others who could one day help him. Tom Tullock of New Hampshire offered to help and even sent Lincoln a campaign worker, Frank Fuller. He wrote, "We remember with much satisfaction your visit to the Granite State."[345]

The mail also kept him up to date on how the campaign was going in far distant states where logistics prohibited the dispatch of Davis, Swett, or Judd, such as those in the South or far West, like Oregon and California.

Amory Holbrook, the former U.S. attorney for Oregon, let him know that he was speaking for him in every county and every backwoods precinct, that "hard and zealous work" was being done, and that the state "will be carried."[346] Holbrook told him that the Republicans had picked up three more state legislative seats in Oregon in 1859, giving them twelve of thirty-eight, and seemed on the ascendancy. The thirty-eight Democratic legislative seats were split between the Douglas men (sixteen) and the Buchanan clique (twenty-two).[347]

Republican Congressman Elbridge Spaulding in New York told him in late July that the Empire State was "regarded as safe for the Republican ticket."[348]

Levi Powell of Clarksburg, Virginia, kept Lincoln abreast of activity there, a state where he had no chance but hoped operatives could create mischief with the opposition. Powell wrote: "Your friends here...keep it a warm contest between the friends of Douglas and Breckinridge in order to give the state to Bell... We can help you only by dividing the enemy."[349]

Lincoln's nephew, John Hanks, who left Springfield in 1850 and had become an Oregonian, explained to him that Douglas, not Breckinridge, was the strongest Democrat in Oregon and the candidate to be stopped, adding that "Douglas will be hard to beat."[350]

This was exactly what Lincoln wanted to hear. California and Oregon had a few electoral votes (just seven between them), but if he won both and then added them to a large state such as Pennsylvania or Indiana, those far west states could be the difference between victory and defeat in November.

Others suggested that tactics that worked in appealing to workingmen in one area would work for others in different parts of the country, such as the efforts to legislate protective tariffs to protect ironworkers in the East. William Bourne of New York urged the Republicans to push hard on the rights of the workers in the western states. He wrote: "Let the working men of the country be well informed of the iron platform movement of united working men. Keep it before them. Help us to help you. (For you)...an iron platform for Pennsylvania, built of American iron!"[351]

Politicians in the border states kept Lincoln up to date on their efforts. By late September, Republicans in Missouri were finally making a dent in the two Democratic tickets there. "We are working some results from Douglas men. I am really surprised at our success," wrote Sam Glover about one Democratic ticket. He added with glee about the other—the Breckinridge ticket—that it was turning off thousands. He said, "The Buchanan Democrats are violent and appeal to the worst passion in the multitude."[352]

Politicians Lincoln met who did not actively campaign for him were helpful in telling him how the election was going in their district so that he could send money or campaign literature. Ed Pierce was one. He had met Lincoln during 1857, when Lincoln campaigned for John Wentworth in Chicago. The two were introduced at the offices of the *Chicago Press and Tribune* after a Lincoln speech. Pierce met Lincoln again when Lincoln gave his Cooper Union speech in New York during the winter of 1860.

"Everything looks well here," Pierce wrote of his district in Massachusetts, where there was much Seward support that Lincoln was trying to tap. "There was some disappointment at Mr. Seward's not being nominated, but his friends were generally the best friends of the cause."[353]

Locals helped relieve Lincoln's concerns when they provided accurate data about the Douglas campaign, reporting what they believed were the actual sizes of crowds after the Democratic newspapers reported much larger numbers. They also gave Lincoln a more balanced view of crowd reaction to Douglas as he campaigned across the nation. Former Congressman Joe Casey, one of Lincoln's Pennsylvania operatives, followed Douglas through his state. He reported that "crowds guffawed at Douglas in Harrisburg when Douglas lamented the defeat of the tariff."[354]

These reports enabled Lincoln to ascertain how the Republican campaign was going in each state and to adjust the party's efforts. Even the far-flung Republican Party could not cover every town and village in every state, but these letters and reports could serve as their eyes and ears.

Of course, tumbling out of the middle of the stacks of hundreds of important political and policy letters were notes from job seekers, con men, entrepreneurs, prognosticators, and "long lost relatives." A photographer tried to interest Lincoln in sitting for photos that the nominee could purchase later at a nominal fee. One letter writer, who had heard so much about the candidate's travels over back roads in the Midwest to try legal cases, attempted to sell him a horse. Attorney/author/abolitionist Henry Sherman sent him a copy of his latest book, *Slavery in the United States of America*.[355] Another man sent Lincoln a Welsh translation of his Cooper Union speech. George Card of Illinois was so confident that Lincoln would win that, shortly after the campaign began, he asked him for a presidential appointment to West Point.[356]

He had letters from people telling him of the odd places where they learned of his nomination. One man was sailing on the steamship *Arabia*, off the coast of Nova Scotia, when he heard the news.[357]

Then there were the ardent Republicans on the campaign trail who kept asking Lincoln for expense money, such as R. H. Brooke of Para, Illinois.[358] Sam Field had a bargain for Lincoln. He told the nominee that a wealthy Douglas supporter in his hometown in Westchester County, New York, had offered him $100 a month to campaign for the Little Giant. He believed in the Republicans, though, and would ignore the offer and campaign for Lincoln instead for the bargain price of just $33 a month.[359]

And, as always, there were job seekers. "I will deliver two hundred votes if you can assure me I can have a position in the custom house," wrote former newspaper reporter John Carson of Philadelphia, who said he needed an immediate answer.[360]

John Pickell, who fought in the Black Hawk War at the same time that Lincoln did, thought that bond deserved employment. The apparently multitalented Pickell, at the time a newspaperman, wrote Lincoln that he would like a job in Baltimore either as a government coal inspector, surveyor, or naval agent.[361] Ben James of Chicago had loftier ambitions. He wrote Lincoln that he wanted to be the president's private secretary. Another man said that if Lincoln gave him a job in a U.S. Custom House, he would guarantee two hundred votes.[362]

Lincoln had to suffer the pessimists, such as young Medill in Chicago, whom Lincoln's men said listened to too many people. In a depressing letter, Medill wrote Lincoln that "friends tell me it's a close race in October (several state elections), and chances are against us. The Democrats are going to give us a harder race than we anticipated a few weeks ago…in Illinois, I fear Sangamon, other north and central counties will be lost. My (hope) of carrying the state legislature is subsiding."[363] Lincoln did not respond.

The mail brought a twenty-four–year-old bill. E. C. Blankenship of Upper Alton, Illinois, contended that in 1836 Lincoln represented a family's trust fund, which was supposed to pay Blankenship $143. He claimed he never received the funds, and now, since Lincoln was going to be president, he wanted his money.[364]

The Republican nominee was sent letters from eccentrics who wanted him to start federal murder investigations as soon as he moved into the White House. Morton Bradley of Peoria, Illinois, who spent three days with President William Henry Harrison when he was inaugurated in

1840, and was absolutely certain that Harrison's death was due to poison. Lincoln, he felt, should look into the claim immediately.[365] That murder conspiracy was expanded by Oliver Parker, who wrote Lincoln a long letter carefully explaining that Harrison *and* President Zachary Taylor had both been poisoned in office so that their vice presidents, from slave states, could become president and defend that institution. He added that an effort was made to murder President Buchanan because he did not support slavery strongly enough, and he cited the fact that five hundred people at a convention Buchanan attended came down with food poisoning. Parker said that the slavers would surely try to murder Lincoln for the same reason. Parker had it on good authority that both Harrison and Taylor were killed by poison sprinkled into brown sugar that they used with their coffee. He urged Lincoln never to use brown sugar, or any kind of sugar, when he drank coffee (Lincoln bristled at the numerous letters about his assassination and by dozens of visitors to his Springfield office who warned him of plots against his life).[366]

Peter Wyckoff, a casual acquaintance in Chicago, wrote to ask Lincoln if he could use his name on his business cards as a character reference.[367] Joe Colbert, another friend, asked Lincoln, the staunchest antislavery man in America, to write a letter of recommendation for him that he could use to increase his business with slaveholders in Kentucky.[368] George Savidge wrote a very serious letter explaining in great detail how he had recently passed through Springfield on his way to New York and left a package of some kind in the baggage room of the railroad station. He knew no one in Springfield except Lincoln, whom he constantly read about in the newspapers, and wondered if Lincoln would be kind enough to walk over to the train depot and try to recover his package for him.[369] Hugh East of Bloomfield, Indiana, a gambler, wrote Lincoln to tell him he had to work extra hard to win the election because a friend of his had bet $10,000 on him.[370] Sam Artus of Quincy, Illinois, caught a large salmon and was so pleased with the size of it that he wrapped his catch up and mailed it to the Republican nominee so that he could enjoy a fine dinner while working on his campaign.[371]

L. Clapham mailed him a large box of grapes.[372] Zenas Robbins of Washington DC offered Lincoln the use of his home until the inauguration, explaining that he had a large living room that the nominee could use for his cabinet meetings and that, most important, "Mrs. Robbins will be most cordial to Mrs. Lincoln."[373]

William Knoer, from Pennsylvania, wrote Lincoln that he was quite ill and needed money from Lincoln to get better.[374] Another man said he needed money because he could not work; he had spent so much time on the Lincoln campaign that he could not find a job.[375] One man in New Jersey claimed that a fireworks display he was operating in a Lincoln rally exploded, and he needed money for his recovery.[376] A woman named Libbie Bailey, of Irvington, New Jersey, told him that she and her sisters were the long lost sisters that Lincoln never knew.[377] George Lincoln of Alabama told him that he always had to prove to Southerners who hated Lincoln that he was not related to the nominee.[378]

One bold entrepreneur explained that he had somehow purchased and was now selling dozens of wood canes that Lincoln had made thirty years before with John Hanks. He attached a photo of Lincoln to each cane and was now writing the nominee to ask if he could send him dozens of strands of his hair to include with the picture in the sale.[379]

Some of the letters brought a smile to Lincoln's lips, such as a charming note from Grace Bedell, eleven years old, of New York. She wrote: "Let your whiskers grow. You would look a great deal better, for your face is so thin. All the ladies like whiskers, and they would tease their husbands to vote for you and then you would be president."[380]

In a macabre note, an insurance salesman for D. L. Olmstead and Co. offered him a discounted life insurance policy.[381]

The boldest letter of all was from William Hemstreet, owner of the Adams Express Company in Philadelphia. He read that Lincoln wrote hundreds of letters and tried to sell him his company's short-hand writing system at just $10 per week, telling the nominee that he could save "four fifths of your valuable time" with the system. "Escaping the drudgery and brain retardation of the pen and business can be dispatched with five times the speed," he added in his pitch.[382]

The one thing that Lincoln enjoyed in the campaign was bits of gossip that came his way. There was plenty of it. Midwesterners gossiped madly about Thurlow Weed, and the New Yorkers gossiped about the Pennsylvania Democrats. "Forney has given a terrible stab to Foster," wrote Alexander McClure of the newspaper columns of John Forney about Democratic gubernatorial candidate Henry Foster.[383]

Lincoln learned from the mail, too, that people were saving letters from him as "autographs."[384]

Inns and hotels around America invited him to stay with them now that he was president-elect.[385]

The one unfortunate result of all the letters he read was that hundreds of them told him what he wanted to hear—he was going to win the election. Could the correspondents from so many different states, counties, and towns be wrong? He grew overconfident from his mail. He was so certain, early in July, that he wrote Hannibal Hamlin that they would be victorious. In early August, he repeated that claim to Caleb Smith of Indiana. Again, in August, he wrote to Simeon Francis in Oregon:

I hesitate to say it, but it really appears now, as if the success of the Republican ticket is inevitable. We have no reason to doubt any of the states that voted for Fremont. Add to these Minnesota, Pennsylvania, and New Jersey, and the thing is done.[386]

He had to settle numerous intraparty disputes over campaign funds. The biggest squabble was between Pennsylvanians and New Yorkers, who loathed each other. Lincoln asked Weed to send Pennsylvania money expressly because Pennsylvanians Simon Cameron and Alex McClure asked for more cash, complaining that they had no funds and could not mail any circulars or pamphlets for the Philadelphia mayor's election. As soon as Lincoln did what he was asked to do, the Pennsylvanians howled in complaint because the money came from Weed in New York.

Russell Errett of Pennsylvania, who was running for comptroller of Pittsburgh, wailed to Lincoln through his friend Medill of the feud. He said Philadelphians were furious that they had to beg for money from Weed and the New Yorkers.[387]

An exasperated Lincoln then had to add this peacemaking mission to all the other conflicts he wanted Judge Davis to settle on his next trip to Philadelphia.

These disputes and jealousies between party leaders in different states did not surprise him. Back in 1857, just three years after the Republican Party was formed, he had predicted they would argue. "We were a collection of individuals, but recently in political hostility, one to another, and then subject to all that distrust and suspicion and jealousy could do."[388]

He frequently used local campaign chiefs to smooth over feuds or help correct what he thought was a gross distortion of his views in newspapers. Sometimes this worked and sometimes it did not. In the middle of the summer, he told George Fogg, his man in New York City, to get James Gordon Bennett, editor of the *New York Herald*, to not only correct a mistake in his paper, but have the reporter write an entire correction story, with his name on it. Fogg was persuasive. So was Bennett. The *Herald* was Bennett's paper, not Lincoln's, the editor, an old ally of Seward, told Fogg. All the *Herald* would do is print a two-paragraph correction, buried inside. No more. Lincoln dropped the matter.[389]

There was correspondence that must have warmed Lincoln's heart, such as letters from and about the elderly who had been born in the last century, seen the American Revolution and the War of 1812, and supported the Founding Fathers. One of the most touching was from D. C. Gillespie, of Bearbille, Pennsylvania. He wrote, "My father is eighty-four. He was crippled at Lundy's Lane (War of 1812). He has not voted for a number of years. He told me he shall vote for you (if he must) out of a carriage."[390]

On other occasions, Lincoln found that letters directly from him were much more effective than notes from aides. He believed a story written about him in a Midwest newspaper was full of mistakes and wrote a long letter to the editor about it. The result was a very apologetic story in the paper, correcting the errors.

Lincoln also used the mail to write forceful letters to stamp out untrue rumors about him, rumors that could wreck the campaign. He was successful in a series of letters to a man who had started a rumor that Lincoln had stayed at an inn where known American Party/Know-Nothings routinely met and had become friendly with them. In a long note, Lincoln emphasized that the inn was merely a stopover where he kept warm while waiting for a stagecoach. The letter ended the rumor. On another occasion, he reassured Abe Jonas that he was not and had never been a Know-Nothing but admitted that he, and other Republicans, had adopted a new policy of not publicly criticizing the Know-Nothings and asked Jonas to pass on that information. Lincoln wrote, "It must not publicly appear that I am paying any attention to the charges."[391]

He also kept up with friends who were watching other friends. Lower-level Republican officials constantly wrote him on what other higher-level officials were doing for him in their state. Notes to him showed that someone was fulfilling, or not fulfilling, promises, such as a July letter from James Lesley of Philadelphia, who informed the candidate that Simon Cameron had given a fine speech on his behalf earlier in the week.[392]

There was jealousy and dislike between the Republicans in New York and Pennsylvania that Lincoln was never able to resolve. Their dispute started in Chicago, where New Yorkers blamed Pennsylvanians for ruining Seward's chances for the presidency. There was hatred in New York for New Yorkers, such as the rift between Seward/Weed and Horace Greeley. Dozens of New York politicians told Lincoln he had to be wary of anybody from their state. "The politicians in this state (are) beyond dispute the most corrupt, selfish clan that was ever banded together," wrote George Davis, an upstate New York Republican.[393]

California Republicans hated California Democrats, but it often seemed they hated members of their own party even more. James Churchman wrote that there was hostility between two groups of Republicans (they ran separate tickets in the San Francisco area against each other) that threatened Lincoln's election chances. Churchman felt the county Republicans were despicable. He wrote, "We are so villainously and corruptly ruled that our people have forgotten that working for principle is a popular thing."[394]

Another spat broke out in early September between Judge Davis, Hannibal Hamlin, and Schuyler Colfax. Davis told Lincoln that Hamlin told Colfax that two Republican congressional candidates might be beaten. Letters then flew from Lincoln to Hamlin and the national committee to hold the line in Maine. An angry Hamlin then wrote Lincoln that he had never said any such thing to Colfax, and that he was certain the two congressmen in question would win.[395]

Judge Davis was fed up with all the feuding politicians by early July and worried that the factions would bring the party down. He said, "Jealousies are great disturbances to party contests."[396]

Would all those disputes and jealousies wreck the campaign?

★ CHAPTER 12 ★

The Wide Awakes

Our Friends in Maine led off the van,

The Keystone followed, true,

And now we'll try, with might and main

What "Jersey Blues" can do.

—TRENTON, NEW JERSEY, WIDE AWAKES PAMPHLET

The planning of the Lincoln campaign was simple and brilliant. Because of the unpopularity of the Republicans and Lincoln in the South and fear of the contest being thrown into the House and Senate, Lincoln decided to ignore the Southern slave states and concentrate his campaign on the northern half of the country, plus Oregon and California in the far West. In the North, they mapped out the campaign geographically and chronologically. Although Breckinridge and Bell would be contenders in most Northern states, the Lincoln team decided correctly that their chief rival was still Douglas. Thurlow Weed wrote Lincoln of the Democratic convention, "(It) was madness.... Democratic destruction. This is our opportunity."[397]

They decided that they had to hold the states John Frémont took in the presidential election of 1856 and win in four states he had lost—Illinois, Indiana, Pennsylvania, and New Jersey. They had a westerner running, and therefore had to win the West—Iowa, Wisconsin, and Michigan. Most important, they had to capture New York with its huge thirty-five electoral votes (21 percent of the winning total).

Chronologically, they wanted to win the Maine statewide races in September to give the entire campaign needed momentum. One month after that, in October, they wanted to win the statewide races in Indiana, Ohio, and Pennsylvania to earn even more traction and convince voters in other states to get on their bandwagon.

The Lincoln team, familiar with the rush of German immigrants into central Illinois and the Midwest, decided to seek the immigrant vote and created a "foreign" division, headed up by German American leader Carl Schurz, who would speak in immigrant districts in the various Northern states. At the same time, others would try to get the former Know-Nothings, the ardent enemies of the immigrants, to back Lincoln because he never said anything bad about them in public, a plan Lincoln seemed to accept since he approved the early, tentative idea of making Henry Winter Davis, an influential American Party leader and Judge Davis' cousin, his vice president to pull in the Know-Nothing vote. Fortunately for Lincoln, Henry Davis dismissed the idea because he thought it would ruin his career and end his friendships in his home state of Maryland, a slave state. A vice president who was a Know-Nothing might have won many Millard Fillmore and American Party votes, but he surely would have cost Lincoln the important immigrant blocks that would be crucial for victory in several large states.[398]

Party leaders predicted the Republicans would get about half of the Know-Nothing vote, but throughout the summer the support of the

Know-Nothings was "not settled," as Judge Davis put it. Lincoln wondered which way their multitude of members would vote.[399]

From the start, the campaign sought the youth vote. Friends often referred to Lincoln as "Old Abe," but the fifty-one-year-old candidate saw himself as a young man in charge of a young party. His years working to found and develop the Republican Party in Illinois convinced him that the Republicans were mostly young men. That is why Lincoln and his advisers decided to build on the momentum created by the vibrant Wide Awake clubs. The nominee first heard of the clubs just days after the first was organized in Hartford, Connecticut, in early March 1860 as a young men's Republican club. He addressed their rally on March 5 and delighted in a torchlight escort of young men wearing capes who accompanied him back to his hotel after his speech that evening.[400]

The Republicans made plans to develop Wide Awakes in every city and state and to use them to spearhead large voter registration drives, knowing that new voters and young voters tended to embrace new and young parties.[401] The Wide Awakes were applauded by an editor at the *Hartford Daily Courant*, who wrote, "The young Republicans are an organized… young laboring men…and feel their strength."[402] Republicans loved them. William Seward said, "Each successive year brings into its ranks an increasing proportion of the young men of this country."[403]

From 1840 to 1856, the number of Democrats in the country remained pretty much the same, rising by a single percent. Almost all Democrats repeatedly voted for their party's presidential nominee. The key for Republicans was not to woo Democrats but to entice more brand-new voters to the polls and get them to vote Republican.[404] By November, various sources put the number of Wide Awakes at nearly 500,000. The Wide Awakes held weekly meetings, elected officers, gave each member a lavish membership certificate, and published their own pamphlets and newspapers, all with the ominous "wide awake" single eye on the stationery. Clubs mailed out thousands of invitations to join the Wide Awakes. The Trenton, New Jersey, invitation mixed state and national patriotism in its poetic invite: "Our Friends in Maine led off the van/ The Keystone followed, true/ And now we'll try, with might and main/ What 'Jersey Blues' can do."[405]

Their marches were major events for their towns and cities; they also tried to have a total of one thousand young men, each carrying a torch, in parade. One of their members wrote:

> *Young men dressed in brilliant martial uniforms and carrying torches of red, white, or blue marched in unison as they lustily sang campaign songs and cheered their candidates. On cue, the Wide Awakes in parade would shift ranks to form "rails" that were part of fences to symbolize "the rail-splitter." With drums beating, trumpets blaring, flags flying, torches gleaming, candles flickering, and rockets soaring, spectators thrilled to such demonstrations.*[406]

A man who founded yet another "Lincoln Club" in Boston believed the rail-splitter legend so completely that he asked Lincoln to send his club some of the rails he had split as a young man.[407]

The young Wide Awakes carried hundreds of banners in their rallies and parades. They were adorned with simplistic slogans, but one after the other, for several city blocks, they drove home the Republican philosophy: THE PILGRIMS DID NOT FOUND OUR EMPIRE FOR SLAVERY. FREE LABOR AND FREE MEN. NO MORE SLAVE TERRITORIES. GOD NEVER MADE A TYRANT OR A SLAVE. EQUAL PRIVILEGES TO ALL CITIZENS. And to support other issues, banners were unfurled with slogans such as PROTECTION TO AMERICAN INDUSTRIES and HOMESTEADS FOR ACTUAL SETTLERS.

There were even Wide Awake chapters of all-black freedmen in the North. They always carried numerous antislavery banners.[408]

The Wide Awakes became a brotherhood and marched in each other's torchlight parades. On July 25, five hundred members of the Wide Awake chapter in Newark, New Jersey, in full uniform, boarded trains and traveled to Hartford, Connecticut, to march in the weekly Wide Awake parade there.[409] Each young Republican felt he belonged to a group, psychologically and emotionally important for young men supporting Abe Lincoln. For the Wide Awakes, the Lincoln campaign was a crusade, not just an election.

They continued their marches even though they were met by countermarchers supporting other candidates and were often jeered by Democratic spectators, some of whom hurled stones at the Wide Awakes as they paraded through city streets.[410]

They were effective too. At the end of September, a Republican leader bragged to Lincoln of "the ardent Wide Awake efforts which the Connecticut Republicans are putting forth to give you the state." On October 3, in New York, the Republicans staged one of their largest parades and rallies; newspapers reported that the parade included 19,334 Wide Awake young men with torches.[411] By the middle of the campaign, the Republicans bragged that they had Wide Awake chapters of Republican clubs in every county in every Northern state.[412]

The Power of the Press

Lincoln knew how helpful the media could be for a politician. Several newspaper editors–politicians from Pennsylvania and other states asked for a biography that could be published in newspapers so that people who knew little about the nominee could become familiar with his background. In it, Lincoln described his years as a flatboat operator earning $10 a month, a local postmaster, and a general store clerk. He framed himself as a workingman, with calluses and tired muscles, a common man seeking the support of all the common men. The three-thousand-word self-portrait was tight, well organized, and constantly highlighted the careful rail-splitter image Judge Davis was trying to market. Lincoln then made certain that it was mailed to every Republican newspaper in the country. Most ran it and received a huge reader response. More than any other publication, that newspaper autobiography helped cast him in the role he desired. The biography was so successful because it was short, honest, modest, and a clearly written story penned by the candidate. Most campaign biographies were long, bombastic, vain, and glorious tomes produced by campaign aides. Lincoln's biography connected directly with the people who read it, many of whom saw their own story in his.[413]

He also intervened with the Republican newspapers toward the end of June to stop them from painting him as a fire-breathing abolitionist (Lincoln refused to be associated with abolitionists and considered them radicals). Republicans in Pennsylvania and other states complained that party newspapers were printing copies of his legendary 1858 "House Divided" speech and feared that it convinced readers that he was a radical on the slavery issue. Lincoln quietly convinced editors to stop printing the speech.[414]

He was approached by a New York publisher, through Weed, to print his biography in book form. At the same time, the editors of the *Chicago Press and Tribune* asked him to authorize them to publish it. Lincoln would have liked to do a favor for Weed, but he also remembered that it was the *Chicago Press and Tribune*, during the convention, that backed his candidacy and endorsed him. His newspaper friends Charles Ray and Joe Medill worked for the *Chicago Press and Tribune* too. He gave permission to the *Chicago Press and Tribune.*[415] The brief biography, highly publicized by the newspaper, was put together from Lincoln's notes and speeches and a lot of paperwork from aides. It sold hundreds of thousands of copies, approaching sales of *Uncle Tom's Cabin.* It outsold the bestselling compendium of his debates with Douglas issued the previous year.[416]

That book was followed by twelve more campaign biographies of Lincoln, three printed in German and two in Welsh. In addition, Horace Greeley published his *Political Textbook of 1860,* which was so popular it went through fourteen printings. The Republican Party also began selling *The Republican Campaign Textbook* to get out the party message.[417]

The Evangelicals

Lincoln was a deeply religious man and understood more than any politician of his time how religious the American people had become over the last thirty years. One of the main reasons the evangelical movement, known as the Second Great Awakening succeeded, he knew, was their leaders' ability to stage large outdoor events such as torchlight parades and place speakers on the slopes of sprawling meadows, where crowds of ten thousand and more could hear them. At these gatherings, hymns were sung by thousands of people. Lincoln knew this made everyone attending feel a sense of participation. He and his team planned identical events for the Republicans, substituting politics for religion in an effort to make thousands at a rally—cheering, singing songs, listening to speakers—see everyone around them as Republicans too. Some of these rallies attracted over forty thousand people. Lincoln had seen this work firsthand through the outdoor revival meetings of John Wesley Redfield, one of the founders of the Free Methodist Church, who organized a series of revival meetings during his years in Illinois.[418] Lincoln and his aides improved the early torchlight parades that had been so successful for the Republicans in 1856, where large groups of men walked down city streets chanting "Free men, free labor, free soil, Frémont."

Lincoln and Seward

The support of William H. Seward was critical. Lincoln had to win moderate votes, but he also had to hold the radical abolitionist voters that belonged to Seward. The New York senator was also important for other reasons. He was a beloved figure in New York, where he had served two terms as a U.S. senator and two terms as governor. Seward was just too popular a figure in New York to have as an opponent. He was the bridge to New York boss Thurlow Weed, whose political machine was not only needed to win New York but all the Northern states. Weed also personally controlled vast sums of money he raised for each election and was capable of landing contributions of up to $100,000 from single individuals and companies. This money could be spent in New York, Lincoln thought, and, importantly, channeled to other, marginal states where it could make the difference between victory and defeat.

Seward's bitterness at the loss of the nomination and betrayal by Simon Cameron and others ebbed over the summer. He wanted to help Lincoln get elected because he would become the secretary of state. He was also certain that Lincoln would not be able to handle the presidency and that he would, in effect, run the country for him. The cabinet post would also open the door to a Seward administration in 1864. He could easily run for president as secretary of state.

The Seward and Lincoln forces went through a delicate dance from May through the middle of the summer. Lincoln let Seward know right away that he wanted his support by inviting Weed to Lincoln's home after the convention. With his meeting with Weed, he showed that there was no enmity between the winner and Seward, the man whom so many thought should have been nominated. It was an olive branch that put everyone in the party at ease.

Lincoln's aides were wary of Weed, as they should have been. He had maneuvered in murky political waters for more than three decades with great success, and he controlled hundreds of politician, tens of thousands of votes, and enormous amounts of money in contributions. Norman Judd wrote to Lincoln: "Weed & Co. are bitter, but they cannot afford to give you the cold shoulder.... I suppose Weed has been to see you, and I imagine he took nothing by his motion."[419]

Lyman Trumbull also told Lincoln to watch out for the New Yorker. He wrote: "It was reported here a few days ago that Mr. Weed had been to see you.... He is known to be a very shrewd, fascinating man, but I remarked to the gentlemen who spoke to me on the subject that you were too prudent and cautious a man to get complicated by promises to anybody."[420]

Some worried that the New Yorkers would seize everything they could. Caleb Smith of Indiana wrote Judge Davis, "The New Yorkers will demand about half of Lincoln's patronage, and I hope they show that they deserve it."[421]

Some Republicans told Lincoln to avoid Weed no matter how much help he could give to the nominee. George Sparrow of New York was one. He wrote of "Weed and his mercenaries" that "there are many thousands who will vote the (Republican) ticket, but they will not touch anything that Weed and his gang of robbers have anything to do with."[422]

The meeting in Springfield was a duel of wary politicians, with Weed asking for nothing and Lincoln offering nothing.

Weed and Lincoln made quite a pair. Physically, Lincoln was six foot four, thin, and unusually strong. Weed was one of the few tall men in the country for whom Lincoln did not have to lean down to talk to. The New Yorker was a large-framed, muscular man, slightly taller than six foot one. He was one of the few men Lincoln knew who approached him in size and strength, and Lincoln immediately felt comfortable with him. Weed was also a consummate politician who remembered the first names of just about everyone who counted and knew intimate details of their lives, as did Lincoln. Weed was a practical man who understood that no political philosophies were enacted by people out of office. Lincoln was the same. Both men understood that politics, not political theory, ran the country. Both realized that public figures won some elections and lost others. They both understood that victorious politicians had to appeal to the great political center of the voting population, that extremists on either end of the political spectrum lost elections. Both were veteran strategists and campaigners; they traded political war stories with each other and liked each other.

A deal between the two men that would eventually result in Seward as secretary of state was in the works.

Lincoln and his brain trust courted the egomaniacal Seward. Lavish praise was heaped upon him whenever Seward spoke for Lincoln at a rally, whether it was in his native New York or at one of the many cities he visited during his national speaking tour for his party's candidate. Letters inviting him to speak were filled with syrupy praise and deference. One from James Dwight, a Republican organizer in Michigan who wanted him to stump for Lincoln there, was typical. Dwight wrote, "There are thousands here, Mr. Seward, who would deem it an *era* in their lives to have seen you or to have grasped your hand."[423]

The Wide Awakes, especially, stroked Seward, as an invitation to speak in Wisconsin indicates. Norman Eastman, the head of the La Crosse, Wisconsin, Wide Awake club wrote him: "The valleys of Wisconsin and

Minnesota will send out thousands of hardy pioneers, winning friends, to greet you. They will come far to even see you."[424]

Politicians in Connecticut were just as laudatory. William Burkingham wrote Seward, "Your many friends in the vicinity will be highly grateful if they can manifest their personal regard for you (with a visit)."[425]

The Republican nominee and his team also carefully mapped out the Northern states they needed to win according to the issues that concerned them. They pushed hard in the western states of Indiana, Iowa, Michigan, and Wisconsin on the Homestead Act, which guaranteed cheap western state land for farmers who had toiled the land for several years. Residents there all wanted the Homestead Act. A delegate to the Republican convention had written, "This Homestead measure overshadows everything with us and throughout the West."[426]

They pushed hard on slavery in the northeastern states that had high numbers of abolitionists, such as Massachusetts, Vermont, and New Hampshire. They campaigned for the tariff just about everywhere, especially in Pennsylvania, Ohio, New Jersey, and Illinois. By 1860, the protective tariff, taxes charged to foreign goods to keep American producers competitive, was a raging issue throughout America and had been since the first U.S. government was formed in 1789. America was no longer as dependent on foreign goods as it had once been, but moderate tariffs made foreign goods cheaper than similar American products and were holding down American sales. For years the Republicans had tried to raise the tariff to protect local manufacturers and add jobs for American workers, particularly factory workers, but the Democrats had steadfastly held to the older, lower tariff.

The Republicans did not understand why the Democrats insisted on the lower tariff even though it meant trouble for so many voters. They had made it a campaign issue. The Democrats never wavered on their defense of the lower tariff; it was a colossal political blunder for them in that election year, and throughout the year many had pleaded with them, publicly and privately, to pass it.[427]

The tariff was an especially hot issue in Pennsylvania, with its nearly one million ironworkers, and in the western states. Workers and manufacturers in those states saw the tariff as an economic noose that was slowly strangling them and would soon kill them. It was such a key issue that many newspapers, such as the *Cleveland Plain Dealer*, and newspapers in cities that depended on Great Lakes shipping, warned delegates to both Democratic and Republican conventions that they should only nominate candidates who would push hard for a much higher tariff.[428]

Illinois newspapers, too, backed candidates who favored a tariff. This had been a key issue with newspapers in that and other western states long before the conventions of 1860. "The tariff men, like Abe Lincoln, (will help) the finish of American commercial and independent projects and development and the people are becoming convinced of that fact," wrote the editor of the *Chicago Journal* as early as 1858.[429]

The tariff was a major issue in Michigan, too, where jobs as well as trade were at stake. "The difference between the Democratic party and the Republican Party is that the Democrats would have all the labor done in England, while the Republicans would have it close here at home, by our own laborers," wrote the editor of the *Detroit Advertiser*.[430]

It was this combination of issues, in addition to their antislavery beliefs, that made the Republicans strong.[431]

Mark Delahay of Kansas said, "I feel it in my bones that we'll bust the Democracy this time."[432]

Lincoln and his team did their best to help doubtful states and took money from prosperous, "safe" states and funneled it to them. They addressed everyone's concerns in the Northern states, answered all their mail, cemented relations with the press, and mobilized hundreds of thousands of new voters. They did everything a shrewd campaign team should have done.

But would it be enough?

CHAPTER 13

Disdain for the Secessionists

The South could no more unite upon a scheme of secession than a company of lunatics could conspire to break out of bedlam.

—HORACE GREELEY, *NEW YORK TRIBUNE*

The leaders of the Southern states had threatened to secede from the United States as early as the 1780s, when the country was just a postwar confederation. In 1811, a congressman, Josiah Quincy, from Massachusetts, told Southerners in Congress that he would not object if their states seceded, even "violently, if they must." Secession was discussed during the nullification crisis of the early 1830s.[433] From 1854 on, when they saw the enormity of the antislavery feeling in the North expressed over the Kansas-Nebraska Act, Southerners incessantly called for secession.

The secessionists used every angry phrase they could find to drive home their point. A writer for the *Southern Confederacy* wrote:

The South will never permit Abraham Lincoln to be inaugurated president of the United States. This is a settled and sealed fact. It is the determination of all parties in the South. Let the consequences be what they may, whether the Potomac is crimsoned in human gore and Pennsylvania Avenue is paved ten fathoms deep with mangled bodies or whether the last vestige of liberty is swept from the face of the American continent. The South, the loyal South, the constitutional South, will never submit to such humiliation and degradation as the inauguration of Abraham Lincoln.[434]

Moreover, many Southern radicals feared that the campaigns of two Southern democrats would anger Lincoln and make him even more prejudiced against the Southern states and slavery.[435]

Lincoln and his men saw the appeal for secession as just one more chapter of political blackmail in which the South always got what it wanted by threatening to leave the Union. When a Southerner broached the subject on the floor of the House of Representatives, Republicans would laugh in unison and break out in a song called "Goodbye, John."[436]

Northern newspaper editors humiliated Southern secessionists. John Forney, editor of the *Philadelphia Press*, wailed, "(The) people are thoroughly sickened and disgusted with the treachery and trickery of the faithless guards who wish to betray them into the hands of their worst enemy—the secessionists!"[437]

Carl Schurz joked that whenever Southern politicians threatened to secede in Congress they would leave the chamber, have a drink, and then come back. He said that if Lincoln was elected, the Southerners would be so upset that they would leave the chamber, have two drinks, and then return to the chamber.[438]

An editor at the *New York Tribune* scoffed that the Southerners did not agree on secession and that "the South could no more unite upon a scheme of secession than a company of lunatics could conspire to break out of bedlam."[439] William Seward joined the chorus of disbelievers. He said, "Who's afraid? Nobody's afraid!"[440]

A New York newspapers editor sneered "that game has been played out" and suggested that, after Lincoln's election, he would be pestered for jobs by far more "secessionists" in Georgia and Virginia than from all the free states combined.[441]

Lincoln himself saw the secessionists as a radical minority. Only 25 percent of Southerners owned slaves. How could they inspire the rest to secede? He also felt that many old Whigs, now in the various parties in the South, would overrule the secessionist radicals, such as Robert Rhett, the editor of the *Charleston Mercury*, who called for a "Southern confederacy" on October 4, 1860.[442] The entire Constitutional Union movement was proof that many old-line Democrats were still Unionists. As early as 1856, Lincoln dismissed threats of secession, often with ridicule, telling one newspaper reporter that his belief that the South would secede if Lincoln was elected was brought on by his alarm at the drop in pork prices.[443] Lincoln added, "All this talk about dissolution of the Union is humbug, nothing but folly."[444]

Lincoln dismissed the depth of Southerners' feelings on the expansion of slavery. The editor of the *New Orleans Daily Delta* wrote: "Slavery cannot long endure without this right of expansion. Everyone acknowledges this. To consent to give it up is to say that we consent to regard this institution, which is 'flesh of our flesh' as temporary."[445]

In the middle of the 1860 campaign, Lincoln told one reporter that "the people of the South have too much of good sense, and good temper, to attempt the ruining of the government."[446] And he emphatically reminded all that he did not run for president for the purpose of ending slavery. He wrote to Horace Greeley later:

My paramount object is to save the Union, and it is not either to save or to destroy slavery. What I do about slavery and the colored race, I do because I believe it helps to save the Union, and what I forbear, I forbear because I do not believe it would help to save the Union.[447]

Journalist Donn Piatt, who talked to him in the middle of the campaign, wrote that Lincoln said all of the secession talk was just a "bluff," merely talk to "frighten the North." He paid no attention to the hate mail sent to him or the news that he was continually burned in effigy throughout the South.[448]

The Republican nominee dismissed published statements by Democrats in large Northern newspapers that vilified him, such as one in a New York paper that called him the "undisguised enemy of the people."[449]

Lincoln was right in believing that a small band of secessionist politicians or former politicians, such as William Yancey, could not persuade the people to leave the Union. In his view, the South had ample opportunity to secede and had not done so. Despite his friendships with Southerners and his wife, Lincoln failed to realize that the close social, cultural, and political ties of the non-slaveholding middle and lower classes throughout the South were often identical to the slaveholders of the master class.

The itinerant dirt farmers who lived in the hills of Southern states had nothing in common with the rich planter who owned two hundred slaves, yet they almost always allied themselves with the rich planters. They did so for several reasons. They believed that if slaves were free, they would ruin the dirt farmer because they would work for much less. They insisted the freed blacks might develop sexual relationships with white women and taint the race. Since half the people in the South were black, freed slaves—four million of the eight million residents of the South—would turn the South into a black society with no room for poor white dirt farmers. And finally, they declared that blacks were an inferior race.

In contrast, the Republicans insisted that as long as the status quo was maintained for poor whites, they had no reason to agree to secession, which hurt them economically by reducing markets for their work in the North.

However, there were other ties between the rich and poor in the South that Northerners did not understand. Many of the planters themselves had been poor at one time. They had started as small farmers, buying up more land and slaves until they were respected planters themselves. Every county had a former poor farmer who had "made good." Other farmers did not envy the planter his comfortable world because they were certain that with hard work it might be their world too. If that seemed an odd view in the North, where a lowly blacksmith could never become a rich banker, it was not so in the agrarian South, where farming gave all a better chance at sudden success.

Poor white Southerners also saw the rich planters as fellow whites in a land half black and felt they had to unite in order to hold the four million blacks in bondage, where they believed slaves belonged. Some feared that the disagreement between rich and poor whites on the issue of slavery might open the door to emancipation. The poor whites also looked up to the planters as educated and politically savvy and believed they knew what was best for them. They viewed them as kinsmen of a sort, the relations who succeeded. The success of the rich slaveholders became their success, and the causes of the rich slaveholders became their cause. This alliance had been cemented through many generations and the political events of the 1850s.[450]

In fact, Southerners would explain in arguments defending slavery that the Republicans wanted "to take *our* slaves," even if they did not own any.[451] Political scientist David Thomas wrote of the poor non-slaveholders:

> *The man without money and without slaves was thus generally without education. Such people usually follow a leader. In political parties, they had no choice except between the Whigs and Democrats, both slavery parties, until the advent of the Republican Party. Of this party, the poor whites in the lower South knew nothing except what they heard from their slaveholding neighbors, and they had no chance to vote with it.*[452]

There was a professional middle class of white Southerners who held no slaves. They were doctors, lawyers, engineers, and merchants who had no need to own slaves to support their livelihoods. Yet they, too, sided with the slaveholders in political issues and defended the right of the slaveholders to maintain their human property. They did so because they all had longtime business dealings with planters. It was to the advantage of that middle class and the lower-income whites to vote with the slaveholders.[453]

The Republicans did not understand, either, that Southerners believed the Constitution worthless by 1860. Northerners paid no attention to anything the South said about slavery or the individual rights of Southern states or their residents.[454]

Southerners were certain they could no longer successfully hold off the antislavery people in Congress. It was possible that Lincoln would be elected president and that the Black Republicans would gain control of both the House and Senate and end slavery.[455] There was no doubt in their minds that the Northern Republicans, not the Southerners, were the "sectional" party and that they were the root of all the troubles between the North and South. Moreover, the Republicans were a minority party, too. Frémont had only captured 34 percent of the vote in the 1856 presidential election against James Buchanan, and Lincoln was projected to win less than 40 percent. The Republicans, they charged again and again, had it all upside down.[456]

Northern newspapers never gauged the depths of Southern unhappiness and told readers that the few radical secessionists were unable to convince the overwhelming majority of Southerners to leave the Union. The papers dismissed all Southern secessionist speeches. The editors of both Northern and Southern newspapers insulted the candidates of both regions, in all parties, and used crude language in describing many of them. The Northern editors laughed at Southern editors' insistence that no slavery meant no union.[457]

It was not unknown Southerners who threatened secession, but well-known, experienced political figures, such as Senators Jefferson Davis of Mississippi, Alexander Stephens of Georgia, and James Hammond of South Carolina. Stephens fired up his crowds by telling them that the results of a Lincoln election would cause "an attempt at secession and revolution." Hammond called Lincoln an "instant hazard."[458]

Dozens of men traveled to Springfield to see Lincoln, or wrote to him, pleading that he acknowledge the secessionist threat and make some kind of mollifying public statement to prevent it. Lincoln shrugged off their pleas.

"I'll cross that ditch when I come to it," he said, adding that those secessionist threats were "the trick by which the South breaks down every Northern man" and that if he agreed to them he would be "as powerless as a block of buckeye wood."[459]

Lincoln received numerous Southern newspapers that promoted secession. The newspapers warned Lincoln that he would be a powerless president without the South and that no Southerners would serve in his administration. George Prentice, editor of the *Louisville Journal,* wrote, "No man will dare to accept office under him in any slaveholding states."[460] The editor of the *Georgia Star* even bluntly declared that "any Southerner who worked for Lincoln should be outlawed and killed." The editor of the *Charleston Mercury* exclaimed that Lincoln was "a bloodthirsty tyrant."[461]

Political clubs pushed secession. When the Montgomery, Alabama, Young Man's Club was formed in 1860, it printed this slogan on broadsides and letterheads: RESISTANCE TO LINCOLN IS OBEDIENCE TO GOD.[462]

Southern politicians threatened secession as early as August 1860. Virginia Governor Henry Wise wrote a friend: "Have we the purpose, will, and sense of honor sufficient for revolution? If we have, Breckinridge and Lane will be elected; if not, God spare the sight of the consequences."[463]

In July, J. D. Ashmore, a South Carolina political figure, called for immediate secession. He wrote: "Lincoln and Hamlin will be elected. I go for preparation first and dissolution afterwards on the first favorable opportunity."[464]

Former U.S. attorney for Georgia Robert Gourdin wrote in mid-July that he hoped his state would secede if the Republicans were elected.[465] Laurence Keitt, one of the South Carolina extremists, used historic analogies for secession and a new government. He exclaimed:

> *The concentration of absolute power in the hands of the North will develop the wildest democracy ever seen on this earth—unless it should have been matched in Paris in 1789 (French Revolution). What of conservatism? What of order? What of social security or financial prosperity can withstand Northern license?... I see no alternative but the sword.*[466]

W.W. Boyce, in a letter to the *Charleston Courier*, wrote that the entire South should secede if Lincoln won, but if some Southern states resisted, then just a handful should leave. If all of them resisted, then just South Carolina should secede and form its own country.[467]

Some Southern editors even blamed Lincoln for the falling price of slaves. The *Charleston Mercury* reported that the election of Lincoln would reduce the price of each slave in the South by $100.[468] The *Nashville Banner* went further, claiming in December 1860, that the price of a slave had dropped by 20 percent.[469]

Democratic newspapers argued, too, that if elected, Lincoln would permit all of the freed slaves in the North to join the Republican Party and turn the United States into a black and white nation. They added the familiar scenario that thousands of black men would taint the white race by having sex with white women.[470]

Lincoln's views on secession, and his disdain for those who discussed it, inspired his advisers to urge him to remain silent during the campaign. They cringed when they remembered some of his previous speeches that touched on secession. During his 1859 campaign swing in Ohio, he nearly challenged the entire South to declare war against him over secession in a speech that shocked his friends and backers. Lincoln gave the speech in Cincinnati, across the Ohio River from Kentucky, a slave state, and directly opposite one of the South's largest slave markets. Many in the crowd were Southern slaveholders who had ferried across the river to hear Lincoln. Some irked him by urging secession while he spoke.

An irritated Lincoln responded:

Will you make war upon us and kill us all? Why, gentlemen, I think you are as gallant and as brave men as live; that you can fight as bravely

in a good cause, man for man, as any other people living; that you have
shown yourselves capable of this upon various occasions; but men for
men, you are not better than we are, and there are not so many of you
as there are of us. You will never make much of a hand at whipping
us. Were we fewer in number than you, I think you could whip us; if
we were equal, it would likely be a drawn battle, but being inferior in
numbers, you will make nothing attempting to master us.[471]

By mid-October, Lincoln could daily hear the voices of ardent secessionists. Few threatened to lead a secessionist movement themselves, but all warned of others they knew—reputable, influential Southerners in almost every state—who would. After all, they told the Republicans, on October 20, the Light Infantry of Charleston, South Carolina had been mobilized, and on October 27 prominent South Carolinians had met at the home of South Carolina Senator James Hammond to agree on legal procedures for secession.[472]

On October 10, just two days after the elections in some states, William Hodge of Washington DC urged Lincoln to make a formal statement to the people within forty-eight hours of the November 6 election to assure them that he would hold the Union together and to put several Southerners in his cabinet.

Editor George Prentice in Louisville thought a public letter, printed in every newspaper, North and South, would work. If the president-elect did not issue a letter, Prentice warned that "as soon as you are elected…blow will be struck for dismemberment of the Union."[473]

Charles Gibson of St. Louis warned O. H. Browning, a friend of Lincoln, "evil spirits are at Washington" and that the "conservative men of the South" (slaveholders) were worried about Lincoln and his appointees. Gibson added that "the secessionist movement would at once be extinguished" if Lincoln wrote such a letter for public consumption.[474]

W. T. Early of Pen Park, Virginia, wanted an entire "manifesto" on slavery to be issued by Lincoln right after election day. He told him in threatening tones that "(if there are no guarantees on slavery)…the whole South will be bullied into a measure which will result in our own union…destruction of our government…the Negroes would be put to the sword."[475]

Throughout the South, pressure increased for a mollifying stand by Lincoln. On October 20, three weeks before the election, a group headed by Louisiana's B. L. Hodge posted hundreds of broadsides throughout the state asking the governor to call a secession convention. Hodge wrote, "The fate of the Union is sealed. It must be dissolved!" Others began to write pamphlets on secession that would begin to appear within three weeks of the election.[476]

Robert Rhett, the editor of the *Charleston Mercury*, said simply, "Emancipation or revolution is now upon us."[477]

These cries came not only from Southerners or border state residents. Businessmen, particularly those in New York and other Northern cities who did so much commerce in the South, worried that the Southerners would secede and pleaded with Lincoln to prevent them from doing so. Philadelphia's Thomas Sweney argued that he had extensive business with Southern clients and they wanted assurances that there would be peace, not a civil war.[478]

George Davis wrote Jesse Dubois that he constantly heard rumors that Southern businessmen would cause a stock panic if Lincoln did nothing to pacify them. Davis' friends on Wall Street were also fearful that Southern trade would collapse. They lobbied Lincoln. Davis said that "a letter would prove one of the greatest blessings he could confer on this country; (it) would crush in its incipient stages a most wicked combination to (create) a financial panic."[479]

Others argued just as strongly that Lincoln should not make any kind of a speech right after the election. After all, he did have four months to sort out his ideas and programs before his inauguration. They felt that a speech on slavery right after the vote would make him look like he was being coerced by the slaveholders.

Besides, some argued, president-elects have never made public speeches. Presidents up until the 1860s didn't care for public speeches, either. They made numerous public appearances, where they inevitably delivered "happy to be here" talks. They rarely spoke on politics, though. Martin Van Buren made no public speeches for three years during his one term as president. At the end of his term, he decided to make a speech in New York City and then speeches in three more New York cities on his way home to Kinderhook. James Polk and John Tyler gave no addresses, either. James Buchanan, Lincoln's predecessor, never spoke in public until his farewell address. No president-elect had ever delivered a campaign speech, either, and none ever left his own home until the election was over.[480]

One of the strongest advocates of stonewalling was William Cullen Bryant, the influential editor of the *New York Post*, who argued that anything Lincoln said would be misinterpreted.[481] The members of the politically influential Blair family of Maryland were against it, too. Francis Blair wrote in a letter signed by five other important politicians in his state that a speech would not appease the South, but rather anger it. "(They are) even now ready to apply the torch which will light the fire of civil discord."[482]

But the politically savvy Blairs and their friends thought civil war could easily be avoided by time-honored political means, that if elected, Lincoln would name Southerners to his cabinet.

Some of Lincoln's advisers wanted him to waffle. George Davis told him that he should be noncommittal and make no promises. He wrote, "(Just) emphasize the rights of all sections."[483] Republican National Committee officer George Fogg agreed. The *New York Times* reported that William Seward had told friends that Lincoln would make a conciliatory speech to the South right after his election.[484]

Besides, Fogg added: "There will be time enough for you to 'quiet the fears of the South' when you have power and the responsibility that power brings. You can afford to maintain…inactivity for the four months preceding your inauguration.[485]

Throughout the election Lincoln himself made clear he was completely against any kind of speech that offered concessions to the South. After ignoring dozens of letters on conciliation, he wrote one correspondent, "It would do no good. I have already done this many, many times…in print. Those who will not read what I have already probably said will not read or listen to repetition…. (The Bible says) 'If they hear not the prophets, neither will they be persuaded though I rose from the dead.'"[486]

A week later, again badgered by people from the North and South, Lincoln chose to make his strongest statement in a letter to the *Louisville Journal.* Lincoln told its editor:

> *Would it do any good? If I was to labor a month, I could not express my conservative views and intentions more clearly and strongly than they were expressed in our platform and in my many speeches. Even you give no prominence to those oft-repeated expressions. This impression (convinces) your readers that I am the very worst man living. If what I have already said has failed to convince you, no repetition of it would…the good men of the South (and I regard the majority as such) (understand). The bad men…are eager to have something new upon which to base new misrepresentations.*[487]

Lincoln completely misjudged the Southern mood.

In a surprising letter to Alexander Stephens, a Georgia senator who had been a fellow congressman with him in the late 1840s, Lincoln wrote, "Do the people of the South really entertain fear that a Republican administration would, directly or indirectly, interfere with their slaves?... There is no cause for such fears."[488]

Lincoln had ample warning of secession, understood it, and ignored it, as did all of his advisers.[489]

Lincoln's trusted campaign manager, Judge Davis, was told by his own cousin, former American Party leader Henry Winter Davis, that there would be no secession. He told Davis, "The opposition in the Southern states will stand by your (Lincoln's) administration, and it can perpetuate itself for several successive presidential elections." No one should have been more sure of that than the well-connected Henry Davis, right?[490]

Dan Roberts of Centreville, Virginia, reiterated what Davis said in plain language. He wrote: "We the people are getting tired of the old oligarchy. Some men say that no one will accept offices under you, but that is old moonshine."[491]

Many Lincoln supporters argued that the secessionist warnings came only from firebrand Southern politicians or hotheaded newspaper editors.

But Lincoln did have proof of secession.

He had in his possession two long, detailed letters from Abner Doubleday, a well-educated and reliable U.S. Army colonel stationed at Fort Sumter, in the harbor of Charleston, South Carolina. Doubleday flatly stated that the city would not only secede if Lincoln was elected but would go to war. He also said that the commandant of the garrison had such orders in the event of secession. Doubleday said the mood in Charleston was ugly. Doubleday had written the letters to his brother Ulysses at the end of September. His brother, alarmed, sent the correspondence, insisting to Lincoln in a cover letter that his brother Abner was a professional soldier and that although a Republican, he had no strong views on any political matter. He said he forwarded the letters to Lincoln so that he could "save the country from the disgrace" of an attack on Fort Sumter.[492]

Abner Doubleday wrote that "secession with every one I meet seems to be a foregone conclusion. They all say as a matter of course that they must have the forts (in the harbor). The army would withdraw the troops…and give up the forts to the South if secession takes place."

Doubleday added that officers who came from the South planned to leave the military and fight for a Southern army if, following secession, a war broke out. Two days later, an even more upset Doubleday wrote that he was convinced there would soon be war. He told his brother that the movement of U.S. troops from another facility in the harbor, Fort Moultrie, to Sumter and the rumor of ships carrying more troops to Charleston had fueled the fears of the local residents.

Doubleday wrote:

> *I hear (federal) troops are on the way. (South Carolinians) distrust us…do not like to see additional strength given to the forts. Secession is a foregone conclusion in them and they would have no hesitation at stepping in here any moment. The danger we anticipate will proceed from the decision of the secessionists to commence the campaign by driving us out to give themselves prestige…for their decision (to act at once)—a reasonable proof that Lincoln will be elected. They will not wait for the action of their own legislature.*

Lincoln ignored him as well.[493]

He received letters from George Keith, too, that warned him of authentic, fierce Southern feelings against him. Keith lived in Ohio but had a second home in the South. He wrote Lincoln in the summer that many Southern communities were getting ready to secede and "form a Southern confederacy." The Republican nominee ignored him too.[494]

"If agitation on the subject is continued for three months longer, we will be compelled to arm our militia and hunt down our (slaves) in the field." wrote an angry J. W. H. Underwood that year to Howell Cobb, one of the young secessionists who would later become a leading figure in Confederate Congress.[495]

But Abner Doubleday's warning was not the only one. Lincoln paid no attention to long and lengthy correspondence from U.S. Army colonels and generals about secession, based on firsthand reports. In just one week, October 20–27, Lincoln received reports from respected military men in Kansas, Ohio, and Washington DC predicting civil war.

U.S. Army Capt. George Hazzard, stationed in Cincinnati, told Lincoln that the latest army reports indicated that all of the army arsenals in Southern and western states and territories were just supplied with their full quotas of rifles, muskets, and ammunition and that the Southern arsenals, in particular, were filled to the tops of their storage bins. He added that the arsenals in all of the states, particularly in the South, had few guards or no guards at all, and the weapons could easily be seized during an insurrection (the arsenals at Baton Rouge and Augusta alone, he said, could supply an instant army of some twelve thousand men). Hazzard said an armed party of just twelve men could seize any U.S. arsenal. He also warned that army officers might lead them. He noted, "Most officers in the South and Southern (enlisted) men are on intimate relations with Southern politicians."[496]

A week later, on October 29, Gen. Winfield Scott, the nation's highest-ranking commander, wrote Lincoln a long confidential letter in which he predicted civil war and said that it would make the Mexican War "look like mere child's play."

General Scott quoted William Paley's "Moral of Philosophy" in arguing that the federal government had to put down any state insurrection and that, legally, states had no right to secede from any larger government. Scott was certain Paley was right and that war was at hand. Scott outlined in rather astute detail ways in which the seceding states might form a new government with four different scenarios involving different states, but he concluded that somehow, someway, there would be a confederacy. He urged Lincoln to begin functioning as commander in chief before he even took office. Scott told him:

> *(There is) danger of an early act of rashness, preliminary to secession: the seizure of the following posts—Jackson and St. Phillip, Morgan, Pickens, McKee, Pensacola Harbor, Pulaski, Moultrie (and Sumter), Monroe, and Hampton navy yards. These should be immediately garrisoned.*[497]

He received word on October 26 that U.S. soldiers at Fort Kearney in Kansas would leave the army and help begin an armed resistance movement against the Northern states. During the first week of November, Lincoln was burned in effigy at Pensacola, Florida. In the middle of the campaign, his friend Samuel Haycraft suggested that, as a publicity stunt, Lincoln travel to his birthplace in Kentucky. The candidate, well aware of the political climate there, wrote back, "Would not the people (there) lynch me?"[498]

The direction of the campaign and its secessionist overtones began to take a dangerous turn in early October, when letters warning Lincoln of his assassination began arriving. They were ominous.

On October 5, a minister, the Reverend W. B. Orvis, wrote Lincoln that he heard rumors from Southern sympathizers that "political enemies may endanger your life. Take heed to guard."[499]

On October 16, Maj. Thomas Phil wrote the nominee that he heard that if he was elected, "we should not have a president more than five days" and told him that "many of your friends have an apprehension of your personal safety."[500]

The very next day, F. R. Shoemaker of Pennsylvania told Lincoln that he should be wary when he traveled to Washington DC to take office. "When you cross the Mason-Dixon line, keep your eyes open and look out for your enemies or they will poison you."[501]

Others warned him that there were "people looking for him" and that he would be poisoned at some state dinner. "We are surrounded by danger," wrote George Thompson, a Republican from Wheeling, Virginia.[502]

Officers in the army who dealt with substantial information and not wild rumor gave Lincoln similar warnings. Col. David Hunter, based in Leavenworth, Kansas, told him that on a recent trip to Virginia, a respected and credible woman there informed him that gangs of young men were plotting to assassinate Lincoln—and had taken bizarre secret oaths to complete the task—if he was elected. Hunter warned Lincoln that "on the institution (slavery), these good people are most certainly demented."[503]

The Republican nominee and the leaders of his party also ignored signs of turmoil in Southern counties and cities, activities that escalated from name-calling to assault and battery.[504] Just three days after General Scott's warning, a mob of Southerners descended on a parade of Wide Awakes on their way to a Republican rally in Baltimore. Southerners pelted the Republicans with eggs, and after a few moments, bricks began to fly through the night air. Some in the crowd severely beat some Republicans, and others fought in a melee that finally had to be broken up by the police. "Little police help," lamented one eyewitness. Another eyewitness said the marchers were not merely hit with a few eggs but "showers" of them.[505]

Lincoln's decision to pay no attention to the prospective secessionists at the end of the campaign was a mistake. The Lincoln campaign was, in all other respects, one of the most brilliantly managed in American political history. Yet the candidate and his key advisers scorned the overriding issue of the campaign, the issue that later tore the Union apart. Why?

First, Lincoln could not, as a man who hated slavery, compromise on his views. The winds of fortune that had swept across Abe Lincoln's Illinois had made him the moral leader of a crusade to restrict or eliminate slavery, and he could not now abandon the issue.

His moral convictions were probably secondary in his thinking. Most important, he knew that if he pandered to the secessionists during the campaign, he would have lost the support of the enormous block of antislavery voters, who would have seen him as just another candidate willing to compromise, another Douglas, and he would have lost the election. His strategy from the last day of the convention through November was to downplay his personal feelings on slavery so that he could be viewed as a moderate while others talked about the issue in more inflammatory terms. As a moderate, he still held in his hands hundreds of thousands of die-hard antislavery voters, whether they were out-and-out abolitionists or moderates who may have been agreeable to leaving slavery alone where it existed in 1860 but wanted to eliminate it at some point in the near future. The Republicans could couch their views on slavery in as moderate a fashion as they wanted, but everybody knew that it was the single driving issue that brought their party into creation and made it strong.

Also, Lincoln may have felt, why make slavery and secession an issue and risk constant questions about it that might lead him into an election-threatening gaffe?[506]

Lincoln had lured Douglas into the exact same kind of blunder in 1858, and he was fearful someone might force him to make a similar mistake. He certainly would not win any Southern states by offering an olive branch to the South.

He was also not in the mood to worry about anything that might happen after the election. Many people might have believed he was going to be elected, but he knew differently. He realized that it was going to be a very tight election and that there was a good chance he would lose. After all, he had to carry each of the midwestern states, and the polls in them showed that the vote was extremely close. He was behind in New York and running out of time. The race might still wind up in the House of Representatives. Why, then, waste time worrying about secession now?

The reaction of many people to his aloof demeanor was expressed in a chilly note from S. Spencer of Chestertown, Maryland. He wrote Lincoln just days before the election, "The wolf is really upon us now."[507]

CHAPTER 14

The Keys to Victory

It is going to be a desperate struggle.

—REPUBLICAN PENNSYLVANIA ORGANIZER

ALEXANDER McCLURE

Pennsylvania

Pennsylvania would be pivotal for Lincoln, but a victory there would not be easy for him because it was the home state of President James Buchanan, who bitterly opposed the Republicans. The fifteenth president was born and raised in Franklin County, whose residents had friends, relatives, and business associates a few miles away in slaveholding Virginia and Maryland. The unpopular president, a longtime politician and officeholder, filled the local, state, and federal job rolls with his cronies, friends, political allies, and relatives, particularly in the hundreds of post offices in the state, which were so crucial to parties that depended on them for swift (and safe) delivery of circulars and pamphlets. Some angry postmaster could throw out thousands of pamphlets a party thought were being mailed. Buchanan, in 1860, controlled that vast army of patronage workers at different government levels in Pennsylvania. He also had the power, as president, to remove any workers whom he appointed but favored his archenemy, Stephen Douglas, and he had done so in Illinois.

Prior to election as president, Buchanan was so popular that most of the politicians he stumped for also won. Still, he was not as popular as he should have been. He had carried the state, barely, in the 1856 election. The Republicans had made significant gains there in the 1858 elections. Still, Pennsylvania was a Democratic state, and its southern counties made it difficult for the antislavery Republicans to carry.

Everyone told Lincoln that Pennsylvania was crucial. "Without Pennsylvania's vote, you cannot be elected president. You are going to need every assistance you can possibly command," wrote Milo Holcomb, a Republican from Hartford, Connecticut.[508]

History made clear the difficulties Lincoln faced in Pennsylvania. Republican Frémont only won 32 percent of the popular vote there in 1856. Buchanan won the state, but former president Millard Fillmore, running on a fusion Whig–American Party ticket, pulled eighty-two thousand votes (17 percent).[509] That same year the Democrats won fifteen of the twenty-five congressional seats and captured a majority in the state legislature.

The late realignment the Republicans hoped for began in 1856. Following the elections, several key Democrats bolted the party and became Republicans They included the influential heads of the Philadelphia and Allegheny bar associations, John Read and William Moorhead, and Congressman David Wilmot, author of the controversial antislavery Wilmot Proviso. They not only had many friends but were successful organizers.[510] Local Republicans rallied as a unit to support the national platform without any dissent and, at their own state convention, leaders called it "perfect for all."[511] That year also marked the apogee of Know-Nothingism in Pennsylvania. By 1857, the Know-Nothings (American Party) began to fade as they had in Massachusetts and other Northern states. Their candidate for governor that year, William Hazlehurst, drew only twenty-eight thousand votes, just one-third as many as Fillmore and his Know-Nothings combined the year before. The state remained quirky, however. In the state legislature, the Republicans gained several assembly seats. (Opposition candidates of all stripes had twelve seats to twenty-one for the Democrats, but lagged thirty-one to thirty-nine in the state senate).

The Republicans fared better in the elections of 1858 and 1859, when they ran a fusion ticket that included Know-Nothings and former Whigs. All eleven of their state senate candidates won in 1859, and they gained their first majority, twenty-two to eleven, over the Democrats. They won thirty-five seats in the assembly in 1858 to tie the total there at thirty-five. The Republicans took a commanding twenty-one-to-four lead in congressional seats in 1858. In both 1858 and 1859 the Democrats hung on to the key southern border counties that would be critical in the 1860 presidential election. The Democrats had won in 1856 by an impressive 73,000 votes over the Republicans and 148,000 votes over Fillmore's American–Whig ticket.[512]

To win in 1860, the Republicans had to win the Know-Nothing vote. Who knew what they could achieve on election day? They were so critical that Lincoln's advisers told him to alert his men throughout the county not to criticize the Know-Nothings for any reason.[513] It would be an uphill fight in the Keystone State.[514]

Like well-organized Republicans everywhere, the Republicans in Pennsylvania had worked hard since the Kansas-Nebraska Act to organize their brand-new party. Their efforts started to pay off in 1856. Frémont did not win the state, but his votes were distributed evenly in just about every county, building a balanced foundation for the 1860 election.[515] They did carry the state senate in 1858 and achieved a tie in the assembly. They shrewdly played up to the Know-Nothings by demanding immigration laws that kept out criminals and paupers but stopped far short of what the Know-Nothings demanded in their seemingly senseless war against immigrants and Catholics.[516] Lincoln's advisers convinced him that he should not even mention the fourteenth plank in the Republican Platform, which supported immigration, in any conversations.[517] His advisers reminded Know-Nothing supporters that Lincoln had never spoken out against them. Lincoln was neutral and would treat them fairly if elected.

Lincoln was assured of strength in Pennsylvania as summer began. "Politically, Lincoln is looking as good as could be expected," wrote newspaper editor Morton McMichael from Philadelphia on June 10.[518] A week before, Thurlow Weed wrote that he met a leading Democrat from Pennsylvania traveling through New York and "he says they are without hope."[519]

The most important thing local Republicans in Pennsylvania did was work with the national committee to pledge the party to push for a strong tariff to protect the state's iron, coal, and salt industries, which employed over one million workers. The endless speeches about the tariff won over thousands of supporters in the labor-intensive state in 1856 and would again in 1860. Everyone knew the tariff was a volatile issue in Pennsylvania. A tariff party, the People's Party, was formed there and in neighboring New Jersey in the late 1850s and in 1858 captured a number of seats in the legislatures of both houses and a handful of congressional seats. The Democrats, too, realized that the tariff was the key to a Pennsylvania victory but were lukewarm in supporting it.

The Pennsylvania Republicans grabbed the issue, wooing many tariff men into their party and promising to make the tariff the central issue of the 1860 presidential election.[520] By 1860, the ironworks in Pennsylvania had grown to the point where the state supplied half of the nation's iron. Ironworker jobs were threatened by any imported iron or coal. High tariffs on foreign iron and coal protected the businesses and jobs. The higher the tariff, the greater protection Pennsylvania received.

One of the Republican operatives working in Pennsylvania, William Reynolds, was specifically assigned the coal and iron counties of Lancaster and Cambria. He had been sent there personally by Lincoln to assure the residents that the Republican nominee supported higher tariffs. On July 25 he wrote Lincoln that voters were shaky about his views on the tariff. They were "wishing they had something more satisfactory from you," he wrote and added that "the tariff is the all-absorbing question in Pennsylvania." He asked Lincoln to send him copies of his 1840s pro-tariff statements. Reynolds' request had been prearranged between the two men when Lincoln gave Reynolds explicit instructions in Springfield just before he departed to forward the pro-tariff statement.[521]

The Republicans pushed for higher tariffs throughout the summer and fall of 1860 on the state and national level and ordered their congressmen, from all states, to vote for any protective tariff bills. They scored a major victory in their Pennsylvania efforts in June when the Justin Morrill bill was introduced. The bill would raise tariffs even higher, offering Pennsylvania's iron and coal industries better protection. Of the 113 Republican congressmen, only 3 voted against it. Of the 57 Democratic congressmen, only 3 voted for it. The bill, passed by the Republicans in the House despite loud Democratic objections that annoyed voters in Pennsylvania, who needed the bill, then went to the Senate.

The Morrill Tariff became a litmus test in Pennsylvania. "If a proper tariff bill passes the United States Senate, it will make a difference of 20,000 votes in Pennsylvania to the Democratic party. If it is defeated, we cannot hope to succeed. This is conceded by all who know the feelings of the people," wrote one Pottsville, Pennsylvania, Democrat to Senator R. M. T. Hunter (D-Virginia), chairman of the Committee on Finance, which had to recommend passage or tabling of the bill.[522]

Douglas and Breckinridge forces also pushed Hunter to pass the bill so they could gain support in Pennsylvania. Democrat Hunter refused. He reported the bill out of committee with the recommendation that it not be voted on until after the November election. Pennsylvanians were furious.

The Republicans were joyous. The issue was clear-cut, and so was the outcome. The Democratic Senate had killed a bill the Republican House had passed and had thus endangered all iron and coal workers in Pennsylvania and the thousands of others in that state who were related or connected to them. It was a rousing victory for the Lincoln effort in Pennsylvania and gave the Republicans the opportunity to denounce the Democrats and tie both Douglas and Breckinridge to the defeat of the bill.[523] The Republicans' staunch support of the Morrill Tariff and all tariffs also helped blunt any feelings against them on the part of the Know-Nothings since many of the Know-Nothings worked in the iron and coal industries. It was a master stroke of legislative electioneering for the Republicans while, at the same time, a stupendous blunder for the Democrats.

The tariff was not enough, though, because in midsummer the Pennsylvania Republican Party appeared ready to break apart when two factions began to bicker. The largest faction in the state was led by Senator Simon Cameron, who was promised a cabinet post if he could deliver Pennsylvania's votes in the convention. Cameron was the political boss of Pennsylvania and had enormous power. He was feuding with Alexander McClure, thirty-two years old, a newspaper editor who had just been elected state Republican chairman. Cameron threatened to form his own state committee and asked Lincoln to send two of his top aides to the state to visit him to talk about McClure. McClure wanted to talk to them too.[524]

Weed, in New York, who kept track of events everywhere, suggested that Lincoln himself visit the state to end the sizzling feuds between the Republican leaders there. Weed told him that "the Pennsylvanians say that the state is sure for Lincoln and it looks (that way to me)," and he added that he should take the train there. Weed urged him to go to New Jersey, too, a state that could go either way in November.[525] Feuds were breaking out in New Jersey as factions accused each other of doing little. "The state committee is doing nothing of any account," one New Jersey leader complained to Judge Davis.[526]

And Lincoln, too, wondered if the party's great scheme to add unhappy Democrats and former American Party members into its fold in Pennsylvania would help them gain votes or just create more discord.[527]

George Fogg warned early that New Jersey could wind up in anybody's column. "The Republicans *must* carry both New Jersey and Pennsylvania by large pluralities," he told Lincoln.[528]

The nominee, however, never listened to pleas about New Jersey. Later in the summer, the head of the New Jersey state committee asked Lincoln to send Senator Lyman Trumbull to the state to stump for Lincoln in six towns. Lincoln turned him down.

Weed also believed that the men Lincoln was dispatching around the country to heal rifts in the party and to campaign were not good enough. In late July, he sent his own political wizard, Elliot Sheppard, to Springfield to help out in the campaign. Weed told him that "Mr. Sheppard is a gentleman of high character and reliable political principals," but Lincoln's aides received their unwelcome "expert" coldly.[529]

Lincoln declined all invitations because he feared visits to one state would wind up meaning visits to all, which would then include pleas for public speeches when he arrived. He did agree with Weed on the urgency of the problems in Pennsylvania and sent Judge Davis, with explicit instructions. Davis, traveling as Lincoln's fence mender, arrived a few days later and saw Cameron at his mansion. It was their first meeting. Davis was careful. The senator had to be treated with great respect. Davis brought with him, as requested, scraps of paper that were outtakes from Lincoln's more than fifty 1844 speeches on his beliefs on high tariffs delivered when Lincoln ran as a presidential elector. They were pages from his speech. Lincoln was so unknown in 1844 that no newspaper wrote any story about his tariff speeches that he could have used as a handout later. This was the assurance Cameron, so edgy about the protective tariff, needed.[530] Davis delivered the same assurances to McClure and his state committee a few days later. Davis assumed all would then be well and told Lincoln the two warring party chiefs now got along "harmoniously." They did not.

Davis wrote that "any quarreling between the committees ought to be stopped," and he asked Weed to send money to Pennsylvania once again. He did.[531]

This infuriated Cameron, who was independently wealthy. No political boss in New York was needed to help him out, he told Davis. He wrote that he would supply his own money and then, in a bizarre finish to his letter, made a blatant offer to "bribe" Lincoln, perhaps to ensure the promised cabinet post. He wrote, "Mr. Lincoln may need a few thousand dollars for his own private purposes, as a loan, and if so, I will cheerfully provide it."[532]

Lincoln immediately turned it down and begged the warring Pennsylvanians to work together.[533]

Intraparty spats in Pennsylvania proved endless. Letters between Pennsylvania politicians and Lincoln show that not only did the Cameron people despise the McClure people, but they could not stand their own nominee for governor, Andrew Curtin.

Cameron saw Curtin as a hopeless bungler. He declared, "Curtin will be elected, unless he defeats himself, which we must try to prevent him from doing."[534]

Others told Lincoln that he would probably be elected, despite Curtin, who was universally despised by the Cameron people. "I have seen a great many men who will vote for you who will not support him," Charles Leib, a former Democratic organizer, told the nominee.[535] Others complained about the Cameron people. Both sides told Lincoln the political bosses would betray him and back Bell or Breckinridge.

Republican political boss John Sanderson told Lincoln that Curtin's men were driving everyone crazy. He said, "Curtin has for two weeks been on a tour of the northern counties, and if he will only stay away from here, we may do very well. If he comes back and is surrounded by his very obnoxious friends, he may spoil all the good that we are now doing."[536]

The heated disputes within Pennsylvania, and between the Pennsylvanians and New Yorkers, convinced Weed to stay out of Pennsylvania ("I don't want to raise jealousies") and to decide, finally, that "I think it will become necessary to work with both (Pennsylvania) committees."[537]

Lincoln never did end the feud between Cameron and McClure, but both state committees, endlessly stroked by Lincoln and Davis, worked tirelessly on his behalf. On his own, Lincoln began a strenuous campaign to get Curtin elected. Time was running out and the state elections were coming up. Several states voted in their governors and state legislatures in late September and early October. Maine voted for its governor in September;

Pennsylvania and Indiana did so in October. The vote totals were a barometer for the presidential election in November. If the people in a state swept in the Republicans to statewide offices, they could be counted on to vote Republican for president. The three early state races had a domino effect in other states. Voters, seeing the three early birds vote a certain way, might consider that a trend and vote the same way. Victory in October often meant victory in November too.

Lincoln convinced important national Republican figures to go to Pennsylvania to campaign for Curtin, including Andrew Reeder, the former territorial governor of Kansas, and ethnic speakers. They were effective.[538]

One coup for the Republicans was to convince William Hazlehurst, leader of the American Know-Nothing Party in Pennsylvania, to stump for Lincoln. He was one of many former Know-Nothing leaders who switched to Lincoln. Hazlehurst jumped into the campaign in late September and gave speeches every day or night throughout the state, emphasizing the Republican support of high protective tariffs. Cameron said of Hazlehurst, "He will speak for you in every county which gave him a large vote in 1857. They (voter interest) will indicate the movement of the people in your behalf."[539]

Lincoln then sought money for Pennsylvania through the Republican National Committee. Massachusetts' John Goodrich, the top fund-raiser in that state, pulled out all the stops for the final push to generate money for Pennsylvania and raised money everywhere he could.[540]

At the same time, the Republican National Committee poured money into Pennsylvania. The *New York Herald* reported that $5,000 was earmarked specifically for Curtin's gubernatorial campaign and another $100,000, much of it from Weed in New York, for other races throughout that state.[541]

A letter from a nervous Judge Davis to Weed in August, again begging for money, summed it up best. He wrote: "Their expenses are heavy. It is difficult to raise enough money to keep campaign speakers in the field. They want a number of speakers and they have to be paid."[542]

Despite their continual money troubles, the Republicans in Pennsylvania were superbly organized. They were building the vote in rural valleys, small towns, and large cities. They were growing as rapidly in urban Pittsburgh as in rural York County. John Forney wrote of their progress, "Every opposition newspaper in Philadelphia was arrayed against us (in 1856)... now we have a strong organization."[543]

Still, even the optimists of early summer were gloomy as the state elections approached. "It is going to be a desperate struggle," wrote McClure. The key, he felt, was a successful voter registration drive that would result in a huge vote with new voters voting Republican. McClure feared that outcome would not happen.[544]

Others, though, told Lincoln that his rallies were attracting larger and larger crowds. J. E. Breerly wrote that he had just returned from a rally in Pittsburgh. It was, he wrote, "a great success and a mighty outpouring of the people. In all my political campaigning, I have seen nothing to compare with it."[545]

Breckinridge and Bell were certain that if they could win Pennsylvania, they could not only stop Lincoln but bury Douglas too. They pounded each other publicly through their newspapers. Bell, wanting as much newspaper support as he could get, started publication of his own newspaper, which was widely distributed in the state and elsewhere. Breckinridge relied on Pennsylvania newspapers and Southern newspapers, whose stories and editorials were reprinted in Pennsylvania papers. The Bell and Breckinridge papers flayed each other. Their efforts to unite the three candidates on a fusion ticket failed.

"We have reached the end of fusion in this state now," Republican McClure happily told Lincoln.[546] Efforts at fusion tickets in each state failed that summer and throughout most of the fall.[547]

The battle over the fusion tickets nationwide became so crazed that at one point a Republican suggested that his party deliberately arrange to let Bell win Virginia in order to make it impossible for Breckinridge to sweep the whole South.[548] At another point, there was a tentative agreement that Breckinridge would get sixteen of the Democratic electors in one state and Douglas nine. It was, a Democratic newspaper complained, "a suicidal act...too ridiculous to admit of anything but laughter and scorn."[549]

Douglas supporters went so far as to beg Virginians to give up both Bell and Breckinridge there and get behind the Little Giant. The editor of the *Richmond Enquirer* wrote, "Meet the Douglas men of Virginia kindly. Deal with them in a spirit of friendship and conciliation... (We are) friends at heart. They will vote with you (fusion) in November."[550]

As soon as Lincoln saw that the Democratic Party would field three candidates, he made his decision to give up the South and concentrated on the North for victory. The Republicans, he told them, had to campaign to win all of the Northern states but one, regardless of any fusion tickets against them. On election day, they could not count on anything except their own hard work. That was the plan, and they had to stick to it.

He had inadvertently changed the nature of electoral politics that year. Lincoln's nation-divided plan resulted in two elections, one in the North and one in the South. The elections meant that candidates and voters in each did not know what was going on in the other. The result was that the two sections of the country drifted farther apart during the election.[551]

There would be no strong fusion ticket in Pennsylvania, but the Republican Party there was not convinced they had gathered enough votes to overcome the huge gap between Frémont and Buchanan just four years before. Could they keep their fragile alliance with the Know-Nothings as the election turned more and more on slavery? Could they make any dents in the steel belt of southern counties along the Maryland and Virginia borders that repeatedly went Democratic and would be targeted by Breckinridge? Could they beat both Douglas and Breckinridge, plus political history, all at the same time?

Indiana

Indiana, too, was a big question mark. Lincoln faced different problems in Indiana, his neighboring state. There, Frémont had been beaten by Buchanan in 1856, 50 percent to 40 percent, but the remaining 10 percent of the votes, which went to Fillmore, were up for grabs in 1860.[552]

Unlike the New England states, Indiana was relatively conservative on the slavery question, so the Republicans hammered away at the Homestead Act with the slogan FREE LAND FOR FREE LABOR.

Lincoln and his advisers put together a team of nationally famous speakers to stump through Indiana in mid-July. One was Cassius Clay, an abolitionist and powerful political figure from Kentucky whose support, as a Southerner, was important. Lincoln wrote Clay, "I sincerely thank you for this."[553]

Clay told Lincoln that "I must trust you to the fullest extent," and then he added, "I can't help myself!"[554]

Clay, a good campaigner, went on a stump tour in Indiana that lasted from August 28 to September 9 and was then sent into Pennsylvania for speeches in the southern counties. He reported earlier that the Democratic Party was in disarray. "The whole Fillmore vote is dissolved," he said, and added, "You are surely a winner in Indiana."[555]

Judge Davis decided more German speakers were needed to hold the German vote for Lincoln. Several German orators, including the influential

Carl Schurz, who charged his dear friend Lincoln $600 for his campaign services, then stumped through the state for the Republicans. They targeted heavy German areas with German speakers to prevent the old Know-Nothings, kept in the Republican ranks by the thinnest of threads, from bolting because of the Republican efforts to secure the German vote. They were walking a political tightrope.

The hardest-working speaker in Indiana was Schuyler Colfax, a longtime political figure in the state, who delivered more than 120 speeches for Lincoln, an average of one per day. Perhaps the most influential was Pennsylvania Congressman John Covode, the chair of the committee that investigated the corruption in the Buchanan administration. He was electric, telling crowds that "offices were bought and sold in the ante room of the Senate and the executive mansion was open as a butcher shop."[556]

Davis organized large outdoor rallies for Lincoln in the major cities, including a wild affair at Indianapolis on August 29. Local Republican organizers attracted a crowd of over fifty thousand to watch one of the biggest demonstrations of the campaign, a festive rally that featured speeches by a dozen state and national leaders, including Edwin Stanton (Lincoln would later name him secretary of war). Thousands of Wide Awakes paraded through the streets of Indianapolis. They were joined by two new Lincoln groups, "Abe's Boys" and the "Rail Maulers," who, like the Wide Awakes, were comprised of new, young voting men (the Wide Awake uniforms were mass produced and only cost each man $1.15).[557]

"Our friends have gone home inspired with new zeal," said Lincoln supporter Caleb Smith after the rally.[558]

Still, things were not going well. "To injure our prospects in November, I am afraid a majority of Bell men will vote against us in our state in

November…. We need money very much," John DeFrees, chairman of the Indiana state Republican committee, wired Weed.[559]

Unexpectedly, Lincoln received help from the unlikeliest of sources, the regular Democratic Party and Indiana's Democratic senator, Jesse Bright, and Constitutional Unionist and leading American Party leader Richard Thompson. Bright and Douglas began a feud during the 1858 and 1859 arguments over the Kansas constitution. Bright was determined to deny Douglas the presidency, and in September he denounced the Little Giant, his Democratic colleague in the Senate, and stumped throughout Indiana for Breckinridge and Bell. Bright's Democratic friends joked that he was not running against Lincoln but Douglas.[560]

Thompson was disappointed at the small turnout for the state's Bell convention and became convinced that the presidential election would be thrown into the House of Representatives and that a Constitutional quirk might make Joe Lane, whom he despised, the president. He thought about leaving the American Party and working for Lincoln.

What followed was another example of shrewd politicking by Lincoln. He knew that Thompson was a fellow Whig congressman in the 1840s and had been cordial to him when Thompson first wrote him about a possible defection. Thompson had reminded him that "you and I were good Whigs" and that he would "defend you at all times against the villainous assaults of the Democracy." Lincoln then decided to connect Thompson with another American Party leader, Henry Winter Davis, a new Lincoln supporter, explaining to Thompson that he and Davis had never met or corresponded and assuring him that he would get an impartial view from Davis.[561]

Thompson and Davis did correspond, and Davis told Thompson to back Lincoln. Thompson then wrote Lincoln to discuss the campaign and suggested that he send him letters via express riders because he feared that local Buchanan post office managers were opening his mail. Instead, in a master stroke of political diplomacy, Lincoln sent John Nicolay, an associate who would later become his private secretary, to Indiana to personally meet with Thompson because, Lincoln indicated to the ex–American Party leader, Thompson was a very important person. The impressed Indiana leader completely supported Lincoln after he met with Nicolay.[562]

Thompson began to campaign for the Republicans in late summer, giving an average of seven speeches every two weeks and, wherever he spoke, bitterly denounced the editorials against Lincoln in the *Louisville Journal*.[563] He brought thousands of Bell men over to Lincoln with him.[564] Many of them found Lincoln palatable because of what the party kept insisting was his moderate stand on slavery. "Lincoln…in my mind is so much better than Seward and Co. that I have no opposition to him," wrote one Constitutional Unionist.[565]

And, too, disgruntled Democrats were talking of crossing the line and voting for the Republicans, such as William Sharp of Cambridge City, who had voted Democratic all of his life and switched.[566]

The Bell movement faded by the middle of October, but led by several newspapers, the Breckinridge forces were growing in the southern counties of Indiana, and Douglas was still strong there. Although Indiana had elected a Republican governor in 1858, it still had a tied state legislature, seventy-five Republicans and seventy-five Democrats, and still had four of eleven congressional seats held by Democrats—all in the southern part of the state.[567] Judge Davis felt that Indiana was very doubtful in October. So did Caleb Smith, their campaign manager in the state, who told Lincoln at the end of the summer that "some of our folks are more uneasy here."[568]

No one in Springfield believed they would know how Indiana would vote until the ballots were tallied on election day.

Illinois

Lincoln had to worry about his own backyard too. Although Lincoln's defeat of Douglas in the popular vote in the 1858 Senate race in Illinois gave Lincoln national exposure and was a major reason for his presidential nomination, the Little Giant had important job patronage at his disposal, which he used to promote his 1860 presidential candidacy. In the fall of 1860 reports sent to Lincoln indicated that the two were running neck and neck and that Douglas had a firm hold on the southern counties.

The campaign in Illinois required Lincoln's skills as a politician. Judge Davis learned in the summer that Illinois' American Party leader John Wilson might favor Lincoln. He asked Lincoln's permission to let him visit Chicago to help convert Wilson. Lincoln asked him not to go, fearful that the often blunt Davis might turn off the quirky Wilson. Instead, he used his newfound ally, American Party leader Richard Thompson of Indiana, to work as a diplomat with his next intended ally, Wilson.

Lincoln wrote Thompson, "I wish you would watch Chicago a little. They are getting up a full (Bell) movement.... I believe a line from you to John Wilson, late of the Gen'l Land Office (I guess you know him well) would fix the matter."[569]

It did. Thompson won Wilson over to the Lincoln side. Wilson, though, wanted public affiliation with Lincoln and asked to meet with him. Davis, seeing an opportunity to completely win over Wilson, not only arranged for him to meet Lincoln, but asked him to deliver a speech for Lincoln at a large rally planned for August 8 in Springfield. Wilson was not only an American Party leader but had close ties to Fillmore and to many politicians in both parties in Chicago. He would be a huge plus for the campaign.

Davis explained to Lincoln how his aides should deal with Wilson. The American Party leader was one of the vainest men in America and enjoyed being fawned over. Davis wrote, "You should impress upon them the necessity of personal attention to him. He is sensitive. Kindness wins him. Someone should be put in personal charge of him. He has a good deal of personal vanity." When Wilson arrived in Springfield, he was wined and dined and deferred to as visiting royalty. [570]

But Illinois continued to worry Lincoln. The Republicans had managed to assimilate many Know-Nothings into their party without turning Lincoln into a Know-Nothing supporter. Lincoln had to continually refute the charges that while he waited for a stagecoach one night he went to a meeting in a well-known Know-Nothing hotel in Quincy, Illinois ("I never was in one, in Quincy or anywhere else," he shot back at the charges).[571] Throughout the campaign, he was always correcting people who said he supported or belonged to the Know-Nothing (American) Party. "I belonged to the Whig Party from its origin to its close. I never belonged to the American Party," he told letter writers.[572] Lincoln managed to beat the popular Douglas in 1858. The Republicans won the governor's mansion and a near majority in the state legislature in 1858 too. The entry of Breckinridge into the 1860 race helped in Chicago. Davis wrote Lincoln that it "killed all the Douglas men in the city."[573]

Yet the Illinois presidential vote often ended differently from its state balloting. The Frémont election was an example. At the same time that Republicans were doing well in congressional and state elections there in 1856, Frémont lost the state by twenty-four thousand votes.[574] His pattern of voters alarmed Lincoln. Frémont had been successful in the northern part of the state but only won 23 percent of the vote in the southern counties that were near the slave states. Worse, Frémont took only 37 percent of the vote in the central swing counties, where the Republicans did better in the state races. If Lincoln was only to receive 30 percent or less from those southern counties, he had to do much better than Frémont in the central counties.[575] He had done better in the central counties in his 1858 Senate race against Douglas, but only breaking even with him. Douglas defeated him badly in the southern counties, and Lincoln won the northern counties handily.

By 1858, and more so by 1860, more German immigrants, with whom Lincoln was popular, had moved to Illinois. More residents had settled there thanks to the Illinois Central Railroad, now operating through that part of the state. Tens of thousands of transplanted New Englanders and immigrants built towns and ran farms in that area now. The sparsely settled area in the central part of Illinois now boasted 411,000 people, making up one–quarter of the state's population. That demography should help Lincoln, but no one knew that meant he would be elected. He could not take any chances.[576]

Lincoln had started work on the Illinois campaign after Frémont's election. He had been instrumental in keeping Owen Lovejoy on the ticket as the Republican nominee for Congress in 1856 and 1858, thwarting efforts of his own brain trust (Davis and Swett) to dump the fiery abolitionist. Although Lincoln kept his distance from abolitionists, he did so to bolster his own strength and to heighten his popularity in McClean County, a central county that he saw as crucial in the years ahead. He wrote Ward Lamon, "Running an independent candidate against Lovejoy will not do. (It will) result in nothing but disaster all around.... (The candidate) will lose us the district.... (He) can get a majority of the voters to which *all* look for an election."[577]

Lincoln had another reason for his support of Lovejoy—beyond a foothold and support in McLean County. Lovejoy's brother Elijah, an abolitionist newspaper editor, was murdered by proslavery vigilantes in Alton, Illinois, in 1837 and became a martyr to newspaper editors and reporters across the country. To support Lovejoy was to build good relations with the Illinois and national press for the years ahead.[578]

The year 1858 also saw Lincoln making repeated trips to Tazewell County, another swing county in the central area of Illinois. Tazewell had not been friendly to the Republicans. The old Whigs always carried Tazewell by two-to-one margins, but in 1856 the county went Democratic at 56 percent.[579] Lincoln campaigned there throughout 1858 and visited often in 1859 and 1860 in an effort to bolster the Republican vote.

He and Davis were determined to build the Republican vote throughout Illinois. The soaring increases in registered voters and high turnouts at the polls, tied to the general population boom in Illinois (its size doubled between 1844 and 1860), corresponded directly to Republican success in the state. The Republicans were born, as a party and opposition group, in 1854, shortly after the Kansas-Nebraska Act was introduced. Turnout jumped from 71,000 in 1850 to 133,000 in 1854 to 238,000 in 1856 and to 353,000 in 1858. More voters meant more Republicans and, in a state with 1.7 million voters in 1860, more of a chance to not only win the state but pile up national strength.[580] Republican leaders went from town to town to register more voters and published more Republican-backed newspapers.

Still, the election in Illinois would be very close. As summer turned into fall, local pollsters reported dead heats between Lincoln and Douglas in many towns and counties. In late September, Edwin Morgan, of the Republican National Committee, glumly reported to Lincoln that projections showed the Republicans were going to fail to achieve a majority in the Illinois legislature, one of their primary goals in the 1860 race. Morgan told Lincoln that the legislative vote did not reflect the presidential vote, but Lincoln was worried.[581]

Lincoln decided to push even harder in his home state. Plans were made in late summer to flood Illinois with politicians who had already won their races in other states in order to promote Lincoln and to show support for him around the nation. Judge Davis said, "We will get several governors into Illinois to campaign after the October elections."[582]

Lincoln had won Illinois by forty-five hundred votes in his 1858 Senate race with Douglas. He had to win it in 1860. He could not lose the presidency because he had lost his own home state. As the autumn began, though, the chances of carrying Illinois against Douglas seemed slim.

New York

Finally, there was New York—the growling electoral behemoth.

The Empire State's thirty-five electoral votes represented nearly 25 percent of the national total. Lincoln had to win New York, a state that Republican Frémont barely captured in 1856. Lincoln's strategy was to win all of the Northern states but one, but if that state was New York, he would lose the election. New York had a strong Democratic Party and had most of the key leaders in the Whig Party, but the sprawling state had been a puzzle throughout its history. It went Democratic in 1836, Whig in 1840, Democratic in 1844, Whig in 1848 (with 123,000 votes for the Free Soilers), Democratic in 1852, and Republican in 1856 (with 124,000 for Fillmore).[583] How would it vote in 1860?

The key in New York was the 1856 American Party vote for Fillmore. Its strength was hard to assess. Fillmore was a longtime political leader in

New York State and an archfoe of Seward and Weed when he was a Whig.
Was much of that vote from old-line Whig supporters? Fillmore, who
became president when Zachary Taylor died and served three years, was
not particularly interested in running for president in 1856 as an American
Party candidate. When nominated, he was traveling in Europe. So how
strong was his American Party support in New York? Fillmore was hated
by the antislavery faction in New York because he signed the Fugitive Slave
Act into law. Those mysterious Fillmore voters had to vote Republican, not
Democratic. The Democrats also were fearful of losing the election because
of New York. Wrote one, "New York is the key to the White House, and if
not seized to shut out Lincoln, it will be used to let him in."[584]

In midsummer, New York seemed safe. Lincoln heard from a number of
local congressmen that he would win it. Representative Francis Spinner told
him he could promise a nine-thousand-vote majority in his district alone.[585]
Buffalo Congressman Elbridge Spaulding wrote that he had conducted a
"conciliatory" campaign to woo American Party voters into the Republican
camp and was certain that, in upstate New York at least, nearly 70 percent
of them would vote for Lincoln in November.[586] Friend Lyman Trumbull,
who knew many New Yorkers, told him in June that "New York is…certain
for you."[587] Lincoln knew these men were overly optimistic, though. He had
to turn to Weed for accurate information. He trusted Weed, even though
he sometimes referred to him as "the intriguer." Weed wrote Lincoln that
"as things stand…we are abundantly safe. Nothing short of the withdrawal
of *both* the Democrats now running for president can change the aspect of
the campaign."[588]

New York had problems, though, and the nominee recognized them.
New York's importance was no secret, and he knew the Democrats would
campaign hard there. He wrote Weed in the middle of September: "I think

there will be the most extraordinary effort ever made to carry New York for the Democrats. You and all others who write me from your state think the effort cannot succeed and I hope you are right. Still, it will require close watching...great effort."[589]

And he realized that, like Pennsylvania, New York had been torn apart by internal feuding among Republicans. At the beginning of summer, Trumbull wrote him from Washington that all the New Yorkers he knew felt that they were being treated as outsiders by the National Republican Committee and by Lincoln and were angry about this scorn.[590]

Horace Greeley, the prominent editor of the *New York Tribune*, opposed Lincoln, as did all the Democratic newspapers. New York City was a Democratic stronghold and had been for years. Its hundreds of thousands of Irish hated the American Party Know-Nothings and detested Lincoln's efforts to placate them. There was a growing rift between several large Democratic machines in New York, especially the endless feud between Mozart Hall and Tammany Hall, still angry with each other over the chaos at the Democratic Convention in Charleston, but that feud would end by election day and both could deliver the Democratic vote. The American Party voters were reluctant to jump on the Lincoln bandwagon because he was close to the German voters in Illinois. Many downstate New York voters remembered Lincoln's much-publicized Cooper Union speech and thought him a wide-eyed radical on slavery.

The Democrats were very strong in New York and named New York millionaire August Belmont, a longtime Douglas supporter, their national party chairman, confident he could pry loose the money they would need for the race. He made New York City his national headquarters. Douglas also had friends at the New York Central Railroad, a huge financial contributor to political campaigns.

The tightening of the race in New York remained a mystery to most people throughout the United States. The *New York World*, as an example, said the election was the tamest since that of James Monroe in 1816. They had no idea how intense the election really was. Even James Russell Lowell, the well-connected editor of the *Atlantic* magazine, did not understand the backstage complexity of the race. He wrote in the October 1860 issue of his magazine of "the remarkable moderation which has thus far characterized the presidential canvass."[591]

He was not alone. Based on national straw polls taken during the last week of September, the *Chicago Tribune and Press* predicted a Lincoln victory. Other Republican journals were just as optimistic.[592]

On August 18, Judge Davis met with Weed in Saratoga Springs to win from him an agreement that he would use his considerable national influence to get Lincoln elected and, just as importantly, open up his seemingly bottomless campaign treasure chest to send money to other states, as well as New York, during the fall races. He also wanted guarantees from Weed that Seward, so popular among the radicals, would campaign hard for Lincoln.[593]

In return, Weed demanded that if his organization would do all that was asked, Seward had to be named secretary of state and a number of other New York politicians had to be appointed to federal jobs. Reportedly, Davis agreed.[594]

Seward then promptly went on a speaking tour for Lincoln that lasted several months and crisscrossed the Northern states, greatly assisting the Lincoln candidacy. Seward did the same on a tour of New York State, finishing just four days prior to the election.

Seward said that he liked Lincoln, even though the two barely knew each other. Upon his return to Washington after the convention, Seward began to tell friends how much he admired Lincoln and how well he thought the nominee would do in the upcoming elections. Trumbull wrote Lincoln, "He spoke in the highest terms of you."[595]

The response to the popular Seward, whom everyone thought would be the nominee and believed would be president in 1864, was phenomenal. Enormous crowds waited for hours at train stations to greet him, and even larger throngs gathered around him for his speeches. His speaking venue was often moved from inside halls to wide meadows or outdoor city parks to accommodate the mammoth audiences. Extra police had to be hired to keep order wherever he went. Crowds sang a popular song about his presidency in 1864:

> *In sixty-four, with peace secured;*
> *We will have our William Seward.*[596]

In Chicago, the *Daily Democrat* reported that the thick crowds along the sides of the city streets burst through the police lines and filled the avenues as Seward's carriage slowly made its way through the people to his hotel. A reporter wrote that "it was only after a severe struggle that the police were finally enabled to clear a passage for Gov. Seward, accompanied by Gen. Nye and Mayor Wentworth, from the carriage to the hotel entrance.... The vast assemblage broke into a shout of welcome, which echoed like the voice of many waters through the streets."[597]

Lincoln had wanted to go to Chicago to greet Seward, anticipating the huge welcome, but Davis, fearful that Seward would persuade him to make a short speech, talked him out of it.[598]

Seward, always the star of his own parade, paid little attention to what Davis and Lincoln asked him to say. He was told to be moderate on slavery but disregarded their advice. As soon as he put his hands on the speaker's lectern, he was off on another classic, fire-and-brimstone antislavery speech.

He told audiences in Detroit, Michigan, that they were "on the side of freedom against slavery." He told a crowd in St. Paul, Minnesota, that "slavery today is, for the first time, not only powerless, but without influence in the American republic" and that the great march of Northerners would crush it.[599] He wanted to know, he said near the end of the campaign, "who are its (the Constitution's) friends and who are its enemies?"[600]

Everywhere he went, Seward praised Lincoln and Hamlin. "No truer or firmer defenders of the Republican faith could have been found in the union than the distinguished and esteemed citizens on whom the honors of nomination have fallen," he said repeatedly.[601]

Weed also procured hundreds of speakers, local and national, to stump New York for Lincoln, and in November he reported that over ten thousand speeches had been made for the Republican nominee in New York alone. The political boss also opened his war chest to Republicans in other states but was careful in the way he dispensed money.

A candidate in St. Louis, Missouri, asked for $2,000 in campaign funds, but Weed only gave him $1,000, he told everyone, because he knew the Republicans could not win in Missouri. Why spend the money?[602]

Weed pushed his machine as hard as he could through the summer and autumn and until election day. Why did Weed, Seward's campaign manager, work so hard for Lincoln, a man he hardly knew? He did so because his goal was to make Seward secretary of state and then president in 1864, and Lincoln's election could make that happen. He did so because he was a loyal Republican and wanted to help the party. But Weed also worked so hard for Lincoln because he liked him. The two men struck up a fast friendship when they met in Springfield after the convention. Lincoln had always hoped that if people liked him, they would help him. Weed was another one who did.

But was it enough? The combination American and Democratic tickets would have beaten Frémont by forty-five thousand votes in 1856. The Republicans had swept to victory in upstate counties such as Onondaga (ten thousand votes to four thousand), St. Lawrence by a five-to-one margin, Washington by a five-to-one margin, and Tompkins by a four-to-one margin. They also lost many upstate counties, however, such Albany (home of the state capital), Erie (Buffalo), Rockland, Ulster, Westchester, and Schoharie. They lost New York City by over thirty thousand votes in 1856.[603] Many Republicans in New York were angry at Lincoln for having defeated their darling, Seward. Could Lincoln take New York? Maybe.

The nominee began to seriously worry about New York in early September, when he received discouraging letters from Buffalo political chief James Putnam, whose advice had been accurate throughout the summer. Putnam wrote him on September 8 that "the battle begins to grow hot in New York." Personal friend Elihu Washburne had been to New York and talked to many people. He candidly wrote Lincoln, "I must confess I feel some anxiety about New York."[604]

So did Lincoln.

CHAPTER 15

Breck and Bell and Give 'Em Hell

The Constitutional Union Party will restore harmony to this country and will not do anything that may tend to its destruction or to the introduction of anarchy and the overthrow of our glorious Constitution.

—CONSTITUTIONAL UNION CANDIDATE JOHN BELL

John Bell

Shortly after 8:00 p.m., May 15, 1860, as darkness began to fall on the city of Philadelphia, a crowd of more than six thousand people started to march from the headquarters of the brand-new Constitutional Union Party to the La Pierre House, one of the city's fanciest hotels, about a mile away on Broad Street. They carried hundreds of torches that illuminated the night. There were so many in the crowd that police stopped all horse and carriage traffic on the street, the main avenue of Philadelphia. They marched shoulder to shoulder and elbow to elbow, as they moved toward the hotel. Neighbors hung out of windows to watch.

They stopped at the La Pierre. Their bands serenaded John Bell, the new party's candidate for president, who was dining inside with friends. He had been the nominee for less than a week, and headquarters for him had already been opened in most major cities, publicity officers named, and press releases sent out to every major paper in America.

Bell stood on a second-floor balcony with Joe Ingersoll, who helped nominate him, to the cheers of the crowd. Ingersoll said that Bell was not only in favor of preserving the Union, but he supported a high tariff to protect Pennsylvania workers. He noted Bell had been the first to back the state's ironworkers when he was in Congress. Ingersoll said: "This must be the party of the country, of the Union, of the Constitution. I will call up remembrances that will thrill every heart because it is the cause of the Union, the party of the Union, which we hope the people will ratify."

Bell reminded the crowd that those who nominated him were the same men who had kept the Union together since 1820. He said he would not discuss slavery or any other issue in the campaign. "I do not believe that the agitation of these subjects could lead to any public good. It can lead to nothing but mischief. With me, (the party) will restore harmony to this country and will not do anything that may tend to its destruction or to the introduction of anarchy and the overthrow of our glorious Constitution. I trust the masses, North and South, love the Union as I do."[605]

Bell's reception in Philadelphia was followed by similar enthusiastic welcomes wherever he went in the early days of his campaign that spring. When his train arrived in Nashville a week later, people began to leap onto the platforms behind the cars in order to meet the man who might be the next president of the United States. They jumped into the locomotive cage and supply cars and held on to windows as the train brakes grinded to a halt. Fearful of running over people, the engineers nervously stopped the train. Men were waving hats and shouting, and women yelled as well.

Bell stepped out and thanked everyone for coming. Then someone shouted, "Three cheers for the Union," and the crowd in unison roared the same chant nine times. Bell was nearly in tears.[606] Kentucky Senator John Crittenden, who accompanied him, wrote that Bell was "welcomed like twenty presidents" that day. After the Nashville stop, Bell spent a week campaigning in Tennessee, greeted by large and enthusiastic crowds at each stop.[607]

The Bell campaign stressed the Union, the Constitution, and the people, all tied up into a neat political package shrouded in the memories of Washington, Jefferson, and Jackson. Bell's promoters let everyone know that sound leaders were running the campaign, and they intended to keep the country together, aided by people previously turned off to politics. They promised that America's best days were ahead.

The connection to the American Revolution was popular and used by Douglas as well. He claimed in his speeches that the territories should be allowed to decide whether they wanted slavery because they were just like the American colonies in 1776 that were forbidden to make their own decisions, and as a result of that they went to war. For a while, that argument worked for all of the Democrats.[608]

The Bell campaign had a clear vision of its audience. It was not the extremist Southern politicians such as Robert Toombs, William Yancey, and their followers. It was not the radical Southern newspaper editors howling for secession. The Bell supporters, the people who were going to elect him and save the nation, were those individuals who had shied away from politics because they saw politics as corrupt. They were fearful for the future and wanted to participate in the election. Some owned slaves, but the others were poor farmers who were not concerned about slavery as much as getting a good price for their crops. They were merchants who had no use for debates on states' rights but merely wanted to sell their goods at fair prices. They were rich people who were conservative, but they were also middle class, whether farmers, shopkeepers, or salesmen. They were not the loud few who drew all the attention and received all the press but rather the mass of people who lived quietly and received little attention and made up the body politic.

Bell's followers believed they could stop Lincoln. They did not believe, as so many people told them, that it was too late for moderation, that most of the people of North and South had already been radicalized over slavery.

Bell's men stood for restoring harmony and used it to heal rifts in the Democratic Party. "Rash words have been said, unwise things have been done. The North has been severe upon the South. The South has been severe upon the North. But let us forget and forgive all," said a man named Hilliard of Massachusetts.[609]

Some savaged them for their neutrality on the slave issue. G. H. Young, an old-line Whig, said that "Bell's platform is a cheat, a political omnibus which, in an attempt to carry everybody, will in the end carry nobody.... They can't carry a single state."

The editor of the *Macon (Georgia) County Democrat* asked Bell to make a statement on expanding slavery into the territories, but he refused, and the paper then headlined its story John Bell Is a Dumb Bell.

Others complained loudly that the people who ran the Constitutional Union Party consisted of a bunch of old men who should have been put out to political pasture years ago and had no idea what was going on in the country. Breckinridge supporters, pushing their thirty-nine-year-old nominee, referred to the Constitutional Unionists as "the old man's party." A reporter covering the Constitutionalist convention in Alabama wrote that "many of them are old, gray-haired patricians."[610]

Bell was chided by North and South for refusing to acknowledge the slavery issue and criticized for a platform that did not even take a stand on the Homestead Act, tariffs, or the transcontinental railroad. The press made fun of the "Bell Ringers," who clanged their bells whenever they were around people.

Nobody ignored him, though, because Bell's men not only made plans for a national campaign but organized offices and elector tickets in every state. Early feedback from politicians North and South showed that it was likely that John Bell was going to carry his own state, Tennessee, and Virginia and Maryland. He would beat Breckinridge in Kentucky and stood a good chance to win Missouri and Indiana. By May, Bell's campaign was under way.[611] He had a hardworking organization full of "old men" who had run campaigns a dozen times and knew how to win. Early efforts to create a Constitutional Union Party in every Southern state were successful and much larger throngs than expected gathered at these initial meetings and rallies.[612] Paradoxically, because he voiced no opinion on any issue, Bell became a formidable candidate by turning away voters from Lincoln to himself in the North while keeping the proslavery Southern vote without offending either side. Some anxious Lincoln operatives, who chided Bell for following "a wickedly foolish" course, warned the Republican nominee that he should stop worrying about Douglas and start worrying about Bell.[613]

John Breckinridge

John Breckinridge was the enigmatic boy wonder of American politics, the good-looking, well-spoken, bluegrass Hamlet who could never seem to make up his mind about what he wanted out of life. Now, in 1860, he had suddenly been thrust into the middle of a heated presidential campaign, assured he could win, but uncertain whether he wanted to win. His quixotic personality and questionable drive would determine whether he would, at the same time, stop Abe Lincoln, keep the South in the Union, and at thirty-nine years old become the youngest man ever elected president.

Breckinridge came from a long line of men devoted to public service. His grandfather, John Breckinridge, was a U.S. senator from Kentucky and attorney general in Thomas Jefferson's cabinet. His uncle was a professor of theology at Princeton. Another uncle was superintendent of public schools in Kentucky.

Breckinridge graduated from Centre College, Kentucky, as a lawyer in 1838, and by twenty-eight, he was a Kentucky state legislator. He was a congressman at thirty and vice president under James Buchanan at thirty-five.

Breckinridge carved out a legend for himself as a campaigner in his first congressional contest. He started running in February and continued through the summer and fall, averaging five or six speeches each week. His speeches improved, and by summer, people who did not even plan on voting for him turned out just to hear him work the crowds with his soaring oratory, funny stories, and ebullient personality. The legend of "Breck" as a campaign dynamo grew when he won his first congressional race deep in the heart of Henry Clay's Whig country, handily beating one of the Whig's top politicians, Gen. Leslie Combs.[614]

He grew into one of the most popular politicians of the mid-nineteenth century, At the same time he was serving as vice president of the United States, from 1856 to 1860, he was elected as a U.S. senator from Kentucky, holding both offices at the same time, which was legal in that era. In fact, if he was elected president, he would, for one day, hold the offices of president, vice president, and U.S. senator simultaneously. He was a handsome man with a charming demeanor, a forceful public speaker, a much sought-after socialite, a man of unsullied reputation, honest, candid, and a symbol to the huge youth movement sweeping the nation. He was a happily married family man with several children and had lived an exemplary life untouched by scandal.

And yet John Breckinridge just did not know what he wanted to do or where he wanted to go. He certainly did not want to be president—and in 1859 had written a letter to a newspaper saying so—and he had no great love for the job of vice president, although he did enjoy the Senate. He balked at the seceders' convention nomination and only accepted it because he was certain Jefferson Davis would talk Stephen Douglas out of the race and he could go home to Louisville.

Breckinridge was an odd politician. A man who valued his word above all else, he had made a career of turning down opportunities to honor commitment, and he did not change in 1860. In 1856 he at first supported Franklin Pierce for the Democratic nomination for reelection and then shifted to Stephen Douglas, whom he much admired. He stuck with Douglas through several ballots even though James Buchanan was headed for victory. Late at night, Buchanan's men arrived at his hotel room to make a deal: if he could switch all of Kentucky's votes from Douglas to Buchanan, he could be vice president. Most men would have leaped at the chance. Breckinridge reminded them that he told Douglas he would remain loyal to him and would not ally himself with Buchanan just to be vice president. The shaken politicians left. The next day, the convention nominated Breckinridge anyway; he stood on a chair on the convention floor and declined. He just did not want to be vice president. At the conclusion of his ringing speech forfeiting the nomination, the delegates were convinced that he should be vice president, whether he wanted the job or not, and nominated him.[615] In 1860, he told everyone he knew at the second Democratic convention that he had no interest in the presidency and then, again, turned down the nomination, only to acquiesce when literally forced to do so when Jefferson Davis' plan to nominate Horatio Seymour collapsed.

Breckinridge was an unusual man in an unusual time, and the bolters, when they nominated him, saw in him surface qualities and had an iron confidence in him that he did not share.

They saw a perfect presidential candidate. He was the vice president and well known. On trips north, particularly in New York, he had been impressive and won over much support in both parties. He was a young and vibrant man who would make a strong president who could serve two terms, and then, still young, continue as a national party leader. He was one of the country's best campaigners and was the first vice president to stump for office when he campaigned from city to city in the 1856 race. Most important, he was a former slaveholder from the South who could retain Southern support and still attract Northern voters because he was seen throughout the country as a Unionist.

What most people did not know about Breckinridge was that he detested slavery. He had since boyhood. He expressed his doubts about the system to close friends throughout his life, but never in public, and he told everyone that slavery should be abolished. He never owned more than a few slaves himself, mostly for political reasons in Kentucky, and as a city lawyer, he had no need for them. In 1857 he sold his last slave; he was no longer a slaveholder and never would be again. The Southern Democratic Party, as the bolters now called themselves, had as their champion of slavery a man who did not believe in it.

Breckinridge, in his heart, had always been a Unionist. In 1859 he had shifted his politics to embrace Southern causes, such as expansion of slavery into the territories and the protection of Southern businesses with low tariffs, but he never for a moment backed secession.[616]

So, in the end, the Southern Democrats were supporting a slavery-hating Unionist whom they believed was a slavery-loving secessionist.

The bolters were confident of victory. A resident of Kentucky, Breckinridge could win neighboring Indiana and Iowa. He could capture New York, where the Democrats, never high on Douglas, would unite behind him. The corruption scandals that ruined the Buchanan administration had never touched Breckinridge. They honestly believed Breckinridge could carry all the Southern states and capture two or three Northern states and force an election in the House of Representatives. What they needed from Breckinridge, though, and did not have yet, was a promise to become interested in gaining the highest office in the nation.

The Breckinridge and Bell campaigns followed two common themes: 1) the Southern candidates were in favor of slavery but were staunch Unionists who, if elected, could stop the Southern extremists from seceding, 2) Abe Lincoln was a fire-breathing, abolitionist, anti-Christ, a political Satan who, if elected, would bring about the secession of all the Southern states and the complete wreckage of the United States. They managed to get dozens of newspapers to carry a compendium of Lincoln's antislavery speeches from 1838 to 1860.[617] There was a compelling third theme, too, never mentioned but always implied: the Southern hotheads might convince their states to secede if Lincoln was elected, so everyone should support Breckinridge or Bell to prevent that from happening.

The Bell campaign, started in mid-May, began by attacking Lincoln. Its spokesmen denounced Lincoln's antislavery stand. In one statement, a Bell supporter said:

> *Against the laws of God and against your Constitution you have raised an impious hand. It (antislavery) is an unholy crusade. The God of our fathers frowns upon it and every true American sentiment*

rebukes it. (If elected) you will have succeeded in the basest sacrilege known in all history.[618]

They were furious at the repeated Republican claims that Lincoln was not an abolitionist but a moderate who might be against the expansion of slavery into the territories but would do nothing about slavery where it existed. The Southern Democrats, particularly the Breckinridge men, reminded voters that Lincoln had spoken out against slavery for years, often in vitriolic and radical language. They pointed to his famous "House Divided" speech, of course, but had other well-known incidents. In 1856, when he delivered a speech to a state Republican convention, he had said, "Let us draw a cordon, so to speak, around the slave states, and the hateful institution, like a reptile poisoning itself, will perish by its own infamy."[619]

In an 1855 letter, Lincoln wrote that "there is no peaceful extinction of slavery in prospect for us...so far as peaceful voluntary emancipation is concerned, the condition of the Negro slave in America...is now fixed and hopeless."[620] In another speech that same year, he had said:

> *We shall be in a majority after awhile and then the revolution which we shall accomplish will be none the less radical.... Slavery is a violation of eternal right...detestable crime and ruinous to the nation. Those who deny freedom to others deserve it not for themselves and, under the rule of a just God, cannot long retain it.*[621]

He had said the same thing in his well-publicized Senate debates against Douglas in 1858. "Slavery is the real issue. That is the issue that will continue in this country when these poor tongues of Judge Douglas and myself shall be silent. It is the eternal struggle between two principles: right and wrong."[622]

The Southerners charged, too, that if Lincoln was so dead set against the works of the abolitionists and kept criticizing people who called him one, why did he never publicly complain about the activities of the abolitionists?[623]

The Democrats also skillfully tied the hated Seward, detested far more than Lincoln, to the Republican nominee, creating for Southerners a double target. They even more adroitly positioned Seward, not Lincoln, as the man who would really run the government.[624]

The connection to Lincoln was often stretched to include the despised Horace Greeley and others and to insinuate that all of them, when elected, would skewer the South. The editor of the *Charleston Mercury* wrote:

> *The satanic churches of Beecher, Stowe, Greeley, Seward, Webb, etc. are even now loading the Sharpe rifles, and whetting the bowie knives and buckling on the revolvers for the purpose of gratifying that demonic frenzy, which nothing short of diabolical tragedies of the midnight torch, the poisoned fountains and daily assassination in Virginia, the Carolinas, and Texas (will satisfy).*[625]

The Breckinridge men charged throughout the campaign that not only Lincoln but all of the members of the Republican Party were abolitionists determined to crush slavery in an effort to achieve voter solidarity—South against North—throughout every state in the South.[626]

President Woodrow Wilson later wrote that there was no other way Southerners could interpret the North's words and actions. He said, "Their (Republican) creed, their actions alike were compounded of hostility towards the Southland; the challenge of their success was direct and unmistakable."[627]

Some historians argued that Lincoln had become the last straw on the Southerners' back, and many who did not fear Lincoln became terrified of the people who worked for him. Southern editor Edwin Pollard wrote, "(Southerners) suffered from general apprehension, rather than specific alarm…and the election of Abraham Lincoln was an…addition to their uneasiness rather than a cause of complaint."[628]

Breckinridge supporters also managed to neatly tie Lincoln to the *Impending Crisis* book, an anti-Southern, antislavery work that had inflamed so many Southerners, and they pointed fingers at Republicans who enjoyed the book, such as Ohio Republican Joshua Giddings. "Every sentence of the book finds a response in the hearts of all Republicans," he said proudly.[629]

Beneath all of the newspaper editorials and public denouncements, the people of the North and South had concrete views of each other on the slavery issue that framed the entire election and history for that time. This was best expressed in the letters and feelings of ordinary citizens. An example was the Halsey brothers of Rockaway, New Jersey. Joe, thirty-seven in 1860, had moved to Virginia in 1843, married a wealthy woman, had slaves, and became an extremist. Sam, twenty-five in 1860, stayed in New Jersey and joined the Republican Party. He shared Lincoln's view of permitting slavery where it was but forbidding expansion.

Sam wrote to Joe:

> *There is a difference between the words extension and abolition. But you say the right to prohibit its extension implies the right to prohibit slavery from where it now is—and that this we will do next. Now, we don't desire to do any such thing. We have no constitutional right to do it if we would. Each state has the right of controlling and regulating its own domestic institutions, and we say that slavery never can be abolished in the Southern states until the states themselves bring about the movement.*[630]

Brother Joe, in Virginia, charged that all Republicans were abolitionists and, when they controlled the White House, would not only bar the extension of slavery, but they would eliminate it wherever it currently existed. The older brother had come to hate Republicans and hate Northerners because of the slavery question, and he told Sam he firmly believed that when Lincoln was elected, Northerners would move South in packs to not only free slaves but to murder slaveholders and their families. Both men believed their view was correct.[631]

By 1860 these wildly divergent opinions were firmly held by millions of Americans, and the politicians who understood the way Northerners and Southerners felt about each other would be successful in the election, and those who did not would lose.

There were problems in the Breckinridge campaign. First, he had no organization. The Southern Democrats had no workers, no newspapers, no offices. Breckinridge and his followers had to build a political party from scratch.[632] Another problem concerned perception. He was a moderate on slavery but had been tied to the extremists of the South. They wrapped themselves around him, and Breckinridge was never able to get rid of them. Bell, Douglas, and Lincoln quickly painted him as a disunionist and secessionist, despite his protests. This general perception would hurt him.

Most of the people in the South echoed the views of the extremists, although they probably did not want to secede, just as Breckinridge did not. His association with Yancey and others would probably win him votes. So he turned down the advice of the *San Antonio Express* that "an animal not willing to pass for a pig shouldn't stay in the sty."[633]

Finally, Breckinridge had little heart for the race. He was told again and again that he was a great stump campaigner. He decided not to make any speeches or campaign appearances, denying himself his most powerful weapon.

The only major speech Breckinridge delivered was at Ashland, Kentucky, in early September. It did not kick off the campaign or rally supporters but was given to answer charges made against him by others. It was not a powerful speech, even though he pledged that he was firmly behind the South on the slavery issue.[634]

Breckinridge remained in the race, though, because he became convinced that a united Southern Democratic front, with a huge electoral vote, would convince Northerners that the South was strong and had to be reckoned with, and that the slave system could not be eliminated or curbed against such a tough political alliance, which would fight it repeatedly in any new Congress. And he knew that if Lincoln lost a few Northern states, the election would go to the House of Representatives and he might wind up being president, against his wishes, just because he won most Southern states.

The Bell campaign had no substantive foundation, either. Bell's men felt comfortable in efforts to win in several moderate Northern states and were certain they could win the Southern states, but as the summer rolled into fall, they began to realize the deep hatred that many Southerners felt toward the North and toward any compromise with the North that might mean the immediate or even gradual elimination of the slave economy. Those Southerners may not have supported everything the extremists such as Yancey preached, but they believed enough of it to rule out compromise candidates and started to swing toward Breckinridge and away from Bell.

The Southern Democrats always had money problems. Lincoln shrewdly only campaigned in the North, which meant he could spend all of his campaign funds in just half the country. The Southern Democratic candidates had to beat each other in every Southern state, which meant they were forced to spend money in all of those states. The two Southern Democrats also had to defeat Douglas and Lincoln in the Northern states, and so they also had to pour money into New York, New Jersey, Pennsylvania, Illinois, and other states. Their money was stretched thin by October.

The Southern Democratic races were marred by endless mudslinging, and managers of both were unable to focus on Lincoln. They were also hurt by their single-issue campaign on slavery. Neither had another issue. They might toss off a line or two in a speech about the need for more railroads because railroads carried products farmed in the Southern states, but beyond that they had no real campaign. This did not matter in the South, where slavery was the main issue. But the absence of a meaningful campaign made it very difficult for either man to make inroads in the key Northern states. In those states the Republicans had put together a comprehensive package that included more railroads, the Homestead Act for new farmers, tariff reform to protect ironworkers, harbor and riverfront improvement for shipping, better voting rights laws for millions of immigrants flooding the Northern states, and a defense of unions and workers' rights. These different issues helped attract the voters who were not driven only by slavery—and there were many—as well as keep the support of antislavery issue-driven voters.[635] The inability of Breckinridge and Bell to campaign on any other issue except slavery hurt them badly, as did making Lincoln their lone target. Although in reality running against slavery, the Republicans always seemed to be running for something, and the Southern Democrats always just seemed to be running against Abe Lincoln.

The best way to defeat Lincoln was a fusion ticket. It would set Lincoln himself against a merged Democratic ticket with electors for all three Democratic candidates. Each of the three Democrats felt that he could defeat Lincoln in several Northern states and that Lincoln could not carry any of the Southern states. None felt that they alone could defeat him everywhere.

Even if they could run on fusion tickets in just a few states, such as New York, Pennsylvania, and Indiana, they could stop Lincoln.[636]

The editor of the *Nashville Union and American* wrote on October 12, 1860:

> *There is no resource left than to unite upon one ticket, than for all the Southern states to decide upon casting a united vote for one candidate in this contest and thus present an unbroken front to our sectional oppressors.... We are not so weak, divided, and degenerated that we are ready to surrender to their insolent, tyrannical, and insulting demands without resistance.*[637]

But would the Democrats, who fought against each other so bitterly all summer, be able to form a fusion ticket? Early efforts at fusion failed miserably. The discord grew so great that even when state conventions were able to hammer together a fusion ticket of electors, as Pennsylvania thought it did, the friction caused it to collapse. Could the Democrats do what they knew they had to do—unite to beat the Black Republicans? And could they do so before the election took place?

CHAPTER 16

The Douglas Campaign

*We must take the war boldly against the Northern abolitionists and the Southern
disunionists and give no quarter to either.*

—STEPHEN DOUGLAS

Stephen Douglas arrived in New York City in June 1860, his campaign
in tatters. He was the presidential nominee of the most powerful political
party of the century in the United States. He won a nomination many
thought not worth having at the party's second convention, in Baltimore.
The once-united Democratic Party that had swept to victory so easily in
the past was fractured. Douglas had the nomination of the official wing of
the party, but the traditional wing not only shifted to Breckinridge but had
the support of President James Buchanan. The organization of the party,
key to any victory, was hopelessly split. Douglas now controlled very few
organizers in the South, and the Democratic organizers in many Northern
states, particularly the crucial electoral state of Pennsylvania, were still

controlled by Buchanan. Senator Stephen Douglas, who had sought the presidency for so long, was now just a few months away from election, but it seemed hopeless.

His great difficulty, as he saw it, was that he had to once again run against Abraham Lincoln. He feared Lincoln. He told his aides when Lincoln ran against him in Illinois: "I shall have my hands full. He is the strong man of the party—full of wit, facts, dates—the best stump speaker, with his droll ways and dry jokes.... He is as honest as he is shrewd." Douglas had not changed his mind.[638]

Douglas realized that the main problem as he and his wife, Adele, checked into a swank New York hotel, was not organization but cash. The large amounts the Little Giant needed to run for president were no longer available. Southern contributors were gone, and so were those from many areas in the border states. Longtime friends of Douglas were now committed to Breckinridge and Bell and sent their campaign contributions to those camps.

The new national campaign chairman, August Belmont, had to tell him by early July that he was unable to raise sufficient funds for a campaign in New York State, much less the nation. The New York Central Railroad, counted on for at least $100,000 for Douglas, offered nothing. Individuals expected to contribute thousands of dollars spurned Belmont. Even his fellow millionaires would not offer him any money. The few contributors left who supported the official Democratic nominee were convinced he would lose the election. While they were not giving their money to Breckinridge or Bell, they were not contributing funds to Douglas, and in July, he needed money desperately.

A frustrated Belmont said, "Unless we can give our merchants and politicians some appearance of success, I fear that it will be impossible to raise the necessary funds for a campaign."[639]

As Douglas looked everywhere for funds and Breckinridge and Bell fought each other for every nickel that could be found, Lincoln was awash in money, sending huge sums to the different Northern states to fund party organizations and campaign drives. As Belmont was repeatedly turned down by Democratic New Yorkers, Thurlow Weed raised hundreds of thousands from Republican New Yorkers. Newspapers reported throughout the late summer that at the same time the Little Giant could not raise a dollar in the Democratic ranks in New York, Weed was sending checks ranging from $5,000 to $10,000 to different state campaigns every single week.

Like Douglas, Belmont was certain the Democrats, if they could put together a fusion ticket, could carry New York, even without lavish campaign funds. In July, however, they were the only two politicians between Niagara Falls and Staten Island who believed so. Belmont was angry. He said, "If we could only demonstrate to all these lukewarm and selfish moneybags that we have a strong probability to carry the state of New York, we might get from them the necessary sinews of war."[640]

Fund-raisers in other states fared no better. Democrats from Iowa to Georgia were reluctant to contribute to a campaign they considered hopeless. Miles Taylor, the head of the Douglas congressional campaign committee, who served as an ad hoc national vice chairman working in the Washington DC office and who had friends in all the states, could not raise money in the South, either.[641]

To compound the Little Giant's problems, Belmont was constantly threatening to quit, and Taylor was continually trying to undercut Belmont. At one point, Belmont wrote to Douglas, "It is impossible for me to go on in this way. If the other members of the (national) committee will not assist me in raising funds, the whole machinery has to stop."[642]

Miles Taylor sneered at the New York millionaire's threat to resign. He told Douglas he did not believe for a minute that Belmont, with all of his connections, could not raise money. He told Belmont that he was content to reap all the social and political rewards of being national chairman but was not doing any work.

"It will not do to have our chances of success…diminished by Belmont's incapacity, inefficiency, or worse," Taylor told Douglas.

In the end, the Little Giant, tired of their feuding, ordered Belmont and Taylor to end their differences and work together to help him get elected.[643]

A nervous Belmont called a meeting of the national committee to discuss fund-raising. Interest was so low that only members from Connecticut and Pennsylvania showed up. Belmont then assessed each Democratic district $100 toward the national campaign and, separately, assessed New York districts money for the New York campaign. Belmont sadly told friends in mid-September that in over two months of lobbying, he had not raised a single dollar. Douglas was broke. He would have to run for president on a shoestring budget.

The Little Giant was frustrated.

He spent the early days of July trying to make decisions that no other candidate in history had to make in order to jump-start his campaign. Some of them were good and some were atrocious. Uncertain how he would succeed against three separate candidates and his own party, he often moved in the wrong direction, listened to the wrong people, and made political mistakes that a first-time city council candidate in a small town would never make. He decided to spend too much time in areas where Lincoln could not be beaten and where he could not lose. He accepted as unassailable predictions from political operatives that any rational person would reject. He trusted the opinions of the governors, congressmen, and senators of his party and millionaires and ignored the political bosses who could have told him exactly what he had to do. (Lincoln ignored the public officials and sought out and trusted the bosses.)

Worst of all, from a political point of view, Douglas refused to accept any kind of fusion ticket that would unite two or even three of the Democrats in a single campaign against Lincoln. He continually dismissed any suggestions of fusion, even in Northern states like New York and New Jersey, where a fusion ticket had a good chance of winning, and in July he went as far as issuing a public manifesto to curb any more talk about it.[644] The fusion issue, which dogged Douglas the entire fall, was another example of all his old enemies coming back to undermine his campaign. Douglas was running against two other Democrats because his enemies in the South denied him the nomination in Charleston.

He never forgave the Southerners for walking out of both conventions and shredding his candidacy. Throughout the campaign he blamed them for the divided party and said that they were responsible for the surge of Black Republicanism.

He said in Raleigh, North Carolina, of his enemies:

> *What was the object in bolting? Was it not to beat me? If it was, did they not know that the only way to do it was to divide the Democratic Party in the North and South and allow Lincoln to carry each one of these states by a minority vote? The secession took place for the purpose of defeating me.*[645]

Now, those same enemies in the Northern and Southern states were pressing him into fusion, not so that he could win, but so that all would win some electoral votes in each state, denying Lincoln victory and throwing the election into the House of Representatives, where a Democrat would surely be chosen. That Democrat, Douglas' enemies planned, would not be Douglas, and the Little Giant knew that. So he resisted fusion. He turned down efforts by the Bell and Breckinridge men to create fusion tickets in New York, New Jersey, Pennsylvania, and Indiana in June, even though he realized that fusion tickets in each of those states had a decent chance of winning. Fusion tickets in those states might also show votes and financial supporters in other states that the Democrats were united after all, despite their Charleston and Baltimore squabbles, and bring victory there.

Fusion tickets would also help to shear away the party's divisive image of Douglas and make him a powerful leader. Agreeing to fusion tickets with Breckinridge and Bell would also cast Douglas in a much more favorable light with Southerners. Yet Stephen Douglas, so close to the White House now and so bitter about the conventions and the Southerners, could not do it. It was a decision that might cost him the election.

The other Democrats in the race haunted Douglas, who never believed their presence was his fault. The refusal of Douglas to step down when asked by Jefferson Davis after the second Democratic convention propelled Bell and then Breckinridge back into the race and cemented their own desires to somehow stop Lincoln, in spite of Douglas. The Little Giant's refusal also set an army of opponents in his own party against him. In the end, the enemies of Douglas prevented Douglas, not from helping them, but from helping himself—something Lincoln never had to worry about for he had been so long out of office.

The aborted Davis deal also cost Douglas his running mate. Instead of Ben Fitzpatrick, he turned to Herschel Johnson of Georgia, again in an effort to add a Southern man to the ticket to prove Douglas was not antislavery and to win Southern states. That decision also backfired.

Johnson might have been a slavery moderate in 1860, but in 1850–1851, during the heated debates over the Compromise of 1850 and the slave issue, Herschel Johnson was a proslavery, states' rights firebrand. He still had that reputation, and it scared Northerners. After nominating Breckinridge, the seceders convention put together a list of speakers to send north on his behalf (just before Fitzpatrick resigned). One was Herschel Johnson. He was immediately dropped from the list because even extremist Southerners realized the well-known slaveholder would be poison in the North.

Johnson was a pariah in the South, too, when he became a moderate. As a U.S. senator from Georgia in 1854, he committed the cardinal sin in the South that year—he voted for the Kansas-Nebraska bill, which permitted residents there to vote for or against slavery in the territories.[646] Even though Douglas could only win the election by winning in the South as well as the North, he chose Johnson, a man who was unpopular in both areas, as his running mate. It was another Johnson, Senator Andrew Johnson of Tennessee, whom Douglas originally wanted as his vice presidential candidate. He tried to convince him to join the ticket at the Charleston convention, but Johnson turned him down. Ironically, Andrew Johnson eventually became Lincoln's vice president in his second term and president upon Lincoln's assassination.

Once nominated for the second-highest office in the land, Herschel Johnson complained bitterly to friends back in Georgia that he only had the honor because Fitzpatrick backed out, that he was the second choice, the last doll on the carnival barker's shelf.[647] Johnson lamented his state to fellow Georgian Alexander Stephens throughout the summer and fall and became a doomsayer in the party, constantly telling Douglas whenever they met that Douglas was going to lose the election.

Stephen Douglas mulled over all of these problems in a hotel room in New York City in the summer of 1860. Halfway across the continent from his home in Illinois, Douglas also must have felt trapped by the New Yorkers surrounding him. He was a man from the West who had an eastern millionaire from New York, Belmont, as his national campaign chairman. The man who had assumed the duties of his East Coast campaign manager was none other than Dean Richmond, head of the Albany Regency political machine, the same Dean Richmond who first forced a delay in the adoption of the party platform in Charleston, enabling the Southerners to denounce it and walk out. It was Richmond, too, who demanded the two-thirds voting rule be put into effect, making it impossible for Douglas to be nominated at Charleston and forcing the closing of the convention.[648]

Douglas' national headquarters was in New York, not his native Springfield or nearby Chicago. Politically, the New York Democratic Party was a hopeless mess. It had two feuding groups, the "hard" and "soft" Democrats, constantly at each other's throats, and two warring political machines, Tammany Hall and Mozart Hall, which would not join together to support him—or anybody. The one New Yorker who could help him, flamboyant Mozart machine leader Mayor Fernando Wood of New York, who tried to help at Charleston, still smarted from the way Dean Richmond managed to have him and his delegation booted out of the Charleston convention. Wood blamed the head of the ticket, Douglas, for his dismissal. Douglas knew that as long as the "hards" and "softs" and Tammany and Mozart were at war, he could not capture New York City. There were no signs that peace would ever come to the feud between the two groups.

Mayor Wood's Mozart Hall people were so furious with Tammany Hall and Dean Richmond that they even passed a resolution the week they returned from the Charleston convention that flayed the other half of the Democratic Party, charging that "its corruptions, deceptions, and repeated offenses against the Democratic Party of New York, and more recently of the whole country at Charleston, have sunk it so low that no decent man recognizes its authority."[649]

Douglas' continued presence in the race was enough to keep the two machines battling each other. [650]

Were the New Yorkers really trying their best to drum up the vote for him? Were they really working their hardest to raise money? He had very mixed feelings about New Yorkers. It seemed as though every time he thought he could win in New York, he would get a report that fund-raising had stalled. It seemed, too, that every time he thought he would lose New York, someone there would give a rousing speech on his behalf. On the Fourth of July at a New York rally, Senator Tom Pugh did just that. He concluded his pro-Douglas speech by telling the cheering crowd, "He whipped the Rail-Splitter once, and he can whip him again!"[651] He had to believe that the loyalty of the New Yorkers was tentative, though, and that, in the crunch, they would have to be pushed to either raise money or to get out the vote.

The result of these events was a series of bad decisions and political blunders that, in the last fading days of the campaign, might deny him his chance to be president, blunders probably made because Douglas believed he was politically invincible, that everyone who told him all of his life that he was going to be president was right, that nothing could stop him, that the presidency was his destiny. He so firmly believed that he was destined to be president, that when he arrived for a speech in his 1858 Senate race, he asked the band to play "Hail to the Chief."[652]

The Douglas Stump

When Douglas first arrived in New York, he planned to do no more than attend some parties, chair some meetings, raise funds, and then return to Illinois to await the outcome of the election, just like every other candidate for president was doing and just as every potential president had done since the first election in 1789. Congressmen and governors could campaign in their states, but it was simply not considered appropriate at the presidential level.

"I have no political speeches to make," Douglas said in late June in Philadelphia on his way to New York. "If my political opinions are not known to the people of the United States, it is not worthwhile for me to attempt to explain them now."[653]

As the days passed and the campaign coffers remained empty, the Little Giant became convinced that the only way to win the election was the unprecedented step of taking his campaign directly to the people, region by region, state by state, city by city.[654] He had done so all of his life, whether it was for the state legislature or U.S. Senate back in Illinois, and he would do it again.

There were other reasons as well. If Douglas believed he could win the election outright, he had to go on the road to win in the marginal states. If he believed his only chance was in the House of Representatives, he had to campaign on the road in order to finish in the top three and be eligible for the House vote. He needed to convince all Democratic congressmen and party leaders who would eventually decide how their state would vote in the House that it was Douglas, not Breckinridge or Bell, who should be their choice. To cement that political friendship that could bring him the presidency, he needed to see them, campaign for them, and join in their parades.

After the debacles in Charleston and Baltimore, Douglas may also have been convinced that he could not win in 1860 and Lincoln would be the victor. He needed to go on the campaign trail to strengthen his ties with every Democratic official he could find to reestablish himself as the leader of the party—assuming the Southern wing would collapse after the election as Breckinridge and Bell went down to resounding defeat. He also had to be victorious in as many states as he could in order to prove that although he could not win the 1860 race, he did have national support. Then, as the unquestioned leader of the party, he could capture the White House in 1864.

His decision to campaign was made after his supporter, Illinois governor William Richardson, returned from a swing through Maine and other New England states. He told Douglas that the regular Democratic newspapers in those states still strongly supported him and so did the people. He was convinced that if Douglas campaigned hard in the New England states, he could carry them in November.

"Everything looks well in this state (New York)," Douglas wrote Nathaniel Paschall on the Fourth of July from New York. He told him that Richardson predicted New England victories and reported that the Douglas situation was "better than we hoped for." He then wrote, "The reaction in our favor is immense and we are gaining every day."[655]

The next day, Douglas wrote Charles Lanphier back in Illinois that "the changes in our favor are immense in the East," and he added "we must take the war boldly against the Northern abolitionists and the Southern *Disunionists*, and give no quarter to either."[656]

The prospect, however, was not promising. Why did Douglas think he could win in Maine or Connecticut or Vermont or Massachusetts, states where Republicans had swept to victory in tidal waves in every election since 1856? His decision to go to New England to kick off the first ever national campaign does not seem that odd, though. A deluded Douglas had already decided he would carry the Southern states of Arkansas, Louisiana, Texas, Alabama, and Georgia, plus the border state of Missouri. He told friends that Breckinridge would only carry South Carolina and maybe Mississippi. He penciled in Bell as the sure winner in Kentucky, Tennessee, North Carolina, Virginia, Maryland, and Delaware. The rest, he felt, were up for grabs.

Even in midsummer, Douglas should have realized that Breckinridge, not Bell, was the clear favorite in the South and that he, Douglas, was not only an underdog in the Southern states but was despised and would not capture any state there. If any Democrat was going to pick up votes in the South, it was not going to be Douglas. Yet as the heat rose in July, Senator Douglas was certain he could carry a handful of Southern states. Given that woeful political reading of the South, it is understandable why Douglas headed for New England to start his campaign, carving out a long line of lectures in territory where Abraham Lincoln was practically invincible. It was time he would treasure, time he would remember, and time he would waste. It was yet another example of the many political mistakes Douglas made that stretched back to 1858.

There were, he knew, great benefits in meeting and addressing voters. In an era long before television and radio, direct campaigning was the best way to win votes. People who saw the candidate and liked him voted for him. Politicians then had standard speeches, which rarely changed. Direct campaigning, once begun, was not difficult. It not only helped win votes but cemented ties between a candidate and the people in local organizations and between other politicians as the candidates constantly spoke for each other.

Direct campaigning, successful as it was on a local, county, and state level, was quite different on a national basis because of the size and scope of the electorate. Statewide campaigns never carried the candidate more than a few hundred miles, but national campaigns could take candidates thousands of miles. Travel in the nineteenth century was by train and carriage and hard on the candidates. National campaigns could wear down anyone. Was Stephen Douglas up to a national campaign in a political season that stretched through the warm summer and cold autumn and went from states as far south as Alabama and as far north as Maine?

If Douglas was certain of anything, it was that the rigors of the campaign would not slow him down. He had barnstormed through Illinois the first time when he was twenty-three and the last time when he was forty-five. He withstood the challenges of the campaign trail not only with ease but with style. How difficult could a national trek be? In 1858, when he ran for the Senate against Lincoln, he had impressed politicians around the country with his determination in a campaign that took him to practically every city and town in the state. During that campaign, Douglas gave fifty-nine speeches, each two hours or more in length, seventeen shorter speeches after serenades, and thirty-seven speeches responding to welcomes of some kind. One hundred and one speeches were delivered outdoors and seven in rainstorms. Some were made on hot summer afternoons and some on cool October evenings. He traveled 5,000 miles in four months, using just about every mode of transportation in Illinois. No national campaign could be much more rigorous than the dogged run for the Senate in 1858. He was emotionally, psychologically, and physically ready for the first personal presidential campaign in American history.[657]

Or he thought he was. In the two short years since the 1858 campaign, he had forgotten how strenuous that contest against Lincoln had been. Douglas had started off strong, and during the first half of the race he was full of exuberance and bluster. The strain and travel wore him down, though, and during the last few weeks of the campaign, audiences complained that they could hardly hear him because his voice was weak. He did not get enough sleep and always looked tired. Despite his determination to carry on a national campaign in 1860, he might have other problems to contend with.

Candidate identification was one such problem. People were easily disappointed. Politicians in person were always too short or too tall, too thin or too fat. He was late, did not speak well, did not shake enough hands.

His wife looked too prosperous or not prosperous enough. Many politicians thought their image looked better than they did and stayed home. One reporter wrote of a politician, "He looks well enough, but not at all like a great man, intellectually, physically or morally.... He is a chunky man and looks like a prize fighter, though I am not sure his arms are long enough for that."[658]

Personal campaigns offered too many opportunities for mistakes. Under stress, speaking extemporaneously, politicians sometimes say the wrong thing; Douglas had done that over slavery in the territories when he debated Lincoln in his last Senate race at Freeport, Illinois.

All of these elements should have bothered Douglas. None did. He was confident that he was one of the nation's finest campaigners. He was only forty-seven years old and would be able to withstand the rigors of travel. Besides, in addition, aides and his wife would be with him most of the time, and they would all take care of him. He was certain he would not say the wrong thing because he was, after all, the country's best speaker.

His supporters cheered his decision. Belmont thought it was a brilliant move. He wrote the Little Giant, "I know that my suggestion is not in accordance with what has hitherto been customary in presidential campaigns, but exceptional circumstances demand exceptional exertions."[659]

Several newspapers applauded the idea, calling it "the hour of Mr. Douglas' personal triumph." But others were completely against it. One Iowa editor wrote that Douglas was like "a great polar bear" trying to "secure the gaze and huzzahs of the rabble."[660]

The senator from Illinois was eager to campaign and raced out of New York with the energy of a small locomotive. It was a campaign he was hopeful would make him president, rein in the radicals on both sides, North and South, and preserve the Union. Instead, it turned out to be a campaign that, despite initial surface success, exposed him to ridicule, dissolved the Union, and, in the end, killed him.

The Douglas campaign was the forerunner of just about every presidential campaign that followed. The work was so prodigious that no candidate tried it again until 1896, when William Jennings Bryan campaigned throughout the nation. Douglas traveled via train, and his workers raised crowds to hear him at just about every stop the train made. He spoke in big cities, such as Boston, but also in small hamlets along the way. He spoke at colleges, on warehouse platforms, from hotel balconies, and in city squares. He sometimes gave as many as six speeches in a single day. He toured famous landmarks in cities he visited (the Lexington battlefield and Bunker Hill in Boston). Douglas sometimes traveled with just his wife and a few friends and sometimes with a large entourage. He often rode in a small parade in a carriage, doffing his hat to the crowds, and in long parades he was preceded by the Little Giants, the Democratic young men's marching club counterpart to Lincoln's Wide Awakes. Bands playing patriotic music greeted his train when it arrived in a city or town. His presence electrified the campaign.

Douglas left Massachusetts in mid-July and headed for Vermont, where he gave speeches in Brandon, Burlington, Montpelier, Concord, Manchester, and Nashua, and then he ended the New England tour as the guest at a huge clambake in a tiny town just outside of Providence, Rhode Island. He made some brilliant sallies, such as telling people who wanted to know why he left Vermont as a young man and moved to Illinois, that it was a career move to "encounter less intellectual opposition." He also made some gaffes, such as starting a story about the plight of a farmer so poor he had to split his own rails and having the story halted by shrieks of delighted cheers from Republicans in the crowd who reminded one and all who the real rail-splitter was.[661] He was greeted by large crowds, parades, and bonfires just about everywhere he visited, and these buoyed his spirits.

Douglas had a good laugh over the rail-splitter stories as he traveled across the Northern states. The Democrats denounced the Wide Awakes and others who carried split rails in parades as "jackasses who go around in the hot sun with rails on their backs." Some Southern newspapers charged that the Wide Awakes were a paramilitary organization that would swing into action when Lincoln was elected.[662] Editors of Democratic newspapers asked readers how often presidents were required to split rails when they were in office. The *Chicago Daily Herald* smugly added Lincoln's ability to split rails to his ability to run a grocery store, whittle wooden cigar boxes, and tell dirty jokes to his merits. The *Daily Herald* declared that it had learned from close boyhood friends that Abe Lincoln averaged seventy-six thousand split rails per day during his young adult years. The *Vermont Patriot* disagreed, stating quite categorically that it knew for a fact that Lincoln had split exactly 150,000 rails in his lifetime.

The *New Albany (Ind.) Daily Ledger* said Lincoln had split enough rails to build a rail fence all the way from the South Pole to the North Pole. The *Indianapolis Sentinel* urged its readers to start splitting rails, so they could claim they were Lincoln rails and sell them at high prices. Another wag said Lincoln should forget about the White House and open up a rail-splitting business.[663] On hearing that suggestion, an editor at the *Charleston Mercury* urged readers not to buy any rails split in New York because they would have rotted. The *Mercury* also made fun of Lincoln's log-cabin birthplace and the flatboats he used to operate.[664]

The *New Hampshire Patriot* suggested that the Republicans should have nominated Brigham Young and his seventy-five wives because he, too, was once a rail-splitter. Herschel Johnson, Douglas' running mate, joked that a national rail-splitting contest should be held, including Lincoln and hundreds of blacks, and that anyone who beat Lincoln at rail-splitting should be the next president.[665]

The *Louisville Journal* located a seventy-five-year-old woman from Williamson County, Tennessee, whom a census taker verified had split over 300 yards of rather fine-looking wooden rails for the fence around part of her property and, the census taker bragged, had also carried the rails to the fence line herself. The newspaper said she would make a much better president than Lincoln, who merely split the rails but did not carry them anywhere.[666]

Dozens of political cartoonists made fun of Lincoln and his rail-splitting, portraying him in numerous poses, always carrying large, wooden rails with him.[667]

No one chuckled at the rail-splitter mania more than Lincoln himself, who in his newspaper biography joked that his relative, John Hanks, was "the man who now engineers the rail enterprise at Decatur."[668]

In city after city, whether speaking from a wooden platform or a tiny hotel balcony, Douglas made the same appeal: popular sovereignty, obey the Constitution, hold the Union together.

His speech in Saratoga Springs, New York, was typical. He told the large crowd: "It was in defiance of this system that the battles of the Revolution were fought.... All power not delegated to the federal government is reserved for the states or people."

Later, he moved into the divisive slavery issue and set the tone for just about every speech he would give on the subject. He declared: "The federal government cannot eliminate slavery.... The secessionists want the federal government to protect slavery. The people of the territories will refuse to maintain slavery where they do not want it and will protect it where they desire it."[669]

Douglas tinkered with that speech from town to town, embellishing it a little here and paring it down a little there. A veteran speaker, he knew when to push hard on one issue and when to back off on another. His 1860 stump speech reflected that approach. In New England, the heart of the abolitionist movement, he supported the rights of the people in the territory to choose whether they wanted slavery, but he reminded all that he had a long record against it.

He told a crowd in Concord, New Hampshire:

> *I did fight that Lecompton Constitution (that granted slavery in Kansas) with all the energy and all the power I could command. President Buchanan told me that if I did not obey him and vote to force the Lecompton Constitution, he would take off the heads of every friend I had in office (pause).... Any man who approved the use of executive power did not deserve to be my friend.*[670]

However, in a July speech in Philadelphia, he sought to win the votes of many people who lived in the southern Pennsylvania counties who had no interest in abolitionists. There he toned down his remarks on slavery: "The Constitution has conferred upon the federal government certain power and duties they perform. Let the federal government be confined strictly within the narrow federal duties, leaving the people of the states and territories free to govern themselves."[671]

Douglas and his wife then stopped for a two-week vacation in Newport, Rhode Island, where he rested and conferred with dozens of Democratic leaders. Then he was off on another speaking tour.

There were critics who thought it unseemly for a candidate to campaign for himself. Many newspapers, too, were either amused or alarmed at the

Little Giant's personal journeys into the towns of America in search of the White House; their editors said it was beneath him. The editor of the *New York Times* wrote, "It is not a seemly or a welcome sight to see any man whom a large portion of this countrymen have thought fit for the presidency traversing the country and soliciting his own election thereto."[672]

Some editors harangued him. The editor of the *Bucyrus (Ohio) Weekly Journal* said of Douglas, "Now he boldly vows his purposes and glories in his shameless disregard of the decencies of the canvass." Others made fun of him; one labeled him "the wandering orator."[673]

His aides told him that his New England swing was a great success. Campaign assistant manager Miles Taylor told Douglas that his success meant that Maine and Vermont would vote for the mainstream Democrats in the September elections. That would give his campaign the momentum to carry those two states in November and to draw large crowds of voters from other states. Douglas agreed. He was so excited that he left his wife in Newport and raced to Maine to deliver speeches in Bangor, Augusta, and Portland.[674]

When Douglas departed from Newport for the next leg of his campaign tour, three different campaign biographies of him were published. One was a book written by James Sheahan, and two others were thinner works by party writers. A book about the Lincoln-Douglas debates in 1858 was still selling remarkably well across the country, five hundred copies a day, but an unhappy Douglas thought the book provided a much more appealing portrait of Lincoln.

Douglas left Newport in buoyant spirits. Despite the repeated failures of Belmont and others to raise money, he knew from his New England swing that Lincoln was strongly entrenched there, but he was still convinced he could win a number of Northern states. He felt the books about him would win votes and did not think the support from one New York City newspaper hurt him. He thought he was famous enough to overcome the *Times'* criticism of him.

His running mate, Herschel Johnson, was far more gloomy than the Little Giant in the first few months of the campaign. He told Georgia Senator Alexander Stephens in mid-July that the race was grim. "I have not much hope for the future," he wrote to Stephens, another practical politician who worked hard to dampen the secession fires of Southerners. "The sky is dark. The fires of sectionalism in the South are waxing hot and Black Republicanism in the North already exhibits the insolence of conscious strength. The South is in peril—the Union is in peril—all is in peril that is dear to freemen."[675]

Republicans made a point that while Douglas might have drawn sizable crowds in New England, no major political figure stood by his side to endorse him. One Republican noted that William Sprague, the Republican candidate for governor of Rhode Island, even refused to attend a clambake with Douglas. He wrote, "(The Douglas people) had better leave him alone and go and eat their clams without him."[676]

Even his newly written campaign song, the "Douglas Grand March," seemed tepid compared to the Lincoln campaign tunes.[677]

The second leg of Douglas' campaign trip was far more perilous than his swing through the small towns of Vermont. With assistant campaign manager Miles Taylor's enthusiastic support, Douglas booked a string of campaign appearances throughout the South.

Douglas had made peace with recalcitrant Southern senators and congressmen in the halls of Washington before, and now he would do it again. He was propped up in his belief by the wildly optimistic Taylor, who reminded him that he represented the official Democratic Party and that, on election day, Democrats of all persuasions would return to the official party. Both men were also thrilled by the early August state election returns in Missouri, Kentucky, and North Carolina that seemed to favor Douglas. In Kentucky, Breckinridge's home state, the Bell forces beat the Breckinridge men. They concluded that Breckinridge was not unstoppable, that Bell, not Breckinridge, was their main Democratic opponent, and that Douglas could beat both in a number of Southern states.

Douglas and his men also believed that he had a chance in every state because of the three-way split within the Democratic Party. He might not be the party's choice in a southern county and might not be able to win a majority of the votes, but he did not need a majority. He needed a plurality. He did not have to win 5,001 votes out of 10,000 in a three-way race; he only needed more than the other two opponents.

One of the keys to Douglas' ill-conceived Southern strategy was the non-slaveholder white vote. The Little Giant believed that those people had no vested interest in the slave system. Since they had no interest, the non-slaveholders were not angry with Douglas for his support of the Kansas-Nebraska Act and would vote for him in 1860. His reading of Southern newspapers told him that he also had substantial support among Southern politicians, who would help him campaign and win in their counties and states.

The *Louisville Journal* wrote right after the first Democratic convention, "The truth is, there is and has been all the time amongst the (Southern Democrats) a strong undercurrent of feeling in favor not only of Douglas' policy but of Douglas himself."[678] He also believed that many prominent Southern newspapers, while not directly for him, were not against him.

Douglas still failed to understand that poor whites voted for slavery's preservation, and he should have known this because of his longtime

Southern connections.[679] Douglas' belief that those individuals would support him had no basis in fact; they would vote for Breckinridge or Bell.

Despite some setbacks for Breckinridge, Douglas had to know, and Taylor, too, that the vice president was working closely with President Buchanan, following their political reconciliation, and had, by late summer, complete control of the regular Democratic Party organizations in every Southern state. Douglas had no support or organization in the South.[680]

There was very little reason for optimism over the August state elections, yet they were seen as a major reason for Douglas to campaign in the South and ignore the North, where he could have won some states with direct campaigning, such as Pennsylvania, New Jersey, and New York. He had completely misread the political map of the country.

Douglas' initial stop in the first of two southern swings in the campaign of 1860 turned into political disaster, as equally fatal to the senator as his Freeport debate with Lincoln in 1858. He never realized it, though, and it led to even greater political mistakes later.

Apprehensive about this first foray into the hostile South, Douglas was surprised to see hundreds of people gathered to welcome him with loud cheers at a pier in Norfolk, Virginia. A parade, with dozens of black and white children at its head, led the Little Giant through the city to his rooms at the hotel. That night, after he was the guest of honor at a fine dinner, he emerged to speak to over six thousand people in the city square, the largest crowd ever to assemble there. Huge bonfires at street intersections and lengthy rows of torches around the square illuminated the exuberant crowd. The people inspired Douglas, who predicted victory as soon as he began to speak. He told the crowd that if he was the only Democratic nominee, he would beat Lincoln in every state except Vermont and Maine, "and I'll beat him yet!" he thundered to cheers from the crowd.

He launched into a careful, blunt critique of secession that became heated as he spoke. There was no ambiguity in his words. He was against it. "(My policy is) complete obedience to the Constitution and the constituted authorities," he said. "If Lincoln is elected, then it is the secessionists you will have to blame for it."

He was careful not to paint himself as a radical on slavery or to tie himself to popular sovereignty in the South. He said, "The peace and harmony of this country depends upon destroying both factions (secessionists and abolitionists)."[681]

Douglas told his audience that he only wanted to hold the Union together and added that he would rather lose the election than win and cause secession. However, he constantly asked the crowd if they would help him win election, and they roared back, "We will do it!"[682]

When he finished his well-received speech, the senator, full of self-confidence, asked for questions. As always, he was handed slips of paper with questions from people in the crowd. The first asked him if the Southern states would be justified in seceding from the Union if Lincoln was elected, and the second inquired if the United States government was justified in trying to stop the seceders.

The questions were bombshells, just as Lincoln's debate questions on popular sovereignty had been, and they were exactly the questions Lincoln would have been asked had he campaigned personally. Douglas answered them directly and truthfully, just as he had responded to Lincoln in 1858. "I emphatically answer no," he replied to the first. Douglas declared:

> *The election of a man to the presidency of the United States would not justify any attempt at dissolving this glorious confederacy.*

He then addressed the second, holding his ground.

> *It is the duty of the president of the United States to enforce the laws of*
> *the United States, passed by Congress, and as the courts expound them*
> *and I, as in duty bound by my path of fidelity to the Constitution,*
> *would do all in my power to aid the government of the United States*
> *in maintaining the supremacy of the laws against all resistance to*
> *them, come from whatever quarter it might…no, never on earth!* [683]

The reply, that he would help the Lincoln government fight anyone who wanted to secede, stunned the South. His politically damaging statement soon became known as the "Douglas at Norfolk" remarks and were referred to often by Democrats and Republicans. [684]

The crowds he drew were large, and the receptions at the cities he visited in the South tumultuous. The Illinois senator stopped at six Southern cities for major speeches and delivered nine shorter ones in smaller towns. When he arrived in Petersburg, Virginia, he was greeted by a thirty-three-cannon salute and a swarming crowd of well-wishers. More than fifteen thousand people heard him speak at Richmond, Virginia, on August 31. There, and in every Southern state, he reiterated his stand on popular sovereignty and begged crowds to keep Lincoln out of the White House and to unite the country. [685]

There was a firestorm of criticism from editors of Southern newspapers. Many called Douglas' answers "doctrines of coercion." [686] The *Charleston Mercury* called him "a regular old John Adams federalist." [687] The *Richmond Enquirer* said he should be hanged. [688]

An Alabama newspaper eloquently added that he should be dressed in his morning coat when hanged. A Georgia newspaper editor said he should be tarred and feathered and sent back home to Springfield, where he belonged. The *Washington Constitution* called him the worst name of all, declaring he was a Republican.

Stephen Douglas could not see past the crowds that lined the city squares where he spoke. He paid no attention to the reaction of Southern politicians and the press because everything he could observe with his own eyes told him that he was just as popular as always in the South. He was not jeered at the Norfolk speech and, in fact, was cheered as he left. Hundreds of Norfolk residents saw him off at his boat when he left in the morning.

Just as he stood by his word in 1858 against Lincoln, Douglas stuck by his word in cities he visited following his appearance at Norfolk. The very next day he told the large crowd in Petersburg that no issue, no matter how heated, could cause disunion. His reception there was huge, even though it rained and he had to speak inside a hotel.

Douglas then took a train into the Shenandoah Valley, where secessionist feelings ran high. He whistle-stopped his way up and down the valley, giving hour-long speeches in seven cities. Crowds were surprisingly responsive. At Winchester the crowd was so large and pressed so close to him that his carriage had to proceed down the main street at a snail's pace. A correspondent there wrote that the roars of the crowd drowned out the noise of the marching band that led the procession.[689]

His speeches in the Shenandoah were the same—preserve the Union. When he finally left Virginia, he was ebullient. Audiences had been larger and the receptions very positive. He was ecstatic about his decision to go to the South, where he believed he was a grand success.

Nobody else believed it, though. One journalist said that crowds should have "nothing but contempt for the candidate."[690]

Southern politicians were not pleased, either. During the same week that Douglas arrived in Virginia, the Virginia state Democratic convention failed to approve a fusion ticket. A reporter wrote, "The prospect is darker than its worst enemies could desire."[691]

Reaction to Douglas was far greater at his next stop: Raleigh, North Carolina. There he rode in a long train of carriages filled with local dignitaries who had to inch their way through an immense throng of over fifteen thousand people. A large band of musicians led the procession through the city, and flocks of children raced along the footpaths to follow Douglas' carriage. Hundreds of women hung out of windows in homes to wave their handkerchiefs at the Democratic candidate. The anticipated crowd forced Douglas' men to move the speech to the central city square, where he spoke for an hour and forty-five minutes. People shook his hand and clawed at his coat as he strode to the podium. After a reception like this, he knew that he could carry North Carolina. His speech was interrupted by constant applause, even when he defended the Union against tides of secessionists. A friendly reporter wrote that "the Judge was greeted by a hearty cheer. The majority of people are for him."[692]

There, again, he did not back down but raised the stakes and continued to preach his much-reviled "squatter sovereignty." He told the crowd that not only should the territories decide whether or not the individuals who resided in them wanted slavery but that they would soon intermarry, Southerner with Northerner, and become a whole new people entirely and would insist on a strong Union. He told his North Carolina audience that the right to vote yes or no on slavery in Kansas was the same thing as North Carolina voting yes or no on continued obedience to the British Crown in 1776, but his point missed the mark.

He backtracked to soften his position on slavery in the territories and told his cheering audience what they wanted to hear, that "the Democratic Party is pledged...to nonintervention of Congress with slavery in the territories."

Then, a few moments later, he turned them off by stating that just as he believed slavery belonged in the territories where people wanted it, slavery did not belong where it was not desired and that it could not flourish in cold climates anyway.

He railed against disunionists, North and South. He said, "I would hang every man higher than Haman who would attempt to resist by force the execution of any provisions of the Constitution," including, he added, Lincoln and Breckinridge.

Throughout his speech, he stared out at thousands of North Carolinians while churned inside him all the insults he had suffered at the hands of Breckinridge and Bell. Remembering all the years he worked for Southern interests in the government, a frustrated Douglas bellowed to the crowd, "I am the best friend the South ever had!"[693]

In Harrisburg, Pennsylvania, a few days later, he roared, "Pennsylvania would never support secessionists, disunionists, and traitors!"[694]

Those speeches cost Stephen Douglas the South. Hated already for endorsing the idea of popular sovereignty on slavery in the territories, he was now despised for telling so many people bent on secession that they not only could not do it, but that Abraham Lincoln should stop them, and that he, Stephen Douglas, would help him. The Illinois senator made many enemies with this campaign trip. He became a very visible politician, not just a name in a newspaper or a figure on a broadside. He was a flesh-and-blood politician who was dividing his party. His trip provided endless rounds of ammunition to the Breckinridge and Bell men.

And it never escaped Southerners that Douglas and Lincoln, despite their vast political differences, had been personal friends for more than thirty years. Once a reporter asked Douglas his opinion of Lincoln, certain the Little Giant would be harsh. Douglas paused then told the reporter that "I regard him as a kind, amiable, and intelligent gentleman."[695]

William Yancey of Alabama castigated him in Memphis, Tennessee.

He said:

> *Judge Douglas cares nothing about the Democrats, and his aim is simply to pull down the democracy (because) he knows he has no chance of an election and therefore has opposed all sorts of fusion between the two wings of the Democrats that he may now run in several states and destroy that majority. What sane man believes, for a moment, that he has the least chance of carrying the state of Tennessee?*[696]

What happened to Douglas was exactly what Lincoln had feared would happen to him if he went on a cross-country campaign trip.

Finished in the South, Douglas stayed in Pennsylvania in an effort to campaign in the three weeks remaining before that state's key statewide elections on October 8. Then he went on to New York and Ohio, where he received favorable receptions.[697]

He told crowds, "I believe that this country is in more danger now than at any moment since I have known anything of public life."[698]

It was not a triumphant Little Giant who the overflow crowd of Democrats in Cincinnati saw when the Douglas' train arrived, though. The campaign had taken its toll on Douglas, as Lincoln knew it would. He had given too many speeches and had traveled too many miles in trains that were not particularly conducive to sleeping, talked to too many organizers, hosted too many receptions, and worried for too many hours.[699]

It was on to other stops, but his physical condition worsened in Cleveland. His voice was so raspy and poor that only those standing close to the platform could hear what he had to say.[700]

He started to carry plates of lemons with him, squeezing each last drop down his parched throat just to be able to talk.[701] His physical appearance was dreadful. He had lost weight, his clothes looked rumpled, and deep bags had begun to form under his eyes. A review of photographs of Douglas taken from the early spring to November 1860 show a swift deterioration in his appearance. He had grown into an old man in a single political season.[702]

An observer in Cleveland said his voice had been reduced to a "spasmodic bark, laborious to himself and painful to those who in vain attempted to catch his words." The editor of the *Illinois State Journal* wrote, "The only wonder is that his health does not give under the trials and fatigue he is compelled to endure in order to meet the demands upon his strength."[703]

A man who heard him speak that week was equally worried about the public official who had seemed physically and emotionally robust. "The presidency is no compensation for the physical wear and tear he is suffering," he noted.[704]

Douglas had resumed drinking. Some said he was drinking heavily as his physical condition deteriorated. His wife disputed all such charges, but one observer reported that he was so drunk at one stop that he had to be helped from the train.[705] One night he bullied his way into the sleeping car of Senator William Seward, coincidentally on the same train, drunk, bottle in hand, and demanded that Seward get up and give a speech at the next train stop.[706] A few weeks later, in Alton, Illinois, spectators said he was drunk when he arrived. One noted, "His face is all bloated and looks purple from the effect of whiskey."[707]

The campaign carried Douglas back to Chicago on October 4. He was eager to return home and to stump throughout the Northwestern states of Illinois, Ohio, Indiana, Iowa, Wisconsin, and Michigan. There was fear that the Northwest was abandoning him.[708]

The reception in Chicago was astonishing. Illinois rolled out the

Democratic red carpet for its favorite son, its longtime senator, its Little Giant. The nighttime torchlight parade for Douglas through the teeming streets of Chicago was over four miles long. Tens of thousands of cheering residents lined the parade route, which led to the Tremont Hotel, where Douglas was staying. The next day, the size of the crowd was much larger than even the heartiest Democratic loyalists had predicted, filling up an area larger than five acres. Douglas had to feel that his chances of winning his own state were excellent.

The crowd that gathered for Douglas in Dubuque, Iowa, was also huge. Thousands of people had come into the city from miles away to see him. They gathered on the bluffs overlooking the riverfront as he arrived, and thousands more waited for him in the town square. His evening speech went on for over ninety minutes. Douglas' voice seemed better, his appearance was healthier, and his spirits improved.[709]

A local reporter there wrote of him:

> *He is a man of great dimensions, stands very straight behind (the podium). Indeed, he has the appearance of leaning over backwards, his corporation is large—and one is inclined to think that he wears one half of a bass drum under the waistband of his trousers; he has the appearance of having received a heavy coat of purplish-red paint, covered with good varnish, and the whole strand papered to the highest degree of polish that the material will bear.*[710]

Iowans loved him for his tirade against the secessionists, whom they hated. One historian later wrote that Iowans wanted "to lay the slavery problem in blood and gunsmoke."[711]

Party workers drummed up a large crowd wherever his train stopped, and the Douglas handlers were pleased at their size and response to the Little Giant.[712] The many receptions, like the parade in Chicago and cheers in Dubuque, made Douglas believe that he could win the election. After all, look at the size of these crowds!

Nobody else thought that way, though. Alexander Stephens of Georgia wrote, "I am pained and grieved at the folly which thus demanded the sacrifice of such a noble and gallant spirit as I believe Douglas to be."[713]

Douglas' receptions showed clearly that support for him had not wavered. He knew that his margins in Iowa, Indiana, and Illinois would be close. If he had campaigned more weeks in the Northwest he might have cemented slim victories there, triumphs brought about by the last-minute momentum created by his final campaign, despite his physical appearance. His health, too, he thought, seemed better in Dubuque than in Cedar Rapids. Perhaps the crowds and the torchlight parade there lifted his physical as well as his emotional spirits.

The Little Giant Goes South

Douglas was in Cedar Rapids, Iowa, when he learned that Pennsylvania and Indiana had both gone Republican in the October state elections. Douglas immediately turned to an aide, James Sheridan, and said, "Mr. Lincoln is the next president. We must try to save the Union. I will go South."[714]

It was an abrupt change in plans, a last-ditch effort to both win the election and hold the country together. Instead, he should have returned to New York, where he might have won.

His trip south was doomed from the start. Robert Toombs (who had been calling for secession since late 1859[715]) announced that Douglas would not be permitted to make any pro-Union speeches on Georgia soil. Newspapers began to publish death threats against him. Southern editors erupted in a volcano of verbal abuse. A train on which he was riding crashed (he was certain it was sabotage). Once, about to speak from the second deck of a ship, the flooring collapsed, and he and a dozen people fell 10 feet to the deck below (Douglas suffered bad leg injuries[716]). In Montgomery, Alabama, he was jeered and hit with an egg that also splattered yoke on his wife, Adele.[717]

Critics of his campaign tactics said his entire southern swing was wasted effort because it was far too late. Connecticut editor Gideon Welles wrote, "He had tried to rally the Democrats, but the party was (already) broken up."[718]

He did not speak well in stops there, and a reporter grimaced that "his voice is cut up into spasmodic articulation of two or three words each."[719]

Ironically, what Douglas did in his trip south was gain enough votes in places he visited to become the spoiler between Breckinridge and Bell.[720] As an example, on election day in Tennessee, Bell narrowly defeated Breckinridge, 67,661 to 64,467, but Douglas won 11,410 votes. If he was out of the race, Breckinridge might have captured enough of his votes to defeat Bell.[721]

It was a visit that would, however, bring him no electoral votes, no campaign contributions, and no thanks from anyone. It did bring him even worse health. His voice was hoarser than ever in the South, his strength weak and physical appearance pathetic. In Montgomery, Alabama, he struggled through a three-hour speech, and onlookers said that at times he seemed very confused. On the night before the election, his secretary, James Sheridan, worried and told friends that Douglas looked worse than at anytime during the campaign.[722]

CHAPTER 17

The Polls Never Lied

We can't be beaten...

—REPUBLICAN ORGANIZER ALEXANDER
McCLURE ON PARTY POLLS

The Republicans were confident of victory as early as midsummer. They were certain they could carry Pennsylvania, New York, Illinois, and Indiana, even if by the barest of margins. They felt that way because they had built an incredible campaign organization that had operatives in just about every small town in the Northern states.

Congressman Elbridge Spaulding from upstate New York wrote then that "we are perfecting an efficient organization in all of the states and should be prepared to meet the shattered (Democrats)."[723]

Henry Tanner, a Buffalo supporter, was even more confident. He wrote to Lincoln: "Don't fear for New York. All the 'fusion' they can form will be to them 'confusion' in the end. The goal is now near at hand which I have so long deserved and labored for."[724]

Alexander McClure, in Pennsylvania, by now writing several letters a week to Lincoln, was predicting a sweep of all the cities in Pennsylvania as well as in rural Republican areas. "If we can keep the current moving and swell it, we shall sweep the city of Philadelphia," he wrote on October 3. "Allegheny County now promises 5,500 (votes). Our calculations that the vote (grows) beyond ordinary strength. We can't lose!"[725]

Seward's promised long trek for Lincoln started in his hometown of Auburn, New York, on September 4 and lasted over a month. His arrival at Lansing, Michigan, was typical of the way he was received at every destination on his whistle-stop tour. He was met at the train station and put into a carriage at the end of a long parade. The march was led by over two hundred Wide Awakes, dressed in their traditional costumes, with the words WIDE AWAKES printed boldly on them, carrying their by-then familiar one-eyed signs. They led several bands playing "Ain't You Glad You Joined the Republicans," a procession of farm wagons, and as always in these Republican parades, a wagon upon which several men were set splitting rails and tossing "Lincoln nails" to the crowd.[726]

Seward was at the height of his powers by the time his national tour carried him to Lawrence, Kansas, targeted for him by Lincoln and Judge Davis because it was one of the towns involved in the Bleeding Kansas battles of the 1850s. He arrived in the town at the tail end of a mile-long procession of marchers, Wide Awakes, townspeople, wagons, and floats. Several cannon in the town square thundered as his wagon pulled into view. A crowd of over ten thousand roared its approval as he took the platform to speak.

"You determined in your struggle for Kansas that she shall forever be free—and that settles the question!" Seward said. "The whole battle was ended in the deliverance of Kansas and freedom triumphant in all the territories of the United States.... Slavery in Missouri proved a mockery…that this land was for liberty, that slave power would repent in sack cloth and ashes."[727]

He never held back, as Lincoln had asked him. One of the touchiest issues between North and South was the Dred Scott decision. Lincoln, careful as always, deplored it but said it had to be obeyed because the Supreme Court was the law of the land. Seward went at the Dred Scott decision with a meat cleaver. He made clear his views of it, and in doing so, he raised Southerners' fears of what the government would become under Republican rule. He declared, "We shall reorganize the (Supreme) court and thus reform its political sentiments and practices and bring them into harmony with the Constitution and with the laws of nations."[728]

The old fire-eater could not resist attacking the slave states at the end of all of his speeches. In a typical finish in Chicago, he said, "Nonintervention in the slave states is but one half the Republican platform." Then, pausing for effect, he added, "Nonintervention by the slave states in the territories is the other half."[729] His conclusion was greeted with a huge, thunderous roar from the crowd.

Seward's full-blown oratorical blasts at Southern slaveholders, which made Lincoln and his team of politicos cringe, infuriated Southerners, who long saw Lincoln as a straw horse for Seward. "The fiendlike insidious spirit of the speech had no parallel since the days of Cataline," wrote a reporter for the *Louisville Courier* after one of Seward's strident condemnations of slavery. "(He uses) stealthy incendiary approaches…a midnight assassin, but in blood…. Seward is the most dangerous man of our times."[730]

Seward was not the only Republican criticizing the Southerners from the stump. Henry Wilson of Massachusetts was another. He said the Republicans would "rescue the government from the grasp of slave power. We shall blot out slavery from the national capital. We shall surround the slave states with a cordon of free states.... In a few years we shall give liberty to the millions in bondage."[731]

Abolitionist Wendell Phillips roared too, writing, "The Republican party means to grapple with slavery and strangle it as soon as they can."[732]

These speeches and editorials were met with equally vehement responses from Democrats. An editor at the *Providence (Rhode Island) Post* wrote:

> *The (Republicans) would stand as a wall of fire against the admission of any more slave states.... They would change the Supreme Court. They would, in short, pursue such a course as would instantly unite the South against the general government and make a separation of the states the only remedy.*[733]

Southerners complained. Louisiana Senator Judah Benjamin wrote after the election: "You do not pretend to enter into our states (on slavery). Oh, no! You propose simply to close us in an embrace that will suffocate us."[734]

The Southern view of the slavery expansion issue now meant it meant that Republicans wanted to free slaves anywhere, and for the North it meant that Southerners wanted slaves everywhere.[735]

Douglas campaigned hard, and the Bell campaign moved into high gear, but John Breckinridge did little, and what he did was limited. Stung by the adverse reaction to his early September Ashland speech, he decided to go on a short tour of towns in his home state of Kentucky and deliver thirty-minute speeches at socials. The tour was a disaster because the areas he chose were strongly for Bell. Even in his own state, he could not truly judge the feelings of the people. Shortly afterward, he became ill and left the campaign to his lieutenants.[736]

The Republicans enjoyed a great advantage in efficiency in every Northern state. Pennsylvania's McClure told Lincoln: "We are now perfecting the most thorough organization ever attempted in this state. It extends to every county and in each county to every election district—I mean every election district."[737]

McClure, like Weed, used his local operatives to poll voters in each community throughout the summer and fall and reported the results to Lincoln. His men in each city kept tabs on the pulse of Pennsylvania, as did men in Illinois, Indiana, New York, and other states; within a day, Lincoln would learn how the people there felt about various issues.

All of these state organizations and the political bosses were supervised by the Lincoln team of David Davis, Norman Judd, and Leonard Swett. Judd crisscrossed the Northern states to visit every committee chairman or influential campaigner he could find. In one swing through Pennsylvania by train, Judge Davis visited five cities in five days, cutting his schedule at times to spend just six hours in one place so that he could hurry on to the next. Davis managed to see a political boss or newspaper editor at every stop, along with local residents. He constantly sent their opinions and observations to Lincoln. There was no day from mid-July to November that Abraham Lincoln did not know exactly what was going on in his campaign, what money was being sent where, and what the people in just about every county in the Northern states were thinking. All of the members of his inner circle—Davis, Swett, Joseph Medill, Lyman Trumbull, and Charles Ray—were constantly writing him to ask what they should do next.[738]

Polling became one of the greatest successes of the campaign. Men scattered throughout every town kept local and state leaders posted on polls they conducted throughout their districts. They were probably more accurate than telephone polls taken today. The polling technique of Starr Clark, who lived in the rural town of Mexico in Oswego County, New York, was typical. He described it in one of his reports to the Lincoln team in Springfield:

*I saw every single voter in the village. We have 900 voters in town. I
have found 747 Republicans and 129 Democrats. In 1856, my canvas
gave Fremont 530. He got 535. We see every Republican voter and get
him to promise to vote. Then we send for those on the morning of
election day that are in the habit of coming to the polls late in the day.
We will get each vote. Our majority in Oswego will be 4,500.*[739]

Another Republican pollster in New York, George Davis, not only
polled people in his county to determine what candidate they would
back, but he also separately polled American Party voters who had backed
Fillmore in 1856 to see how they would switch in 1860. To do that, he
held his own meeting of Fillmore voters and had them sign charts of their
new preferences. He told Lincoln that the town of Monroe alone would
produce one thousand Republican voters that had gone to the third party
in the last election.[740]

The Pennsylvania poll results covered six entire pages of projection and
notes (they predicted Andrew Curtin the winner in the gubernatorial race
by twelve thousand).[741]

Polls run by McClure gave Lincoln a five-hundred-vote majority in York,
three hundred in Cumberland, two thousand in Lancaster, one thousand in
Berks, and fifteen hundred in Schuykill. McClure told Lincoln that, based
on his figures, Lincoln would carry Pennsylvania by thirty thousand votes.
"We can't be beaten," he insisted.[742]

Indiana results showed that 80 percent of the Fillmore vote in Indiana's
northern counties and 50 percent of the Fillmore vote in the central counties
would go to Lincoln—for a total of about 10,000 votes. Republicans also
polled people who would be voting for the first time and estimated that
one-half of some 32,000 in Indiana would vote Republican. Caleb Smith

supervised polls in each county and in each city. The overall projection was that Lincoln's final total in Indiana would be just over 137,000, with a winning margin of 6,000.[743]

On August 2, Thurlow Weed wrote Lincoln that according to his men in the field, the New York counties of Oswego, Oneida, Madison, Jefferson, Onondaga, Cayuga, and Wayne would, collectively, give Lincoln a majority of twenty-five thousand votes. He said, "These are based on people I have relied on for thirty-five years."[744]

The Republican polls proved to be remarkably accurate. The collective Republican majority in the combine of Oswego, Oneida, Madison, Jefferson, Onondaga, Cayuga, and Wayne—where Weed projected 25,000—was actually 24,236. Smith's Indiana polls were just as close. He projected a Lincoln vote of just over 137,000, and the actual tally was 139,033.[745]

The Democrats had equally efficient polls. A polling book might have pages with categories such as "Republican," "Democrat," and "Uncertain." An 1863 poll book issued to a party worker in the village of Minden, New York, had categories of "Union" (Republicans renamed their party during the war), "Democracy," and "Leaning" (for undecided voters). The results were sent to Dean Richmond, who could then predict how each race as going in every town in the state.[746]

Lincoln's polls were conducted in a far more reliable manner than most of the commercial polls of the day, most run by newspapers, to project winners in the presidential campaign. These straw polls bordered on the ludicrous. People in Boston could purchase a twenty-five-cent ticket that gave them admission to the Boston Theater, the Music Hall, and Tremont Temple, where they could listen to music and also vote in a straw-poll (five thousand people bought the triple ticket, and they voted Lincoln the winner, also giving some votes to the Prince of Wales). McVicker's Theater, in Chicago, tried the same idea in an effort to boost tickets sales. Trains and riverboats added straw-poll ballots to ticket fares as an inducement for travel. On one train poll there were forty-seven votes for Douglas, forty-three for Lincoln, one for Breckinridge, and one for the devil, and the pollster announced to all that it was neck and neck between Breckinridge and the devil. In most Southern polls it was Lincoln who ran neck and neck with Satan. A poll on the steamship *Alabama* showed sixty-four votes for Breckinridge, thirty-one for Bell, ten for Douglas, and just one for Lincoln. A man who cast the lone ballot for Lincoln in another poll, on a Mississippi riverboat, was grabbed by the other voters, undressed, tarred and feathered, and cast adrift in a canoe in the middle of the river.[747]

The Republican Party knew how to work the immigrant vote, county by county. Carl Schurz wrote:

> *Very little has been done along the Ohio, east of Evansville, and it is absolutely necessary that good speakers are sent there.... The Germans are coming over in shoals whenever they are judiciously worked with. I think I have succeeded in drawing over a great many wherever I have spoken, but I want a good German speaker to go over the same ground and follow up the work.*[748]

The Republicans knew both the value of speakers and the press, and they worked hard to combine the two for maximum effect. They would host a series of weekly or biweekly speeches in large halls in cities in different Northern states and feature prominent Republican personalities from across the country. The selection of speakers was made carefully. If the Republican rally was in an area full of former Whigs, they had a former Whig as a speaker. If it was ironworker country, they had a pro-tariff ironworker congressman speak. Wool workers rode in a wagon with a wool loom, driven by a steam engine. Wagons carried men splitting rails. Other wagons contained blacksmiths, tanners, and other craftsmen doing their work. Some processions were miles long; one in Illinois contained five hundred wagons just from one county and a wagon pulled by twenty-three oxen. Party workers would drum up large crowds to hear the speakers. Halls would be festooned with Lincoln-Hamlin banners and signs for local congressional, gubernatorial, and state legislative candidates. Women in Republican auxiliaries would provide refreshments, bands would play, and at some point in the evening, without fail, all five thousand people in attendance would stand up, at the top of their voices, sing "Ain't You Glad You Joined the Republicans."[749]

The Republican rally broadsides roared, A POLITICAL EARTHQUAKE... THE PRAIRIE'S ON FIRE FOR LINCOLN!... THE BIGGEST DEMONSTRATION EVER HELD IN THE WEST...SEVENTY-FIVE THOUSAND REPUBLICANS... MAGNIFICENT TORCHLIGHT PROCESSION AT NIGHT.[750]

Republican newspapers now reached millions of people. A heavily attended biweekly speaker series was held at the largest hall in Philadelphia between mid-September and early November, and each of the speeches was reprinted in Republican papers in Pennsylvania, New York, Delaware, and New Jersey.[751] The Stuyvesant Institute in New York stated that the speeches of just four speakers in New York State resulted in stories read by more than half a million readers. Speeches were also produced in pamphlet form; Lincoln's Cooper Union speech in pamphlet reached 864,000 people, and his biography, printed in German only, reached 400,000.[752]

Some crafty Republicans would stroke the prominent speakers by telling them afterward that they were so good that there was a demand well beyond the city for their remarks and would then ask them if they would consent to letting the party publish their words of wisdom in the newspapers (some speakers also were paid).[753]

The targeting of speakers was critical in Lincoln's stretch drive. He paid particular attention to the campaign to lure American Party workers, or Know-Nothings, who had supported Fillmore in 1856. Their supporters asked former American Party officials for advice. One wrote: "I should prefer Bell to Lincoln but would throw away my vote. I can't vote for Douglas. What should I do?" Yet another wrote him: "Former Americans can't support Douglas. Bell is not appealing. May I go to Lincoln?"[754]

One of the biggest targets of the Lincoln campaign was Daniel Ullman. He was a longtime politician in New York who ran a strong race for governor there in 1854 and had the support of tens of thousands of Know-Nothings throughout the Empire State. He was persuaded to join the Republicans in the early summer of 1860 and promised to stump for them wherever they might need him.

He was a big catch, and they treated him gingerly, constantly stroking him and thanking him profusely for anything he did. One Republican leader wrote him, "With your cooperation, our success is sure." The head of a Wide Awake club told him he would receive "a hearty welcome" if he spoke in his city. An organizer who brought him to Delaware told him that Lincoln would win the state but that "we need your help to do it."[755]

Ullman, like many other Know-Nothings who turned Republican, campaigned hard for Lincoln. An example of his hectic stump tour was his proposed speaking schedule in Pennsylvania: fourteen speeches in fourteen days from mid-September to early October.[756]

Speakers were told what to say for maximum effect in each county and each state in order to target specific issues. Ullman, for example, was told to hit hard on the tariff issue in Pennsylvania.[757]

Judge Davis traveled to Pennsylvania to meet with both Simon Cameron and Alexander McClure in August; he showed them Lincoln's original speech notes outlining his support of a tariff to protect Pennsylvania ironworkers. Davis told Lincoln that Pennsylvanians had been "deceived" so often by Democrats on the tariff that it was no wonder they were eager to get behind a Republican who supported one.[758]

The Republicans targeted German, Dutch, and other immigrant communities, campaigning hard there and sending as many foreign-language speakers as they could to push hard for Lincoln and the state and local tickets.

In many areas of the northwestern states, particularly Michigan, Wisconsin, and Illinois, they thought they could be successful and capture key immigrant communities. An example was Lake Prairie Township, a small, heavily Dutch community in Marion County, Iowa. Lake Prairie's Dutch had gone Democratic in every national, county, state, and local election since 1853 by huge majorities (89 percent in 1855). The Republicans only captured 17 percent of the vote there in the 1857 county elections and just 16.3 percent of the vote in the 1857 state elections. In 1858, though, they did better, rising up to win 27 percent of the vote in the county elections and increasing that to 28.6 percent of the vote in the 1859 state elections. If they could push that up even higher in 1860, to the 33–40 percent range, and do just as well in immigrant towns they often lost, their overall vote, combined with other immigrant regions where they were victorious, could carry Iowa.[759]

The Lincoln team took advantage of Douglas' fight against the administration and the Southern Democrats. McClure said, "Douglas is a factionist in this state, and this will cost him thousands of votes." Cameron agreed, writing Lincoln, "Douglas and Breckinridge now have more battles against each other than they are against us."[760]

Once the campaign began, the two Southern candidates forgot Lincoln and started a mudslinging campaign against each other. Lincoln was left alone, a critical mistake by the Democratic candidates.

They fired arrows into Douglas too:

- He was a secret Know-Nothing and hated all Catholics and immigrants.
- He was a sectional, Northern candidate, not national. "We don't want a geographic party with sectional interests to run the government—as did Fremont and the Republicans in 1854," said one Breckinridge man.[761]
- Douglas' goal was not the White House. A newspaper editor wrote, "The defeat of the Democratic Party is the object of Douglas, and for this he has been laboring in season and out of season."[762]
- He was the Rail-Splitter in disguise. "A vote for Douglas is a vote for Abraham Lincoln," declared one editor.[763]

Local candidates laced into the presidential nominees too. J. Foster Marshall, running for the South Carolina state legislature, a Breckinridge man, branded Bell the symbol of everything short of Satanism (they usually left Satan to Lincoln). He said that John Bell symbolized Native Americanism, Mormonism, Millerism, and abolitionism and that Douglas was Janus-like with three faces, one each for the North, South, and West.[764]

Trivial nominations for small local posts pitted the factions of the party against each other too. A state Democratic convention called to nominate candidates for the clerk of the court of appeals in Kentucky fell apart when the Bell and Breckinridge men refused to sit in any meeting with the Douglas men.[765]

The Southern Democrats squabbled over the most insignificant issues imaginable.[766] Thurlow Weed was told by Democratic friends in Chicago that the feud between Douglas and Breckinridge had grown so hot in the Windy City, fanned by the Republicans in Illinois, "that they (Democrats) would prefer your (Lincoln) election to Douglas or (Breckinridge)."[767] A Republican in Indiana wrote, "There is no hope of a reconciliation between the two factions."[768]

Douglas, frustrated, did not know how to discard the image, and that inability was yet another blunder. He knew that the factionists were Breckinridge and Bell, but because the president, who loathed Douglas, was behind Breckinridge, it was the Little Giant who came off as the factionist. It was another example of how the veteran politicians in the field were hurt by past alliances and feuds, which did not involve Lincoln.

Douglas' position as a factionist hurt him throughout the South. Republican John Richardson wrote from St. Louis: "In the country, I am satisfied the real Democrats will vote for Breckinridge. No sane man can think that Douglas has a ghost of a chance.... I do not see how he can carry a single slave state."[769]

The three Democrats could not agree on a fusion ticket, leading Weed to observe in mid-August that "fusion...will fail."[770]

Syd Kidd from Clarksburg, Virginia, wrote Lincoln on September 9 that he had returned from a Bell-Everett rally and was certain Douglas was finished. He said, "The Bell and Everett speakers here yesterday all said they would rather see you elected than any of the rest."[771]

Douglas received few financial contributions because contributors felt that Breckinridge and Bell were in the race until the end and would drain off votes from Douglas. Henry Winter Davis, the objective third-party (American) observer, said in mid-August that Douglas was finished. "(H. W. Davis) says that Douglas has a considerable body of opposition in all the slave states…enough if they ultimately vote to give several states for Bell," his cousin, Judge Davis, wrote Lincoln.[772]

Throughout the summer, President Buchanan's aides attacked the Douglas forces, which struck back. In response, George Sanders, one of Douglas' fund-raisers in New York, wrote:

> *The Nero-like perfidy to individuals which characterized your administration from the beginning now marks its close by the betrayal of the great and general party that has fostered you by its higher to impregnable (position)…down to your last hours of treasonable ingratitude and disunion. Never did a man owe so much to a party, and never was a party so wantonly betrayed.*[773]

Many rumors floated across the United States as the heated campaign ground toward election day and the very real possibility that no one would win. The wildest, started in Washington DC was that President Buchanan agreed to resign and permit Breckinridge to become president the day after the election if Lincoln won. President Breckinridge, then, after calling out the army, would refuse to let Lincoln take office and declare martial law.[774] People in the South thought it was the only way to stop Lincoln and the Black Republicans, and the people in the North had developed so much mistrust of Southerners that they believed it to be a perfectly sensible move for many Southern politicians. This totally false rumor, thought to be true, was accepted by so many people that it became a political fact and appeared as a news story in the *New York Times* for nearly three weeks.[775]

The rumor was one of many:

- The *Charleston Courier* reported that if the election was tossed into the House of Representatives, there would be no president and no federal government because the states—with one vote each—would never be able to pick a president.[776]

- The *Courier* also reported as fact that William Seward, still a senator in November, would introduce a special bill, secretly written by Abraham Lincoln, to pack the Supreme Court. He would add three to six more judges so that the Court could overturn the Dred Scott decision and the Fugitive Slave Law.[777]

- The *Cincinnati Inquirer* reported that Lincoln had secretly promised to uphold the Fugitive Slave Law and back slavery in Washington DC in exchange for the Virginia vote if the election went to the House. This rumor replaced an earlier rumor that Virginia's congressmen would not attend any presidential voting session of the House, making any selection there invalid.[778]

- The *Charleston Mercury* reported that all of the Douglas Democrats in the House would switch to the Republican Party so that they could vote Douglas' Illinois neighbor into the White House. The *Mercury* later reported that on the morning after the election, a Southern union would be formed as a separate nation with Breckinridge as its first president.[779]

- The *New York Times* told its readers that it had learned from unimpeachable sources that defeated Democratic congressmen planned to rush the newly elected Congress en masse into the House chamber on the first day of their 1861 session and, via fistfights, beat up the Republican victors, take their seats, and void Lincoln's election.

The *New York Times* also reported that the Southern states would all secede so that, legally, the businessmen in those states could be absolved of any all debts to Northern businessmen via special legislation to be passed by the Southern union congress.

In addition, the *New York Times* declared the South would deliberately withhold all shipments of cotton, sugar, tobacco, and other goods to England and Europe, creating a worldwide economic crisis, which would topple the new Lincoln administration.[780]

The Republicans were sending money all over the country per Lincoln's careful and specific directions. The Republicans needed it. Their woes were common to all political campaigns, as illustrated by the dilemma Norman Judd found himself in as he worked with the Illinois campaign. Judd noted with great pride that the local party was mailing out over five thousand circulars and pamphlets a day, a prodigious amount, but the group was broke. He wrote, "(I) am crippled for lack of funds."

Judd appealed to Lincoln for funds: "You must not let your friends neglect (the Illinois state committee). We in this office can see the whole state and can use means (money) with telling effect."[781]

Ominous events cast a shadow over the campaign. Southern legislators began to pass bills to rearm their militias or to create new militias just in case a civil war occurred. Stories about these legislative acts, or the formations of the militias themselves, were published in numerous Southern newspapers and noted in Northern journals. The *Charleston Mercury* warned its readers that the state did not have an adequate militia and suggested that eight thousand men get ready...in case. "This force would be sufficient to maintain its (state) laws, keep down any domestic outbreak, and form an efficient nucleus upon which a larger force could be raised without difficulty," the editor wrote.[782]

In early October, Southern commissioners from a newly appointed militia armaments board traveled to several different gun factories in Northern and Southern states to get estimates on the purchase of rifles and ordered one thousand pistols at $20 each. The commissioners even entertained buying thousands of rifles from British manufactures if Northern producers would not cooperate.[783] Several other states increased the training of their militias and passed legislation to study the purchase of arms.

Many Southerners predicted an overwhelmingly Northern, Republican, abolitionist government that would throttle the South. Northern newspaper editors agreed.

Speculated the *New York Herald*:

> *With men holding these views (antislavery) as judges and officers of the federal courts, as postmasters and collectors of customs, as district attorneys and marshals…there will commence an agitation of the slavery question such as the world has never witnessed.… The abductors of slaves, the formentors of servile incendiarism, and the coming John Browns will pursue their inquisitous labors in the full confidence that, if arrested and brought to trial, it will be by marshals, prosecuting attorneys, juries, and judges that sympathize with them and who believe that the cause in which they are engaged is the cause of righteousness.*[784]

And there was race. Stories about the formation of all-black Wide Awake clubs were run in most Southern newspapers, all under ominous headlines, such as "The Beginning to the End."[785]

Even though polls showed him far behind, Douglas was deluded that he could win in the Southern states.[786] Longtime Democrats stopped supporting Douglas and shifted to Breckinridge or Bell. James Thompson of Ripley, Mississippi, wrote his father in the spring of 1860 that he would vote for Douglas because he was opposed to secession. By October 11, though, he had changed his mind and backed Bell. He declared: "A great deal depends on this presidential election. This Union is no longer a Union if Lincoln is elected."[787]

The campaign went into the stretch with Lincoln far more worried about the outcome in Indiana, Illinois, Pennsylvania, and New York than his overconfident inner circle. Like Weed, he knew the only path to victory in politics was relentless, never-ending campaigning. He had numerous letters warning him to watch out for the Democrats in Pennsylvania. One man wrote him that "the Democracy will expend every influence and energy in Pennsylvania.... (It) is the battleground."[788]

In Oregon and California he was ahead one day and behind the next. Some of his operatives in Indiana told him exactly what he wanted to hear, that he was leading, but others told him that Indiana would be very close.

Swett had grave doubts about Indiana too.

He wrote: "Thompson says...he is carrying Americanism (vote) with his own personal influence. Usher says ten thousand or eleven thousand American votes, maybe three fifths of all of them. (But) in Avram county, our account based on a canvass seems (to have us) even. My judgment—doubtful."[789]

Others agreed. "Douglas is up more than ten thousand votes," wrote John DeFrees from Indianapolis on October 3 after a rally where Douglas fiercely attacked Breckinridge.[790]

Bad news came from Anson Henry in Oregon, who told Lincoln that the Republicans were split there. He wrote: "We were stunned with the proof of treachery in our Republican ranks. Most remarkable political rancor in the history of our government."[791]

Lincoln kept up constant communications with his men in the field in the different states, knowing almost daily how the political winds were shifting. This responsiveness enabled him to make moves almost instantaneously. But despite his rapid moves, advice on campaign activities, and direction of money to different states and counties, Lincoln still considered Ohio, Illinois, Indiana, Pennsylvania, and New York too tentative to call by the middle of October.

CHAPTER 18

Down to the Wire

We have done nobly...

—OHIO REPUBLICAN BELLAMY STORER ON
THE OCTOBER STATE ELECTIONS

The race tightened in the final month of the campaign, and Douglas did better. Over forty thousand turned out for a Douglas speech and rally in Indianapolis in a rousing demonstration of support that struck terror in Lincoln's heart. Douglas was running stronger elsewhere. Reports from the southern counties in Ohio were starting to turn for Douglas. Leonard Swett's team in southern Illinois, which predicted huge victories for Lincoln there, was now reporting dead heats. Lincoln's newspaper friends in Ohio informed him that the Little Giant had picked up strength there. He was not only carrying the southern counties, along the Ohio River and the Kentucky border, but winning in counties alongside the Indiana border such as Putnam, Defiance, Butler, and Darke. He was ahead in Marin, Hocking, Union, Shelby, Monroe, Perry, Noble, Brown, and other Ohio counties. Lincoln was beating him in

Cleveland, but Douglas was now ahead in Columbus and its county, Franklin. Lincoln began to believe that Douglas could beat him if he had enough time.

Lincoln had to deal with conflicting predictions too. In a very optimistic letter written just a week before the Indiana election, Swett noted the American Party's former leader Richard Thompson, working now for Lincoln, predicted that Lincoln would win 60 percent of the American vote and that Henry Lane would be elected governor with a ten-thousand-vote margin. But Judge Davis rejected any optimistic reports. Of Indiana, Davis wrote Thurlow Weed that the Bell and Breckinridge men were working hard there. He said, "In my judgment, that state is in a good deal of danger." Davis complained to his wife that "I am uneasy, very, about the Indiana and Pennsylvania elections."[792]

How important were the state elections? President James Buchanan wrote of the Pennsylvania race, "Never was there a period in our history when so much of good or evil depended upon the results of the elections in the Keystone state."[793]

The October State Elections

The Republicans' hard work helped stem the growing Douglas tide, though. Maine not only saw Republican victories for state offices but also for the six Republican congressional candidates who won there too. "We carried all of our congressmen…like a prairie on fire," wrote a happy Hannibal Hamlin.[794]

Indiana and Pennsylvania went Republican in their state races on October 9, electing Republican governors along with a substantial number of Republican candidates in local elections. The numbers were stunning. In Indiana, Republicans captured eight of eleven congressional seats and swept to majorities in both houses of the state legislature as the Bell, Breckinridge, and Douglas men all feuded with each other.[795] In Pennsylvania, Andrew Curtin not only won the governor's mansion, but the Republicans won twenty-one of the twenty-five congressional seats and both houses of the state legislature.[796] Every congressional seat in Vermont was won by a Republican too. In many voting districts in Maine and Vermont, the Republicans swept to victory with 65 and 70 percent of the vote.

The Republicans took the Maine governor's race by eighteen thousand votes, the Pennsylvania's governor's race by thirty-two thousand, and captured the governor's mansion in Indiana by ten thousand. Earlier, the Republicans elected Frank Blair, an end-slavery-now radical, to the U.S. Senate in Indiana. They also won state races in Ohio by comfortable margins.[797] The Republicans were even victorious in tiny, faraway Oregon, where their man E. D. Baker captured one of the two Senate seats there and wrote back joyfully that Lincoln would now "have a true...friend at your side."[798]

Lincoln received news of the October victories quickly via dozens of notes sent to him by politicians through the Illinois and Mississippi Telegraph Company.[799] He was relieved by the victories in Maine, Indiana, and Pennsylvania. Kudos poured in. "Congratulations to you and the whole country upon this great news," wrote Carl Schurz. Bellamy Storer of Ohio wrote, "We have done nobly."[800] There was news from Maryland, too, that Bell and Everett men were joining the Republicans there. Lincoln wrote Seward, "It now really looks as if the government is about to fall into our hands."[801]

Joe Lane, the Oregonian who might become president if Lincoln could not win in the electoral college, was crushed by the October election news. He told a friend, "Things are looking very bad just now. The entire South, in my judgment, will go for Breckinridge, and the entire North, with the exception of the Pacific States and New York, and they are doubtful, will go for Lincoln."[802]

Lincoln's men in the October states were now certain of presidential victory in the November elections. "I hope this will be a final putting away

278 ★ LINCOLN FOR PRESIDENT

of the Douglas party in Indiana," said Mark Delahay. In Pennsylvania, C. T. Shaw bragged that the party would turn out stronger for Lincoln than it did for gubernatorial winner Curtin.[803]

Schuyler Colfax wrote, "In the entire history of Indiana, the October majority has always been increased in November. No exceptions."[804]

Pennsylvania's Alexander McClure predicted the same thing as Colfax, adding that the Democrats were too burned out to mount much of a presidential fight. He wrote, "The spasmodic efforts of (Democrats) exhausted itself ten days before the election while our extra efforts were continued."[805]

William Bascom, secretary of the Ohio state Republican committee, told Lincoln that he could relax because the October elections would bring him victory later. He declared, "The results in Ohio, Pennsylvania, and Indiana...substantially settle the presidential election and leave no doubt of your election by the people. The people of Ohio will stand by you."[806]

When he heard the election news, Carl Schurz was thrilled. "I feel as though I heard cannon thundering all over the North."[807]

There was no Republican in the country who was happier at the October results than Judge David Davis, who heard the results in a courthouse. "He kicked over the clerk's desk, turned a double somersault, and adjourned court until after the presidential election. He looked straight at his clerk and, eyes narrow as slits, shouted at him in jubilation, 'Douglas will be sorry he didn't die when he was little!'" said a man with him.[808]

It was then that Douglas decided to spend most of the rest of the campaign in the South. It was a gargantuan mistake. Douglas, who had committed blunder after blunder from 1854 to 1860, was intent on going into the Deep South, where he had absolutely no chance of winning a single electoral vote, to seek votes and give speeches while supporters in Northern states where he had a chance were urging him to speak there.

CHAPTER 19

All Roads Lead to New York

There is no resource left but to unite upon one ticket, than for all the Southern states to decide upon casting a united vote for one candidate in this contest and thus present an unbroken front.

—EDITOR, *NASHVILLE UNION AND AMERICAN*

Douglas, Bell, and Breckinridge feuded in New York. Democratic newspapers bemoaned the rift in the party. An editorial writer at the *Washington Press* wrote:

Lincoln will be elected. The friends of Judge Douglas will never consent to vote a ticket on which nearly two thirds of the candidates are against their standard bearer.... They will spurn the attempt of those miserable, spoils-hunting politicians to sell their favorite candidate in the utmost contempt.... The (Democratic) seceders will drive off fifty thousand voters (for Douglas).[809]

Thurlow Weed's operatives enjoyed the merciless criticism of Douglas' trip south in Southern newspapers. Weed lieutenant Elliot Sheppard wrote Lincoln of Douglas, "You also have the singularly good fortune to have your most implacable opponent fight on your side whenever he goes into a slave state."[810]

The Democrats felt Douglas was finished in Pennsylvania because of Republican assaults. John Forney, the pro-Breckinridge leader who also corresponded with Lincoln, wrote that "the unremitting attacks of many of the Republican leaders upon Judge Douglas, in lieu of the fact that he cannot be elected, has done much to drive the Douglas men to (Breckinridge)."[811]

One of the most fervent pleas Douglas ignored in the North came from the critical state of New York, in which he had a good chance to win by late October and, in winning, deny Lincoln the presidency and throw the election to the House of Representatives. New York, Douglas knew, had been a real problem for him. His operatives there were unable to raise any money, and his own organization fought bitterly with local groups; they all battled with Buchanan. He had no single ticket to run on but was facing Bell and Breckinridge tickets, which would surely split the vote. Powerful Mozart Hall and its leader, New York City Mayor Fernando Wood, remained noncommittal to him all fall, as did Tammany Hall and the Albany Regency political machine, controlled by Dean Richmond. But by the end of September, the situation in New York was changing, and Democrats finally realized they might take the state.

Worry began to filter directly to Springfield, where Abraham Lincoln was disturbed about polls published in several New York newspapers in early September that indicated that he and Douglas were in a dead heat if Douglas could run at the head of a fusion ticket.[812]

The *Albany Argus*, a Democratic paper, published a chart that showed that in 1856, the Republican candidate Frémont lost New York by 44,475 votes. The paper said the Democratic vote in New York grew from 195,879 in 1856 to 252,078 in 1859 and that the Republican vote fell from 276,007 in 1856 to 251,139 in that same year. It noted that in many cases the Republicans won races with a minority of the vote since these were three- and four-party contests. That paper also suggested that historically, two-thirds of all new voters in New York elections went Democratic. The paper predicted some 150,000 new voters in 1860 and advised that 100,000 of them would vote Democratic. The *Argus* editor wrote, "They are not for putting at hazard our substance and our institutions or any more speculative theories as to imaginary Negroes in our new territories."[813]

Clark Wheeler, an upstate New York Republican, offered a defense of the Republican efforts, and predicted thousands of American Party votes and the support of disgruntled Democrats. He denounced the *Argus* but admitted that "the foreign vote will be 'against us'" and agreed that "we will lose forty thousand votes in sixty counties."[814]

The new voters, always a source of puzzlement to politicians, worried Lincoln's local men. "The new element in the election, which has never yet voted distinctly, can only be estimated roughly…without reliable basis," said James Harvey, whom Lincoln would later appoint minister to Portugal.[815]

James Webb, a Republican newspaper editor from New York, was just as gloomy and worried about "the extraordinary amount of money the fusionists were using in the interior of the state."[816]

Wheeler told Lincoln that New York was going to be very close. "Do not be discouraged if you discover this part of the state has given very large majorities against us."[817]

Weed was working on his own campaign to win over American Party supporters, though. One of the most influential catches was Amos Briggs, a former state senator and longtime political leader. He endorsed Lincoln in the *Troy Weekly Times* on October 30, just days before the election. He warned everyone that a vote for Douglas was a vote for Joe Lane in the Senate election and concluded that "the Democrats are responsible for all the evils the country has suffered in consequence of their laying their ruthless hands on the (Missouri Compromise)." His endorsement, even at the eleventh hour, carried much weight.[818]

Seward assured the nominee that he would carry New York. He wrote Lincoln, "I find no reason to doubt that this state will redeem all the promises we have made." Weed added on October 18 that "we are in good (shape) here."[819]

Weed acknowledged problems, though. He told Lincoln: "The (Democrats) raised last week $27,000 while $20,000 was put in the country. The conflict…is a fearful one. So far, there is no flinching, nor do I believe there will be any. All looks well. If things go on well one week longer, we shall triumph."[820]

The next day, a nervous Francis Spinner wrote Lincoln from Mohawk, New York, that the Democrats were flooding the upstate counties with money. "(Democratic) money is being passed out like water," he wrote.[821]

And the Republicans had become overconfident of victory in the presidential election following the triumphs in the early October state races. They were celebrating and not working for Lincoln's victory in what was becoming an unbelievably close race in New York.

That overconfidence was obvious everywhere. In Pennsylvania, operative George Parsons wrote in a circular at the end of October that "the gains of the states of Pennsylvania and Indiana, added to the states that cast their vote for Fremont in 1856, will give Lincoln more than enough votes to elect him president."[822] Philander Jones of Indiana promised "to give honest old Abe (victory) on (election day)."[823] Samuel Haycraft of Kentucky told him on October 27 that his election was "a foregone conclusion." Pennsylvania's Alexander McClure told him that the race was over and that Lincoln would carry Pennsylvania in a landslide of over seventy thousand votes. The head of a "Rail Maulers" club in Indiana bragged that Lincoln would carry that state by ten thousand votes. He wrote, "The Douglas ticket now has no face and will not be back with any energy."[824]

Lincoln received a letter on October 12 from John Harris, who said he was on his way to Springfield to shake the hand of the next president. Hiram Payne called him "the great western giant."[825] James Harvey was so certain of Lincoln's election that he told him in late June to start writing his inaugural address. J. E. Hurlbut of Waterbury, Connecticut, wrote that "this state is Republican to the backbone.... This state will go for you in November by five thousand against a combined ticket...twelve thousand if divided." Hugh East said that since Indiana went Republican in the state vote, they would surely elect Lincoln. Judge Davis held a meeting of the national committee in Chicago on the last day of October, and members told him that Lincoln had to start picking men for his cabinet—six days before the election was even held.[826]

Weed and the New York Republicans were so wary of lethargic, overconfident party workers that they sent out an emergency circular reminding everyone that the October state victories did not mean the campaign was over—Lincoln had to be elected. "Nobody would excuse us, nor could we forgive ourselves, if, from apathy, indolence, or mistaken confidence, the cause of freedom should be (defeated)," warned state head Simeon Draper.[827]

And on November 3, Weed sent Lincoln a letter that jarred the candidate and reawakened the great depression that always seemed to linger deep inside him. New York, Week told him, might be lost and the election decided in the House of Representatives.

"Things do not look so good as they did ten days ago. The fusion leaders have largely increased their funds, and they are using money lavishly. Some of our friends are nervous," Weed wrote Lincoln, adding that he now expected to lose New York City by over twenty-five thousand votes. He told Lincoln that his local leaders had spent their budgets too soon and had no money left and that he, Weed, pushed so hard by Lincoln and his men to help finance the campaign in other states, was now broke.[828]

Lincoln knew that New York had tightened because workers there had been overconfident. New York Governor Edwin Morgan blithely assured the Republican nominee, "We can whip them!"[829]

Lincoln was reeling at the last-minute thunderbolt of grim news from Weed that came so close to election eve.

The money men in New York had, by late September, realized that their business interests in the South would suffer if Lincoln was elected and be crippled if any Southern states seceded, as so many threatened to do. Some of them had been panicking about secession all summer. Stocks of numerous companies listed on the New York Stock Exchange began to drop as the talk of secession increased.[830] One of the strangest political events of the summer was the sudden, unannounced arrival of a delegation of New York businessmen at an all-Southern "convention" in Richmond the week before the second Democratic convention in Baltimore. The Southerners were there to plot strategy. The New Yorkers were there to make certain there was no secession because they had vast, multimillion-dollar business dealings with the South. They were led by the colorful Thaddeus Mott, a wealthy merchant who not only had dealings with European countries but served as an adviser to the khedive of Egypt.[831]

A fusion ticket with the Democrats supporting Douglas in New York was being talked about nightly. It would be just Douglas against Lincoln beginning in October. The New York money men had also become convinced, as election day approached, that the election of Lincoln was not inevitable and that if it was thrown into the House, they felt there was a good chance that Douglas could wind up being president because, despite the numbers, huge sums of money in the form of campaign contributions from businessmen to congressmen might influence the House vote.

That was apparent to them from Douglas' huge receptions on his final campaign swing through New York in late September. Douglas campaigned via train. Hundreds of people greeted him at each stop, whether it was a tiny hamlet outside of Albany or a rural village's water tank. Hundreds more lined the route, sitting on top of wooden fences or tree limbs, fathers with arms around sons and mothers carrying babies, just to wave at the car carrying Douglas as it trundled past them.

At Rochester, local newspapers put the size of a Douglas gathering at over thirty thousand. The crowd, which began to assemble hours before the Little Giant's arrival, was so large that dozens of extra police with riot gear were put on duty to prevent injuries and disorder. Enormous red, white, and blue banners with Douglas' picture seemed to hang in every storefront window in town. The streets, filled with supporters, were illuminated by dozens of tall bonfires that could be seen outside the city for miles and whose flames leaped high into the night sky.[832]

At Syracuse, the day before, the *New York Express* correspondent reported that nearly fifty thousand people gathered in Regimental Park there to hear the Little Giant and that even more participated in the rally and torchlight parade later in the evening.[833]

The most impressive demonstration for Douglas took place at Jones Woods in northern Manhattan, in New York City, on September 3 and attracted a boisterous crowd of over thirty thousand people.

People began gathering there early in the morning, most via trains. As they arrived, they drove past enormous Tammany Hall banners, nailed to dozens of trees, which listed all their candidates for office in November. The train cars then passed a large band that serenaded passengers with a lengthy rendition of "Hail Columbia." The trains then unloaded their passengers in a huge grass bowl in the woods where dozens of food tables were set up. Lunch was supposed to be served at 1:00 p.m., but the long line of people waiting for food became restless, and shortly after noon they surged forward, knocking down a restraining fence, and rushed the food tables. A riot was prevented by the police, but not before people scooped up thousands of large, hard crackers and began a festive food fight with them. Order was soon restored, and urged on by the officers, food servers began walking through the crowds carrying huge wooden trays stacked high with slabs of ox, hog, sheep, and pig, all roasted in large dirt pits in the woods.

The crowd was entertained by numerous bands and a highly publicized appearance by world-renowned tightrope walker Charles Blondin, who gained everlasting fame as one of the few people to survive a trip over Niagara Falls in a barrel. Blondin walked across a wire stretched over the crowd to thunderous cheers.

All eyes turned to one of the roads shortly after 2:00 p.m. when a train of carriages made its way toward the large meadow where a high wooden platform for speakers had been built the day before.

"It's Douglas! It's Douglas!" someone yelled, and the throng of people moved forward and then followed the procession to the meadow, walking and running after the Douglas carriage.

August Belmont, thrilled at the size of the audience, happily introduced Judge Douglas. "I know," Belmont said, "we have fearful odds to contend with, but we are fighting for the maintenance of our beloved and blessed union and the sacredness of our cause must give us victory."

Addressing the throng, Douglas thundered, "He who is not willing to carry out in good faith every clause, every word, every letter of the Constitution is a traitor!"[834]

Local Democratic politicians were sent through their counties once again to drum up more votes for Douglas. Erastus Brooks, editor of the *New York Express*, toured throughout the state, speaking at places as far apart as Sag Harbor on Long Island and in Rochester. He gave fifteen speeches in just nineteen days. The Democrats ripped a page out of the Lincoln campaign book, too, sending W. H. Von Wagoner, a blacksmith from Poughkeepsie, on a campaign swing through the upstate counties, which took him to twenty-three towns in thirty-four days. Von Wagoner was the blue-collar blacksmith to Lincoln's blue-collar rail-splitter, and he assured workingmen wherever he spoke that the Democrats, not the Republicans, had their best interests at heart.[835]

George Sanders, editor of the *Democracy Review,* was one of Belmont's top fund-raisers and a man with a deep-seated hatred of James Buchanan. He began to hustle around the state shortly after Douglas' final, boisterous swing through New York ended. Armed with figures on the huge crowds and enthusiastic responses, he was able to raise $100,000 almost immediately and another $100,000 within a few weeks. It was reported that industrialist William B. Astor secretly contributed $1 million to the Douglas campaign, which was spent in a frenzy during the final days of the race in New York. Another $1 million was reportedly raised from other contributors.[836]

The late surge resulted in the long-hoped-for fusion ticket with Douglas at the top. The Little Giant even had the support of former governor Horatio

Seymour, the Democrats' "almost" nominee (if Jefferson Davis had his way), whose popularity in the state helped swing enormous Democratic support for Douglas.[837]

The fusion ticket was announced at a large celebration at Cooper Union Institute, where one banner proclaimed THE COUNTRY IS SAFE. The speeches were preceded by one of the largest outdoor celebrations in New York City history. A long parade through city streets featured the Minute Men and Little Giants, marching for Douglas, and, right behind them, various marching clubs for Bell and Breckinridge. Bonfires were lighted on just about every street corner, and hundreds of rockets were shot into the sky and exploded over the buildings of the city. Marchers even managed to remember the lyrics of a brand-new campaign song written just for the New York fusion ticket called "Hurrah for the Union."[838]

Democratic leaders in New York were certain that a fusion ticket, with Douglas at the top, could carry the Empire State. Two days later, after the Republicans carried Pennsylvania, Indiana, and Ohio, they knew they were the Democrats' last chance. *New York Herald* editor James Gordon Bennett expressed it best when he wrote, "New York is the Democrats' forlorn hope."[839]

★ CHAPTER 20 ★

The Eleventh Hour

See that every Republican voter is at the polls on election day.
—NEW YORK REPUBLICAN CHAIRMAN THURLOW WEED

As soon as Maine, Indiana, and Pennsylvania went Republican in early October, the Democrats sent every speaker they could to campaign in New York, spent every dollar they could find to finance the New York campaign, and held every meeting they could arrange for the three Democratic campaigns there. They took a desperate gamble and invited Alabama's William Yancey, the longtime secessionist, to speak at a huge rally in New York City; he spoke in other cities too.

Yancey appeared at Cooper Union, the hall jammed with people to hear the Southerner at his best. He did not disappoint. He told them that all people had the right to revolution if they were oppressed by a national government they felt no longer represented them and used the serfs in Russia and peasants in Italy as examples. He intertwined the rights of workers with the rights of states, appealing to the huge throngs of workers in the cities of New York, and ended by once again making a pitch for states' rights.

"Ours is a form of government that the people have willed. It is self-government. It is a government where states have willed to make a compact with each other and, whenever that compact is violated, who is there higher than the states?" he asked. With great precision and logic, he defended his position.

"When governments become oppressive and subversive of the objects for which they were formed them, in the language of our fathers, they have the right to form new governments," he said, tying his views into those of Thomas Jefferson and other Founding Fathers.[840]

When he spoke in Cincinnati, the pro-Breckinridge *Cincinnati Press* said there was no difference between Yancey and the Republicans. Republican George Hazzard heard him there and wrote that his speech was "very egotistical and insulting."[841]

Following the Yancey speech, Douglas' men in New York were so confident that they had stemmed the Lincoln tide that George Sanders wired Douglas: "Our city is now at white heat, the result doubtful. We are gaining so rapidly that it is impossible to foretell the result."[842]

The surge to Douglas continued through the next few weeks. Democratic clubs of every stripe sponsored rallies for voters, complete with long lists of speakers. From October 8 until election day on November 6, at least one Democratic rally was held every day in Manhattan. Upstate cities also staged daily rallies. Small towns had two to three Douglas rallies each week. Thousands of circulars and broadsides for Douglas began to appear overnight.

The Douglas New York campaign highlight was a mammoth torchlight parade through the streets of New York City on the night of October 22. The three warring Democratic factions, united now for over three weeks,

The Eleventh Hour ★ 291

put together a rally that drew more than twenty-five thousand participants (even Republican newspapers were impressed at the size and fervor of the Douglas crowd). There were thousands of torches, long lines of Douglas marching clubs, and hundreds of rockets and other fireworks that were launched into the sky throughout the evening.

There were the typical banners supporting Douglas and others hailing some sort of "big" victory for the Little Giant. There were signs targeting those who hated the abolitionists (NIGGERISM THE OVERPOWERING INFLUENCE and NO NIGGERS ALLOWED IN THIS CLUB) that reflected the ugliness of the campaign in New York.

Everyone acknowledged one thing—the New York Democrats now had plenty of money, and they were spending every dollar of it as the close race went down to the wire.[843]

The Republicans in New York had just about run out of money, but they had two weapons money could not buy: William Seward and Thurlow Weed. The men, old political warriors who could sense victory or defeat merely by sniffing the air around a voting booth, understood the situation completely. What the Republican campaign needed in its last desperate hour was what they had done best for forty long years: barnstorming speeches and efficient party organization.

The New York political world was Weed's empire. He had helped elect hundreds of men to office and procured jobs for thousands of their friends. Everybody who breathed in New York politics owed Thurlow Weed something. In the dying days of October and first week of November, he called in every due bill he had accumulated from Buffalo to Long Island in his decades as a political boss. He cajoled some men to speak on Lincoln's behalf in their towns. He talked others into stumping in their own towns and in a village or two nearby. He maneuvered others into visiting every village in their county to speak for Lincoln. He made agreements with national leaders like Salmon Chase and anticorruption congressman John Covode to take trains to New York and stump the state for Lincoln. Chase, Covode, and others became a relentless full-court press by Weed and the Republicans to carry New York for Lincoln as the sands in the electoral hourglass began to run out. On October 13, Weed announced a new batch of fifteen speakers, from as far away as Wisconsin, who would give ninety speeches.[844]

He had so many speakers stumping the state for Lincoln that a typical speaker would appear once a day in five different towns and in two towns on each of the two remaining days, hustled by one of Weed's men on a train or in a carriage from one community to the next. Governor Chase, a crowd favorite, was put on such a busy schedule that on a single day he spoke at a breakfast rally and lunch rally in Binghamton and was then hustled onto a train and taken to Long Island, 300 miles away, for a speech that night.

The Republican itinerary published in just one newspaper for a single week, October 22–29, is representative of the speaker blitz in the Empire State engineered by Weed. J. C. Venton, brought in from Wisconsin, delivered eight speeches in six days.

Other speakers on the stump in upstate New York that week: Henry Wilson (five); Burt Van Horn (four); E. P. Stanton (four); Daniel Ullman (seven); H. B. Stanton (two); F. W. Kelogg (three); Ansel Barcum of Michigan (four); John Covode, chair of the congressional committee that launched the corruption investigation of the Buchanan administration (two); C. Berale (three); George Bisbee (three); James Doolittle (three); Jim Nyue (two); J. M. DePew (one); and Steve Weedforce (three). In addition to the speakers, Burt Cook's New York City Glee Club appeared in concert with speakers at Kinderhook, Syracuse, and Canandaigua. Total (not including New York City): fifty-four major speeches and three concerts in six days.[845]

Weed's speaker blitz included a special attack on the hundreds of thousands of immigrant voters in New York City and other cities in the state, particularly German Americans. Cooper Institute, in Manhattan, was filled with a capacity crowd that overflowed into the streets surrounding the building to listen to speeches by the Republicans' two most prodigious stump speakers in the German community: Carl Schurz and Reinhold Solger. The latter explained in great detail that Lincoln's policy was not the elimination of slavery but its containment. He told listeners that if slavery was ended, and he was certain it would be, the finish would not come for several generations and could only take place if all sections of the country, including the South, agreed to it. Schurz spoke for Lincoln and reminded the audience that if they did not vote, and convince everyone they knew to vote, the election would be lost.[846]

Weed made certain that every Republican newspaper in New York reprinted selections from the 1858 Lincoln-Douglas debates and italicized the many references in which Lincoln reiterated, time after time, that he would do nothing to eliminate slavery where it existed. Weed flooded towns and cities with broadsides and made certain that anyone who could stitch, sew, or paint worked on Lincoln-Hamlin banners that could be hung across streets or from the sides of buildings. Republican newspapers ran daily lists of places where readers could register to vote and lists of polling places so they knew where to cast their votes. Big-city newspapers urged small-farm counties where they circulated to vote and to get their friends and neighbors to vote. Reminding upstate voters that farm-county votes had carried Pennsylvania and Indiana for the party in the October 8 state elections, the *New York Tribune's* editor wrote, "Republicans of rural districts…perfect your organization so as to be *sure* that, rain or shine, every voter will be at the polls."[847]

Newspapers appealed to the hundreds of Wide Awake clubs in the state to make sure that their members voted and encouraged others to vote, in addition to staging more rallies as the election raced to a finish. "Wide Awakes, begin your work today. If all is left until next Tuesday, it will be too late," said the editor of the *New York Tribune*.[848]

Weed spearheaded rallies of every kind throughout New York during the last month of the campaign in an effort to hold the lead his machine had built up in the summer. Rallies were held in big cities and small towns, with the Wide Awakes leading processions in most of them and local Republican organizers working hard to ensure huge crowds. One rally in Rochester, held the same day of the enormous Democratic rally in New York City to celebrate the fusion ticket, drew over forty thousand people. Four thousand New York Wide Awakes hired a cavalry to act as security for their parades and increased their own parade drills in such a sophisticated manner that one man said they moved like "an army."[849]

One of the state's largest Rail-Splitter clubs marched behind the Wide Awakes. There were "Workers for Lincoln," "Farmers for Lincoln," and even a special "Businessmen for Lincoln."[850]

On October 3, Weed arranged transportation for thousands of Wide Awakes from all over the East Coast to converge on New York for a huge rally that drew 12,500 marchers and hundreds of thousands of onlookers. A reporter covering it wrote, "The crowd gathered early and filled not only every elevation, including brick piles, door stops, railings, and gratings—and all the windows in the vicinity, but even sidewalks and streets."[851]

Weed also worked with national committees and Lincoln to shift speakers. He pulled speakers off schedules in relatively safe states and brought them to New York, where every speaker was needed for the final push. One was former American Party leader Daniel Ullman. He had agreed to stump throughout Pennsylvania for Andrew Curtin, but by late September Lincoln felt Curtin was ahead in his race for governor and could win without support from Ullman or the Know-Nothing vote. Weed wanted him in upstate New York, where tens of thousands of Know-Nothings lived. Ullman was yanked out of Pennsylvania and brought back to New York, where he embarked on a grueling schedule. Weed and the Republicans were throwing absolutely everything they had into a dramatic final push for Lincoln.[852]

Printed election-day orders in New York (and in each state) were handed out to Republican party workers, reminding them to keep lists of registered voters and to make certain each voted before noon, giving the party time to round up those who did not and get them to a polling place. "See that every Republican voter is at the polls on election day," it said.[853]

Lincoln worried about everything in New York during the closing days of the election. He worried about Horace Greeley, who hated Seward and, he believed, despised him as well. Operatives there had to calm him down and tell him that Greeley would not cause trouble.[854] He worried about vote fraud and ballot stuffing that were routinely reported to him by operatives around the country.[855]

Many expressed fear that New York's thousands of Republican Seward supporters were still angry that he did not win the nomination and would sit home on election day, costing Lincoln the White House.[856]

The Republicans pushed hard on a number of issues, but they knew that many in New York would vote Republican just because of their antislavery stands. One was Seth Gates. He wrote, "I rejoice greatly that I am permitted to live to see the beginning of the end of all this (slavery)…(for leaders) who will not be the mere tools of the slave power."[857]

Others, such as I. B. McKeehan, said they just wanted to vote against all the "disunionists" to get rid of them.[858]

Many Southern newspapers turned to the state as their last hope. The editor of the *New Orleans Crescent* wrote, "New York is the only remaining hope of our people for deliverance."[859]

The Democratic surge in New York had started in the early part of the month and was capped by a massive evening parade and rally on October 23, attended by supporters of all three Democratic candidates. More than twenty-five thousand men, many carrying torches, marched, and more than one hundred thousand spectators lined the streets to watch them. Thousands more leaned out of their windows above the avenues. Dozens of cannons were fired and rockets shot into the air. Large uniformed bands played at different street corners and in the parade. The *New York Daily News* gushed that it "was a scene that can never be erased from public memory."[860]

Next to Weed, the Republicans' other weapon in New York was Seward. The senator returned from a successful midwestern campaign swing during the second week of October and, after a two-week rest, began a new tour through New York State, haranguing crowds with a staple speech that had grown more passionate in its denunciation of slavery and more mocking of Southerners every time he delivered it. Seward began his tour in his hometown and then, via train, crisscrossed the state, heading for a grand finale in New York City.

In Fredonia, he said that any Southerner who talked of disunion was not only wrong but guilty of treason. Two days later, at Seneca Falls, in front of an overflow and raucous crowd of twenty-eight thousand, he delivered a ninety-minute speech in which he accused Southerners of murdering the Union. He declared, "Now…the national pulse is its healthiest.… To inject slavery into its veins now would be to smite it immediately with poison."[861]

Finally, after several more stops, his train pulled into New York City, and Seward, saving his best for last, delivered a brilliant speech for the Republicans (and himself) at the opulent Palace Gardens. There, in front of a huge crowd, many with signs promoting Seward for president in 1864, the New York senator again warned Republicans that the election had become a dead heat in New York and that if Douglas won the state, Lincoln would lose the election. Aware of the dozens of reporters in front of him, he once again carefully reiterated the Republican approval of slavery in the states where it currently existed.[862]

All of this was necessary, Lincoln reminded his men wherever he reached them via the mail, because the Douglas campaign in the North was catching fire. The number of uncertain voters was dwindling, and many were sticking with the Democratic Party, despite its problems.

By the first week of October, Douglas finally had the money he needed in New York. He had dozens of speakers in the state to help him. Some Bell and Breckinridge newspapers started to support him. A fusion ticket in New York with him at the top had been hammered together. The warring political machines were making peace to support him and only him.

Democratic polls also showed a remarkable trend—Douglas seemed to be getting stronger in those cities and counties in New York where he had barnstormed in the summer and in September. A return swing through those areas and others would boost his statewide vote. All his men needed in New York was one last-stretch run, one last inning of the game. Democratic newspapers in other states were convinced he could carry New York and stop Lincoln. Southern newspaper editors breathed a sigh of relief when the New York fusion ticket was put together and substantial amounts of money were raised in the last few weeks of the campaign. A correspondent for the *Louisville Courier* wrote that Douglas would defeat Lincoln in New York, and the defeat would clear the way for the House of Representatives to elect Breckinridge, their "man of destiny."[863]

A week more of personal barnstorming in New York in late October and early November could bring Douglas victory and deny Lincoln the White House. But instead, Douglas, unwilling to trust the last-minute encouragement of the men who had duped him before, men who had ruined the chance he had to be the Democrats' unity candidate at Charleston, went South. If he had gone back to New York, he might have defeated Lincoln there and changed history.

An analysis shows that Douglas could have captured New York State if he had personally campaigned there again at the end of October and beginning of November. Election results showed that Douglas did much better than Buchanan had in 1856 in all of the cities and counties where he personally campaigned in New York. He received 50 percent more votes than Buchanan in New York City. He pulled 7,259 votes in Onondaga County to Buchanan's 4,227 in 1856; 7,300 in Monroe County against 4,683; and in Albany he won 11,158 votes, up from 7,751 in 1856. Altogether, he won 50 percent more votes than Buchanan in the upstate counties where he personally campaigned. Across the country, he did much better than the Democrats had done in 1856 in those counties he personally visited. His vote in counties he visited was up 29 percent in Iowa, 45 percent in Illinois, 65 percent in New Jersey, 35 percent in Vermont, and 15 percent in both Ohio and Michigan. He increased his totals in places he campaigned in twenty-two of the twenty-four counties.

In actual votes, Douglas received 30,000 more votes in New York City than the party had in 1856 and 10,000 more in upstate counties he visited. He lost the state to Lincoln by 50,136 votes, so a second campaign swing there might have brought him victory and denied Lincoln the presidency.

CHAPTER 21

"Mary, Mary, We Have Been Elected President"

Mr. Lincoln seems as he always does. You would not think that he had just been elected to the highest office in the world.

—JUDGE DAVID DAVIS

Abraham Lincoln, a surprising spring in his step for such a chilly November election night, arrived at his offices in the statehouse in Springfield, Illinois, in the early evening to await the election returns. Several hours later, Lincoln, his political team, and friends moved through a large and ever-growing crowd, filled with well-wishers from around the state, to the town's telegraph office to check on the vote. Lincoln's walk to the telegraph office was interrupted by cheers from many; some had driven great distances to be with him on this historic night. The second-story, brick telegraph office, where the returns came in, was crowded. A huge throng of people stood outside, ready to celebrate. The streets were lit with long strings of bright torches, and large banners with pictures of Lincoln and Hamlin were hung across the streets.

A group of loyal Wide Awakes appeared in the street, as did dozens of Lincoln supporters who had stood by him and voted for him since the 1830s. Across the street from the statehouse, women of the town hosted a church supper that started at 6:00 p.m. but dragged on endlessly as the slow returns from around the nation trickled in and the people began to sense that their friend and neighbor might become the sixteenth president of the United States.[864]

Would the razor-thin margins of victory Lincoln's polls predicted hold up throughout the long night? A shift of just a few thousand votes in one or two states could cost him the election, and the vote appeared to be that close in several states, especially in the Northwest. Could he carry New York? The latest telegram from Thurlow Weed, that he had hid from everyone but his wife, indicated that he might not. Could the Bell, Douglas, and Breckinridge men carry even just one large Northern state, plus a small one, and in so doing, toss the election into the House of Representatives? Would his massive voter registration drive attract enough new voters to the Republican banner to give him a cushion of brand-new votes needed to carry states where the race was supposed to be very close? Would his North-only strategy backfire on him?

In the last weeks of the election, Republican newspapers said Lincoln would win and Democratic journals said he would lose. One Republican writer from the *New York Daily Tribune* said that Lincoln would be inaugurated with "universal consent, amid an era of good feeling." One Democratic wag wrote that if Lincoln won, he would resign after a year because he realized he could not do the job. Which prediction could Lincoln believe?[865]

The election returns arrived via the loud clack…clack…clack sounds of the telegraph key as it pounded against its wooden frame. Lincoln and his close friends, the men who worked so hard to get him the Republican nomination in Chicago back in May, stood around him, all nervous, as the returns started to tumble in from small towns in Maine, large cities in Ohio, farm communities in Illinois, the river cities along the Mississippi in the Deep South, and the rice fields of South Carolina. As men jostled for position next to the telegraph keys in the room, Lincoln, calm and sleepy looking, rested on a sofa in a corner of the office jammed with friends and political associates. His friends shrugged, thinking his old melancholy had embraced him again or that he was just tired from the long campaign and frighteningly long final day. More likely, his depression stemmed from the knowledge that he would probably lose New York and, with it, the election. The November 3 telegram from Weed had crushed him. Except for his wife, Mary, it is unlikely that he told anyone of Weed's dire prediction. Then certain the election was lost, Mary Lincoln stayed home that evening and went to sleep at 11:30 p.m. Lincoln had one last hope—Weed. The New York political boss had promised him he would work hard in the few remaining days to get out the Republican vote. Weed was an old-time grassroots campaigner, just like Lincoln. The two men understood each other like no other politicians in the country. Weed would be true to his word, Lincoln knew, and if anyone could get out enough votes to help him creep past Douglas in New York, it was the mercurial Thurlow Weed.

Even so, Lincoln worried about New York. He mentioned his fears about the vote in the Empire State to friends in the telegraph office several times that evening.[866]

The first news was very good. Voter turnout had been huge; 81.2 percent of the registered voters in the country—4,685,561—went to the polls (second only to the record that would be set in 1876).[867] The Republicans had counted on a big turnout for an increase in their totals, and they got it.

The news from the South, as expected, was all bad. Tennessee: Bell—

69,728, Breckinridge—65,097, Douglas—11,281…Lincoln—0. Virginia: Bell—74,481, Breckinridge—74,325, Douglas—16,198, Lincoln—1,887. It was the same in Mississippi, Texas, Arkansas, Louisiana, Alabama, Georgia, Florida, South Carolina, North Carolina—all Breckinridge. Tennessee, Kentucky, Virginia went all Bell. The border states of Delaware and Maryland went to Breckinridge (Lincoln was drubbed in Maryland, despite the rosy predictions of his men there). The border state of Missouri went to Douglas.[868]

Stephen Douglas was hopeful of winning the South by appealing to the poor white farmers who owned no slaves, but he was badly beaten in every single Southern state. In Issequana County, Mississippi, out of 250 votes, Douglas won just 6.[869]

The Northern states looked better for Lincoln. Michigan: Bell—415, Breckinridge—805, Douglas—65,057, Lincoln—88,481 (Lincoln must have smiled at the returns from Kalamazoo County, where he campaigned in his very first year as a Republican, 1856, and drew big crowds; tonight Kalamazoo went for him with 62 percent of its vote).[870] He must have been pleased, too, with the Michigan towns and counties with large Dutch populations. The Republicans' courting of the Dutch gave them majorities in dozens of communities with large numbers of Netherlanders.[871]

A little while later, Minnesota's returns arrived: Douglas—11,920, Lincoln—22,069. Then it was Rhode Island (where Weed had supervised last-minute campaigning): Lincoln—12,244, Douglas—7,707.[872]

The night wore on. Maine gave Lincoln 62 percent of its vote. New Hampshire, where his son Robert went to school, gave him 56.9 percent. Iowa, despite heavy campaigning by Douglas, went Republican with 54.6 percent. Wisconsin, with its heavy immigrant vote, went solidly Republican, at 56.5 percent.[873]

Then the results began to arrive from the states where he had trudged through town after town to give speeches against slavery and for himself and where he had shaken so many hands and smiled at so many faces the previous winter. Massachusetts backed Lincoln by 62.8 percent. In Connecticut, he had campaigned in the cold and snow in Hartford and New Haven in support of shoe factory workers on strike. Connecticut went for the rail-splitter by more than three to one over his nearest opponent. New Haven county and its factory workers went for him with 72 percent of the vote. Hartford, where he told crowds of blue-collar workers that he believed in their right to strike, gave him over 73 percent of the vote.[874]

In the West, where Southern Democrats and Douglas Democrats were so certain of victory, more hard work paid off. The Republicans carried California by a thin margin of just 643 votes out of 82,000. In Oregon, nephew John Hanks had worked for him, and Amory Holbrook, as promised, had campaigned for him in every county and every town. He won that state by just 214 votes.

Then, later in the evening, reports tumbled in from the states so carefully targeted by Judge Davis, the states that would make Abraham Lincoln president of the United States or throw the election into the House of Representatives for the third time in American history and create an unprecedented constitutional crisis.

Lincoln barely carried Illinois. Then results from Tazewell County (where the Republicans lost in 1856) and McLean (where they barely won in 1856) came in. The Republicans carried McClean with 3,547 votes. Tazewell was a county Lincoln continually visited and in which he politicked since 1858. On this long night Tazewell went Republican. In Cook County, Lincoln had risked a political war with the *Chicago Press and Tribune* to save the job of political boss John Wentworth and helped get him elected the mayor of Chicago. In that county, Lincoln received the highest vote totals in Illinois history, 14,589 votes—5,579 more votes than it gave Frémont in 1856, a nearly 60 percent increase and enough to beat Douglas by almost five thousand votes.

Then the counties full of immigrants came in and the counties where so many had lived to work on the Illinois Central Railroad. Champaign County went Republican by two to one. He won 60 percent of the vote in Livingston, 60 percent in Vermilion, 61 percent in Iroquois, and 75 percent in Ogle. He piled up substantial pluralities in the counties where he confronted Douglas in the great debates of 1858, such as Stephenson and LaSalle. Altogether, Lincoln carried the state by just five thousand votes.[875]

In Indiana, not only did the northern counties of Lake, St. Joseph's, Miami, Montgomery, Putnam, and Marion vote Republican, as expected, but so did the southern counties where Schuyler Colfax and former Know-Nothing Richard Thompson had worked so hard. Bell and Breckinridge together polled only 6 percent of the vote. Lincoln carried Indiana by six thousand votes over his opponents.[876]

The telegrams reporting the results from around the country through the Illinois and Mississippi Telegraph Company arrived at different hours and told a dramatic story.

From Republican chairman John DeFrees in Indianapolis, early: "Large Republican gains. All safe."

From Philadelphia, early: "Returns already received indicate a majority for Lincoln in this city."

From political operative B. J. F. Hanna in Illinois: "We have stood fine. Victory has come. Glory Hallelujah!"

From Pennsylvania, later: "Allegheny Co., Pa. Ten thousand majority for Republican candidate."

From Indiana, later: "Indiana over twenty thousand for honest old Abe."

They did well in little Prairie View Township, in Iowa, too, where they had increased their vote from just 16.3 percent in 1857 to 28.6 percent in 1859 and hoped to reach 30 percent in the 1860 race. On election day, tiny Prairie View gave 34 percent of its vote to Lincoln.[877]

In Pennsylvania, hard work paid off again. Breckinridge did well in some counties, but the Republicans surprisingly won in over a dozen southern border counties along the Mason-Dixon Line. In some, their gains over 1856 were startling, such as in Mifflin, where they went from 216 votes to 1,701, and York, where the tally leaped from 411 to 5,126, and in Centre, where the vote jumped from 390 to 3,021. The iron counties, where Lincoln's support of the protective tariff was deemed so important, went solidly for Lincoln, some by landslides (he won two-thirds of the vote in Susquehanna, 60 percent in Lycoming, and 63 percent in Schuykill). He doubled the Republican vote from 1856.

The crucial southern border counties of Adams, Cambria, Clarion, Cumberland, Fayette, Westmoreland, Wyoming, Northampton, and Northumberland followed the surge. Eight of the nine switched and went for Lincoln, cutting off any possibility of a Breckinridge tide there. Lincoln swept through Pittsburgh with a three-to-one margin and beat Breckinridge in Philadelphia by 39,223 to 21,619, an increase from the Republican total of just 7,993 four years earlier.[878]

The Republicans had three times their 1856 vote in Cambria County in the iron belt, seven times the vote in Blair, three times the vote in Cumberland. By the end of the night, Lincoln had piled up a startling 89,159 plurality in Pennsylvania, nearly doubling Frémont's 1856 total and carrying 56.3 percent of the vote to 37.5 percent for Breckinridge.[879]

Later the Republicans in Springfield learned that Ohio had held again, as it had held in 1856. There, Lincoln piled up a 44,288 plurality, up from the thin 16,000-vote plurality the state gave Frémont four years earlier.[880] Much of that plurality was earned in Dayton, Hamilton, Cincinnati, and Columbus, where local politicians for whom he had campaigned in 1859 reciprocated by working for him in 1860.[881]

The Pennsylvania victory gave Lincoln 145 electoral votes, just 7 shy of the presidency. All that remained was New York. At that hour, Thurlow Weed had finished the longest day of his political life, working from 5:00 a.m. through the darkness of the night to get Lincoln elected. He supervised thousands of workers, all sent an election-eve note (and reprinted in Republican newspapers on election morning) that read like a fire alarm:

> *Close up the work of preparation tonight: leave nothing for tomorrow but direct work. Pick out and station your men.... Let there be an assigned place for every man, and, at sunrise, let every man be in his assigned place. Don't wait until the last hour to bring up delinquents. Consider every man a delinquent who doesn't vote before ten o'clock. At that hour, begin to hunt up voters!*[882]

It was a seesaw race in the Empire State despite Weed's and Seward's Herculean efforts there, despite the money poured into the race, the torchlight parades, picnics, and thousands of speeches—just as it had been in 1856. If Lincoln won New York, he was the next president. If he lost it, he would stall at 145 electoral votes, and the election would be thrown into the House of Representatives, where he would lose. The men in Springfield waited and waited.

The first returns from the Empire State were grim. Douglas had taken New York City by an impressive 30,000-vote plurality. How could anybody overcome a lead like that? Returns showed, too, that Douglas was running far stronger in counties and cities where he campaigned personally than Buchanan had run in 1856. The telegraph continued to bring results from New York. Lincoln defeated Douglas in upstate cities such as Buffalo and Syracuse, where Weed's forces staged a memorable election-day drive to get out the vote totals, in some counties up to nearly 20 percent over the previous year. He won in rural upstate counties such as Oswego, Saratoga, and Schenectady. He won 65 percent of the vote in some counties and 60 percent in others, slowly making up New York City's deficit.

The former American Party voters in the upstate counties, courted so valiantly by Daniel Ullmann, went for Lincoln marginally in some towns and in landslides in others. Towns where Wide Awake clubs had marched all summer and fall and worked to get out the vote went big for Lincoln. Towns with mayors and councilmen who owed their jobs to money and help from Weed went for Lincoln. After 11:00 p.m. Lincoln appeared to pull ahead in New York, and then, as midnight approached, his margins slowly increased.

A telegram from Simon Cameron in Pennsylvania summed it up best: "Hon. Abe Lincoln, Penna seventy thousand for you. New York safe. Glory enough."[883]

Later, when the last returns were in, a little past midnight, on one of the longest nights in American political history, when Lincoln seemed on the brink of victory in the Empire State, Simeon Draper wired the Republican nominee that nearly final results showed that he had taken New York. Lincoln won 53.7 percent of the vote and had a 50,136-vote plurality out of 675,156 votes cast.[884]

Lincoln, who had remained calm all night, was now the sixteenth president of the United States.

There was jubilation in Springfield. Lyman Trumbull, David Davis, Jesse Dubois (who started singing "Ain't You Glad You Joined the Republicans?"

when New York's tally came in), and others hugged each other. Lincoln, who had been working hard toward this night, shook hands all around. The men began to run down the stairs toward a stand of drink and food set up in front of the telegraph office by an exuberant mob of townspeople. Lincoln very slowly walked down the stairs of the telegraph office, behind them, the last man out of the building, a forlorn look on his face. As the others rushed to join the revelers, Lincoln turned the other way and walked home by himself in the wee hours of the November morning.

Everyone in Springfield seemed to be at the celebration near the telegraph office that night, and few saw the tall, gawky man walk quietly through the street toward his home. Judge Davis wrote: "Mr. Lincoln seems as he always does. You would not think that he had been elevated to the highest office in the world."[885]

Lincoln opened the front door of his home slowly, took off his coat, hung it up neatly (his wife always yelled at him if he did not), and quietly climbed the wooden stairs. He walked into Mary's bedroom and gently shook his wife's shoulder.

"Mary, Mary," he whispered, "we've been elected president."[886]

How did the Republicans win? They won the American Party, or Know-Nothing vote, in most states. The Republicans realized an increase in new voting, mostly for Lincoln, of more than seventy-five thousand votes in 1860 over 1856 in New York, a record 13 percent jump. They increased the vote in already-safe upstate counties for them, such as Niagara, Monroe, and Wayne, by 13 to 21 percent and realized 13 to 30 percent increases in the total vote in counties that switched from Democratic to Republican, such as Ulster, Erie, and Franklin.[887]

The Republicans were remarkably successful in winning the immigrant vote in states where they needed it, particularly in the northwestern states.

The immigrant vote was critical in that region, where Lincoln won all of the states by a narrow seventy-four thousand votes. "Without the vote of the foreign-born, Lincoln could not have carried the Northwest, and without the Northwest…he would have been defeated," wrote Donnal Smith.[888]

Perhaps the biggest factor in the Republican victory was not their stand on slavery but on corruption. Republican Senator James Grimes of Iowa said, "Our triumph was achieved more because of Lincoln's reputed honesty and the corruption of the Democrats than because of the Negro question."[889]

The final total showed that Lincoln won 180 electoral votes to 72 for Breckinridge, 39 for Bell, and just 12 for Douglas (he only carried Missouri). Lincoln polled 1,857,610 popular votes to 1,365,967 for Douglas, 847,053 for Breckinridge, and 590,631 for Bell. He carried every Northern state except New Jersey, where he lost to Douglas by 4,500 votes but earned half the electoral votes there in a complicated split. Even though Lincoln only won 39 percent of the popular vote, he had taken the White House thanks to the makeup of the electoral college and his ability to win the targeted states of Pennsylvania, Indiana, Illinois, and New York.

The Republicans did not win by much. They only took 50.7 percent of the vote in Illinois, 51.1 percent in Indiana, and 52.3 percent in Ohio. They were victorious in Oregon by just 254 votes out of 15,000 cast in a three-way race and in California by only 734 out of 120,000 cast in another three-way contest. They did take the critical six states in the Northwest, but only by a grand total of 6 percent. A switch of only 36,000 votes in those six states would have resulted in the loss of them all. A switch of just 2,500 votes in Illinois or 3,000 in Indiana would have lost those states. Any combination of losses in states barely won would have lost the election too. If just 495 people had switched their votes, Lincoln would have lost California and Oregon. If another 2,500 people in Illinois or 3,000 in

Indiana, plus California and Oregon, had also switched, the trio of electoral votes would have meant defeat. In short, the change in feelings of just 0.6 percent of the voters, or the population of a single small village, would have cost Lincoln the presidency.

Lincoln was not the only winner. The Republicans swept through the congressional races, winning a clear majority in the House of Representatives and Northern state legislatures. Since state legislatures at that time elected U.S. senators, it meant the Republicans would also have a majority in the Senate. They controlled most of the Northern governors' mansions and, with a Republican executive, all the patronage in those states. With the House, Senate, and White House, the upstart Republican Party, just five years old, had complete control of the government of the United States for better or worse. It was a revolution in politics.

"The black Republican party...is, in fact, essentially a revolutionary party," scolded the editor of the Democratic *New Orleans Delta*.[890]

Northerners winked in response. "I say God bless the revolution," wrote Republican Horace White.[891]

A campaign worker put it simply, "A united North succeeded over a divided South."[892]

Ominously, Lincoln received less than four thousand votes in each of the border states of Missouri, Kentucky, Delaware, Maryland, and Virginia and did not receive a single vote in all the other states of the South. The country, as Lincoln had predicted, split into North and South on election day.[893]

The Southerners did not like the results and began talking about secession as soon as the vote was counted. Abraham Lincoln's most brilliant moment was soon to become his country's most desperate hour.

CHAPTER 22

The Inauguration of President Lincoln

President-elect Abraham Lincoln rose in his rooms in suite 6 at Washington DC's Willard Hotel after sunup and had breakfast with his family. Outside, they could see thousands of people walking through the streets toward the Capitol along with six hundred U.S. soldiers and two thousand more armed volunteers. They heard the sounds of loud bands playing, followed by thousands of Wide Awakes marching in formation, as they prepared for the parade down Pennsylvania Avenue.

President James Buchanan greeted Lincoln in an open carriage in front of the hotel at 11:00 a.m. Lincoln was wearing a new black suit and stovepipe hat and carried a gold cane. They traveled to the Capitol up Pennsylvania Avenue, which was jammed with well-wishers who cheered them. District of Columbia cavalry rode alongside the carriage, and infantry troops paraded behind it. The pair rode through an unfinished city. The Capitol dome was still under construction. Only one-third of the Washington Monument had been completed. The city streets remained unpaved. Lincoln said little to Buchanan on the trip to the Capitol. Buchanan told Lincoln if he was as satisfied to enter the White House as he was to leave it, the Illinois lawyer would be a very happy man.

The president and president-elect entered the heavily guarded Capitol to watch the inauguration of Hannibal Hamlin as vice president in the Senate chamber and then walked to the Capitol's sun-drenched East Portico for the presidential inauguration.[894]

Lincoln had worked on his inaugural address for weeks. For help, and as a gesture of good will, he asked Salmon Chase and William Seward to read through it and suggest changes. Chase made some changes; Seward wrote much of the soaring finale of the speech. It was a speech that was designed to reassure Northerners that the new president was a confident, strong-willed, hopeful man who, with majorities in the Senate and Congress, would be an effective national leader. At the same time, Lincoln hoped his words would mollify the South and convince the states that had already seceded—South Carolina, Texas, Alabama, Mississippi, Georgia, Louisiana, and Florida—to rejoin the Union.

When Lincoln walked to the podium to deliver his speech, he looked out on one of the largest crowds to ever witness an inauguration to that time, said to be more than twenty-five thousand. Many, unable to find hotel rooms, had slept on the porches of homes and public buildings the night before. The sprawling crowd swarmed around the front of the Capitol, some people sitting on the limbs of trees, others holding on to statues, for the historical event.

To protect Lincoln, who had received numerous death threats, Gen. Winfield Scott set up two artillery batteries in front of the Capitol, where the new president would be sworn in, and positioned dozens of sharpshooters on the rooftops of nearby buildings. Several hundred armed soldiers lined the street leading to the Capitol to hold back the throng of people and protect the carriage carrying Lincoln and the outgoing Buchanan.[895]

The inauguration wrapped up a series of tumultuous months.

After the election in November, Lincoln was pressured by Southerners to make some statement to assure them that he would not eliminate slavery. He was lobbied to do so by Northerners, too, who insisted that the situation had economic as well as political ramifications. Even Thurlow Weed, who helped elect him, begged him to permit some slaves into the territories to please the South and keep peace. Lincoln turned down Weed, telling him that "I will be inflexible on the territorial question," and adding that such a move "would lose us everything we gained by the election."[896]

Lincoln refused to issue any public statement on slavery, insisting that everyone knew he would permit slavery in the South but was against its spread to the territories. As head of the Republican Party, he strongly urged Republicans to stick with him on this line. They did. "Lincoln is the most suitable man of any party for this terrible ordeal through which he has to pass," wrote Bronson Murray of Connecticut.[897]

In a last-minute step to hold the country together, President Buchanan appointed two committees, one in the House and one in the Senate, to work out a compromise agreement to prevent further secession. Calling the United States "the grandest temple which has ever been dedicated to human freedom," Buchanan pleaded with the departed states to return and said the Union had to stay together.[898] His plea failed. Not only did the House and Senate reconciliation committees fail to come up with a plan, but their meetings usually ended in shouting matches. Stephen Douglas said the rancorous debates on the committees would "drive (Southerners) into revolution and disunion."[899]

Looking down through his steel-rimmed glasses at his inaugural notes, Lincoln believed that the departed Southern states would return, but citizens throughout the United States worried. The editor of the *Daily Missouri Republican* put it best when he wrote, "Gloom pervades the country—

despair of a settlement of the differences between the North and the South is taking deep root in the minds of the people."[900]

Buchanan's postmaster general, Joseph Holt, exasperated by events, wrote at the end of November 1860 that "madness rules the hour." He predicted that "the (secessionist) movement has passed beyond the reach of human control."[901]

Southerners hated Northerners and Northerners hated Southerners. An editor at the *Pittsburgh Gazette* even warned that if any Southern politicians voted for secession, "it will be time to string them up."[902]

Lincoln was confident as he prepared to speak on the 50-degree day in front of the crowd that included his cabinet: William Seward, secretary of state; Salmon Chase, the head of the treasury; Simon Cameron, secretary of war; Edwin Bates, attorney general; Montgomery Blair, postmaster general; Caleb Smith, secretary of the interior; and Gideon Welles, secretary of the navy.

He was introduced and walked to the podium, his hat in hand. He did not know where to put it, so Stephen Douglas reached out and took it from him.

He had been greeted by enormous and enthusiastic crowds at all of his stops on his way to Washington, and his speech to the New Jersey legislature had been interrupted by applause numerous times; he was given a standing ovation at the conclusion. He felt that unionists in the nation's capital were behind him, and although a minority president, his Republican Party controlled the House and Senate.

Everywhere he looked, Lincoln saw tension, but he saw promise, too, on the festive day. The *National Intelligencer* called the inaugural "in some respects the most brilliant and imposing pageant ever witnessed in this capital."[903]

Lincoln was sworn in, hand on bible, by Chief Justice Roger Taney. At the conclusion of the new president's oath of office, batteries of artillery boomed out a loud, smoky salute to Lincoln.

In his inaugural address, he took a tough stand at some points, absolutely forbidding secession, and was conciliatory at others, reminding all that while he was opposed to slavery in the territories, he was willing to let it exist in the Southern states.[904]

His speech was emotional. After he told the crowd how much he loved America, and reminded them that God had always protected the country, he told the people in gentle but unambiguous language about secession, that "physically speaking, we cannot separate. We cannot remove our respective sections from each other, nor build an impassable wall between them. A husband and wife may be divorced...but the different parts of our country cannot do that."

He implored the states that had left the Union to return and told Southerners that they had to work with Northerners to hold the nation together. He said, "In your hands, not in mine, is the momentous issue of civil war.... You have no oath registered in heaven to destroy the government, while I shall have the most solemn one to 'preserve, protect, and defend' it." Then, in inspiring language, he added Seward's line, "We are not enemies, but friends.... The mystic chords of memory, stretching from every battlefield, and patriot grave, to every living heart and hearthstone, all over this broad land, will yet swell the chorus of the Union, when again touched, as surely they will be, by the better angels of our nature."[905]

When he finished, he was hopeful that he had given a good speech. He didn't know that right away because, given the circumstances, the applause from the enormous crowd was restrained. The president hoped that the states that had seceded would return and that North and South, despite their problems, could come back together, permitting the nation to move on.[906]

He was wrong.

Five weeks later, on April 12, Southern military forces opened fire on Fort Sumter, a federal facility in the harbor of Charleston, South Carolina. Those were the first shots of the Civil War, the bloodiest conflict in America's history. The war would conclude four years later after the deaths of 620,000 soldiers and the freeing of the slaves…and Lincoln's Union had been saved.

Bibliography

Historical Papers

Papers of August Belmont, Library of Congress

Papers of Jeremiah Black, Library of Congress

Papers of James Buchanan, Princeton University

Papers of Salmon Chase, Library of Congress

Papers of Stephen Douglas, University of Chicago

Papers of Ward Hill Lamon, Huntington Library, San Marino, California

Papers of Abraham Lincoln, Princeton University

Papers of Frank Nash, University of North Carolina

Papers of William Seward, University of Rochester

Papers of Daniel Ullman, New York Historical Society

Journals and Book Chapters

Auchampaugh, P. G. "The Buchanan-Douglas Feud." *Journal of the Illinois Historical Society* (April–July 1932).

Baker, Jean. "Lincoln's Narrative of American Exceptionalism." In *"We Cannot Escape History": Lincoln and the Last Best Hope of Earth,* edited by James McPherson. Urbana: University of Illinois Press, 1995.

Berry, Mildred. "Abraham Lincoln." William Brigance, ed. *A History and Criticism of American Public Address.* New York: McGraw Hill, 1943–1955.

Bonham, Milledge, Jr. "New York and the Election of 1860." *New York History Magazine* (April 1934).

Brown, R. J. "Abe Lincoln's Campaign Newspaper." Historybuff.com, retrieved October 18, 2008. http://www.historybuff.com.

Crocker, Lionel. "The Campaign of Stephen A. Douglas in the South, 1860." Jeffrey Auer, Ed. *Antislavery and Disunion, 1857-1861.* New York: Harper and Row, 1962.

Dodd, William. "The Fight for the Northwest." *American Historical Review.* Vol. XVI (July 1941).

Hamilton, Rouhac. "Lincoln's Election: An Immediate Menace to Slavery in the States?" *American History Review* (July 1932).

Herndon, William. "Analysis of the Character of Abraham Lincoln." *Abraham Lincoln Quarterly* (December 1941).

Hollcroft, Temple. "A Congressman's Letters on the Speaker Election in the Thirty-Fourth Congress." *Mississippi Valley Historical Review* XLIII (1956).

Holliday, Joseph. "The Critical Election of 1860." Paper for the 1996 Cincinnati Civil War Round Table.

"The Lost Speech." In *Life and Works of Abraham Lincoln.* Edited by Marion Miller. 9 vols. New York: Centenary Edition, 1907.

Lowell, James Russell. "The Election in November." *Atlantic* (October, 1860).

Meerse, David. "Buchanan, Corruption, and the Election of 1860." *Civil War History* (March 1966).

Pitkin, Thomas. "Western Republicans and the Tariff in 1860." *Mississippi Valley Historical Review* (December 1940).

Potter, David. "Why the Republicans Rejected Both Compromise and Secession." George Knoles, Ed. *The Crisis of the Union, 1860-1861.* Baton Rouge: Louisiana State University Press, 1965.

Roll, Charles. "Indiana's Part in the Nomination of Abraham Lincoln for President in 1860." *Indiana Magazine of History* XXV (1929).

Rosen, Robert. "Democratic Debate: Another Charleston 'Fandango'?" www.Charleston news.net, retrieved October 20, 2008.

Schafer, Joseph. "Who Elected Lincoln?" *American Historical Review* XLVII (1941).

Smith, Donnal, V. "The Influence of the Foreign-Born of the Northwest in the Election of 1860." *Mississippi Valley Historical Review* XIX (1932).

Smith, William. "A Reporter with Lincoln in 1859 and 1860." Rufus Wilson, Ed., *Intimate Memories of Lincoln*. Elmira: Primavera Press, 1945.

Stampp, Kenneth. "The Republican National Convention of 1860." Jeffrey Auer, ed., *Antislavery and Disunion, 1858-1861*. New York: Harper and Row, 1963.

Swierenga. Robert. "The Ethnic Voter and the First Lincoln Election." *Civil War History Magazine* (March 1965).

Thomas, David. "Southern Non-Slaveholders in the Election of 1860." *Political Science Quarterly* (June 1911).

Tulis, Jeffrey. "On Presidential Character." Jeffrey Tulis, and Joseph Bessette, eds., *The Presidency in the Constitutional Order*. Baton Rouge: Louisiana State University Press, 1981.

Weed, Sam. "Hearing the Returns with Mr. Lincoln." Rufus Wilson, ed., *Intimate Memories of Abraham Lincoln*. Elmira: Primavera Press, 1945.

Books

Adams, Charles Francis, Sr. *Charles Francis Adams Diary, 1835–1915*. 8 vols. Cambridge: Belknap Press of Harvard, 1964–1993.

Allen, Felicity. *Jefferson Davis: Unconquerable Hero*. Columbia: University of Missouri Press, 1999.

Amber, Charles, ed. *Correspondence of Robert M. T. Hunter, 1826–1876.* Washington, DC: U.S. Government Printing Office, 1918.

Angle, Paul. *Lincoln in the Year 1860 and as President-Elect; Being the Day-by-Day Activities of Abraham Lincoln from January 1, 1860 to March 5, 1861.* Springfield, IL: The Lincoln Centennial Association, 1927.

Auchampaugh, Phillip. *James Buchanan and His Cabinet on the Eve of Secession.* Lancaster, PA: Lancaster Press, 1926.

Baker, George, ed. *The Works of William Seward.* 5 vols. Boston: Houghton-Mifflin Co., 1884.

Baker, James. *Abraham Lincoln: The Man and the Myth.* Fort Worth: Harcourt College Publishers, 2000.

Baker, Jean. *"Not Much of Me…" Abraham Lincoln as a Typical American.* Fort Wayne: Louis A. Warren Lincoln Library and Museum, 1988.

———. *Mary Todd Lincoln.* New York: W.W. Norton Co., 1987.

Baringer, William. *Lincoln's Rise to Power.* Boston: Little, Brown and Co., 1937.

Barnes, Gilbert, Ed. *The Letters of Theodore Weld, Angelina Weld, and Sarah Grimke, 1822-1844.* New York: D. Appleton and Co., 1934.

Barnes, Thurlow Weed. *Memoirs of Thurlow Weed.* 2 vols. Boston: Houghton-Mifflin Co., 1884.

Barrett, Joseph H. *Life of Abraham Lincoln, Presenting His Early History, Political Career, and Speeches in and out of Congress; also a General View of His Policy as President of the United States; with His Messages, Proclamations, Letters, etc. and a Concise History of the War.* Cincinnati: Moore, Wilstach & Baldwin, 1864.

Bartlett, Truman, and Carl Schurz. *Abraham Lincoln: Biographical Essay with an Essay on the Portraits of Lincoln.* Boston: Houghton-Mifflin Co., 1896.

Basler, Roy, ed., Marion Pratt, and Lloyd Dunlop, asst. eds. *Collected Works of Abraham Lincoln*. 9 vols. New Brunswick: Rutgers University Press, 1953.

Baxter, Maurice. *Orville Browning: Lincoln's Friend and Critic*. Bloomington: Indiana University Press, 1957.

Black, David. *The King of Fifth Avenue: The Fortunes of August Belmont*. New York: Dial Press, 1981.

Bonham, Jeriah. *Fifty Years Recollections with Observations and Reflections on Historical Events*. Peoria, IL Franks Publishing, 1883.

Boritt, Gabor. *The Historian's Lincoln*. Chicago: University of Illinois Press, 1988.

Bradley, Edwin. *Simon Cameron: Lincoln's Secretary of War*. Philadelphia: University of Pennsylvania Press, 1966.

Brady, David. *Critical Elections and Congressional Policy Making*. Palo Alto, CA: Stanford University Press, 1988.

Brooks, Noah. *Abraham Lincoln and the Downfall of American Slavery*. New York: G. P. Putnam's Sons, 1894.

———. *Lincoln, By Friend and Foe*. New York: Gold Medal Library, 1922.

Buchanan, James. *Mister Buchanan's Administration on the Eve of the Rebellion*. New York: D. Appleton and Co., 1966.

———. *The Works of James Buchanan*. 12 vols. Philadelphia: J. P. Lippincott Co. 1908-1911.

Bunker, Gary. *From Rail-Splitter to Icon: Lincoln's Image in Illustrated Periodicals, 1860-1865*. Kent, OH: Kent State University Press, 2001.

Burlingame, Michael. *The Inner World of Abraham Lincoln*. Chicago: University of Illinois Press, 1994.

Burnham, W. Dean. *Presidential Ballots, 1836–1892*. Baltimore: Johns Hopkins University Press, 1955.

Campaign of 1860, Comprising the Speeches of Abraham Lincoln, William H. Seward, Henry Wilson, Benjamin F. Wade, Carl Schurz, Charles Sumner, William M. Evarts, & c. Albany: Weed, Parsons, and Company, 1860.

Capers, Gerald. *Stephen A. Douglas: Defender of the Union.* Boston: Little, Brown Publishers, 1959.

Carey, Rita. *The First Campaigner: Stephen A. Douglas.* New York: Vantage Press, 1964.

Carwardine, Richard. *Lincoln: A Life of Purpose and Power.* New York: Alfred Knopf, 2006.

Cash, W. J. *The Mind of the South.* New York: Alfred Knopf, 1941.

Cooper, William. *Jefferson Davis: American.* New York: Alfred Knopf, 2000.

Craven, Avery. *The Coming of the Civil War.* Chicago: University of Chicago Press, 1957.

Crenshaw, Ollinger. *The Slave States in the Presidential Election of 1860.* Gloucester, MA: Peter Smith Press, 1969.

Curtis, Francis. *The Republican Party: A History of Its Fifty Years of Existence and a Record of Its Measures and Leaders, 1854–1904.* New York: G. P. Putnam's Sons, 1904.

Davis, Stanton. *Pennsylvania Politics, 1860–1863.* Cleveland: Western Reserve University Press, 1935.

Davis, William. *Breckinridge: Statesman, Soldier, Symbol.* Baton Rouge: Louisiana State University Press, 1974.

——. *Jefferson Davis: The Man and the Hour.* New York: HarperCollins, 1991.

Diamond, Robert, ed. *Congressional Quarterly Guide to U.S. Elections.* Washington, D.C.: Congressional Quarterly Publishing, 1975.

Dittenhoefer, Abram. *How We Elected Lincoln: Personal Recollections.* Philadelphia: University of Pennsylvania Press, 2005.

Donald, David. *Lincoln.* New York: Simon & Schuster, 1995.

——. *Lincoln's Herndon.* New York: Alfred Knopf, 1948.

——. *We Are Lincoln Men.* New York: Simon & Schuster, 2003.

Dumond, Dwight. *Antislavery Origins of the Civil War in the United States.* Ann Arbor: University of Michigan Press, 1939.

——. *The Secession Movement.* New York: Macmillan, 1931.

——. *Southern Editorials on Secession.* New York: Century Co., 1931.

Ecelbarger, Gary. *The Great Comeback: How Abraham Lincoln Beat the Odds to Win the 1860 Republican Nomination.* New York: St. Martin's Press, 2008.

Einhorn, Lois. *Abraham Lincoln: The Orator, Penetrating the Lincoln Legend.* Westport, CT: Greenwood Press, 1982.

Fehrenbacher, Don. *Prelude to Greatness: Abraham Lincoln in the 1850s.* Palo Alto, CA: Stanford University Press, 1962.

Fite, Emerson. *The Presidential Campaign of 1860.* New York: Macmillan Co., 1911.

Folkerts, Jean, and Dwight Teeter Jr. *Voices of a Nation.* Boston: Allyn & Bacon Publishing, 1998.

Freeman, Andrew. *Abraham Lincoln Goes to New York.* New York: Coward-McCann, Inc., 1960.

Geary, Theopain. *A History of Third Parties in Pennsylvania.* Washington, DC: Catholic University of America Press, 1938.

Gienapp, William. *Essays on American Antebellum Politics, 1840–1860.* Arlington, TX: Texas A&M University Press, 1982.

——. *The Origins of the Republican Party, 1852–1856.* New York: Oxford University Press, 1987.

Gillette, William. *Jersey Blue: Civil War Politics in New Jersey, 1854-1865.* New Brunswick, NJ: Rutgers University Press, 1995.

Goodwin, Doris Kearns. *Team of Rivals.* New York: Simon & Schuster, 2005.

Graebner, Norman, ed. *Politics and the Crisis of 1860.* Urbana: University of Illinois Press, 1961.

Guelzo, Allen. *Lincoln and Douglas: The Debates That Defined America.* New York: Simon & Schuster, 2008.

Halstead, Murat. *Three Against Lincoln: The Caucuses of 1860.* Baton Rouge: Louisiana State University Press, 1960.

Harper, Robert. *Lincoln and the Press.* New York: McGraw-Hill, 1951.

Harris, William. *Lincoln's Rise to the Presidency.* Lawrence: University Press of Kansas, 2007.

Hart, Albert Bushnell. *Salmon Portland Chase, American Independent Series of Biographies.* Boston: Houghton-Mifflin, 1899.

Hatch, Nathan O. *The Democratization of American Christianity.* New Haven: Yale University Press, 1989.

Hayes, Melvin. *Mr. Lincoln Runs for President.* New York: Citadel Press, 1960.

Hendrickson, James. *Joe Lane of Oregon: Machine Politics and the Sectional Crisis, 1849–1861.* New Haven: Yale University Press, 1967.

Herndon, William. *Herndon's Lincoln: The True Story of a Great Life.* Indianapolis: Bobbs-Merrill, 1970.

Herndon, William, and Jesse Weik. *Life of Lincoln: The Historical and Personal Recollections of Abraham Lincoln as Originally Written by William Herndon and Jesse Weik, with Introduction and Notes by Paul Angle.* Cleveland: World Publishing, 1949.

Holt, Michael. *The Fate of Their Country: Politicians, Slavery Extension, and the Coming of the Civil War.* New York: Hill and Wang, 2004.

Holzer, Harold. *Lincoln at Cooper Union: The Speech That Made Abraham Lincoln President.* New York: Simon & Schuster, 2004.

Hunt, H. Draper. *Hannibal Hamlin of Maine.* Syracuse: Syracuse University Press, 1969.

Johannsen, Robert. *The Letters of Stephen A. Douglas.* Urbana: University of Illinois Press, 1961.

———. *Lincoln and the South in 1860.* Fort Wayne: A. Warren Lincoln Library and Museum, 1989.

———. *Stephen A. Douglas.* New York: Oxford University Press, 1973.

Johnson, Allen, ed. *Dictionary of American Biography.* New York: Charles Scribner's Sons, 1928–1937.

Johnson, Charles. *Official Proceedings of the Republican National Conventions, 1856, 1869, 1864, and 1892.* Minneapolis: Harrison and Smith, 1892.

Johnson, Ludwell. *Division and Re-Union: America, 1848–1877.* New York: John Wiley and Sons, 1978.

Johnston, R.M. *The Life of Alexander Stephens.* Philadelphia: J. P. Lippincott Co., 1878.

King, Willard. *Lincoln's Manager, David Davis.* Cambridge: Harvard University Press, 1960.

Klein, Philip. *President James Buchanan: A Biography.* Norwalk, CT: Easton Press, 1987.

Koerner, Gustave. *Memoirs of Gustave Koerner, 1809–1896.* Cedar Rapids: Torch Press, 1909.

Lucas, Henry. *The Netherlanders in America: Dutch Immigration to the United States and Canada, 1789–1950.* Ann Arbor: University of Michigan Press, 1955.

Lunde, Erick Sheldon, diss. "The Idea of American Nationalism: A Study in Presidential Campaign Literature, 1860-1876." City University of Michigan, 1971.

Luthin, Reinhard. *The First Lincoln Campaign.* Gloucester, MA: Peter Smith, 1964.

Mansch, Larry. *Abraham Lincoln: President-Elect.* Jefferson, NC: Macfarland Co., 2005.

Mazmanian, David. *Third Parties in Presidential Elections.* Washington, DC: Brookings Institute, 1974.

McClintock, Russell. *Lincoln and the Decision for War: The Northern Response to Secession.* Chapel Hill: University of North Carolina Press, 2008.

McClure, Alexander. *Abraham Lincoln and Men of War-Times: Some Personal Recollections of War and Politics during the Lincoln Administration.* Lincoln: University of Nebraska Press, 1996.

McPherson, James. *The Battle Cry of Freedom.* New York: Oxford University Press, 1988.

McPherson, James, ed. *"We Cannot Escape History": Lincoln and the Last Best Hope of Earth.* Urbana: University of Illinois Press, 1995.

Meserve, Frederick, and Carl Sandburg. *The Photographs of Abraham Lincoln.* New York: Harcourt, Brace and Co., 1944.

Milton, George. *The Eve of Conflict: Stephen A. Douglas and the Needless War.* Boston: Houghton-Mifflin, 1934.

Minden, New York, 1863 Democratic Polling Book. New York: New York Historical Society.

Mitchell, Stewart. *Horatio Seymour of New York.* Cambridge: Harvard University Press, 1938.

Mitgang, Herbert. *Abraham Lincoln: A Press Portrait, His Life and Times from the Original Newspaper Documents of the Union, the Confederacy, and Europe.* Chicago: Quadrangle Press, 1971.

Monaghan, Jay. *The Man Who Elected Lincoln.* Indianapolis: Bobbs-Merrill Co., 1956.

Morehouse, Frances. *The Life of Jesse W. Fell.* Urbana: University of Illinois Press, 1916.

Murphy, Charles. *The Political Career of Jesse D. Bright.* Indianapolis: Indiana Historical Society, 1931.

Nash, Howard, Jr. *Third Parties in American Politics.* Washington, DC: Public Affairs Press, 1959.

Nevins, Allan. *The Emergence of Lincoln.* New York: Charles Scribner's Sons, 1950.

Nichols, Franklin. *The Disruption of American Democracy.* New York: Macmillan Co., 1948.

Nicolay, John, and John Hay. *Abraham Lincoln: A History.* New York: The Century Co., 1890.

Niven, John. *Salmon Chase: A Biography.* New York: Oxford University Press, 1995.

Oates, Stephen. *With Malice Towards None: The Life of Abraham Lincoln.* New York: Harper & Sons, 1977.

Official Proceedings of the Democratic National Convention Held at Charleston and Baltimore, 1860. Cleveland: Neun's Print, 1860.

Oldroyd, Osborn. *Lincoln's Campaign: Or the Political Revolution of 1860.* Chicago: Laird and Lee, 1896.

Parks, Joseph. *John Bell of Tennessee.* Baton Rouge: Louisiana State University Press, 1950.

Phillips, Ulrich. *Correspondence of Robert Tombs, Alexander Stephens, and Howell Cobb.* Washington, DC: U.S. Government Printing Office, 1913.

Piatt, Don. *Memories of Men Who Saved the Union.* New York: Belford, Clarke Co., 1887.

Pollard, Edwin. *The Life of Jefferson Davis.* Freeport, NY: Books for Library Press, 1969.

Potter, David. *The Impending Crisis, 1848–1861.* New York: Harper & Row, 1976.

———. *Lincoln and His Party in the Secession Crisis.* Baton Rouge: Louisiana State University Press, 1942.

Rankin, Henry. *Personal Recollections of Abraham Lincoln.* New York: G.P. Putnam's Sons, 1916.

Ratner, Lorman, and Dwight Teeter Jr. *Fanatics and Fire-Eaters: Newspapers and the Coming of the Civil War.* Urbana: University of Illinois Press, 2003.

Reynolds, Donald. *Editors Make War.* Nashville: Vanderbilt University Press, 1970.

Rhodes, John. *History of the United States from the Compromise of 1850 to the McKinley-Bryan Campaign of 1896.* Port Washington, NY: Kennikat Press, 1917.

Rice, Allen, ed. *Reminiscences of Abraham Lincoln by Distinguished Men of His Times.* New York: North American Review Publishing, 1886.

Rose, Anne. *Victorian American and the Civil War.* New York: Cambridge University Press, 1992.

Rowland, Dunbar. *Jefferson Davis: Constitutionalist: His Letters, Papers, and Speeches.* Oxford, MS: Mississippi Department of Archives, 1923.

Sandburg, Carl. *The Prairie Years II.* New York: Harcourt, Brace and Co., 1926.

Schlesinger, Arthur, ed; Fred Israel and David Frent, assoc. eds. *The Election of 1860 and the Administration of Abraham Lincoln.* Philadelphia: Mason Crest Publishers, 2003.

Schoen, Douglas. *On the Campaign Trail.* New York: Regan Books, 2004.

Schucker, J. W. *Life and Public Service of Salmon Portland Chase.* New York: D. Appleton and Company, 1874.

Scrugham, Mary. *The Peaceable Americans of 1860-1861.* New York: Octagon Books, 1976, reprint of a 1921 edition.

Seitz, Don. *Lincoln the Politician: How the Rail-Splitter and Flatboatman Played the Great American Game.* New York: Coward-McCann, Inc., 1931.

Seward, Frederick, ed. *William H. Seward: An Autobiography from 1801–1834; with a Memoir of His Life; and Selections from His Letters, 1831–1846.* New York: D. Appleton Publishers, 1877.

Shaw, Albert. *Abraham Lincoln: The Year of His Election.* New York: Review of Reviewers Corporation, 1929.

Smith, Richard Norton. *Abraham Lincoln and the Triumph of Politics.* Gettysburg: Gettysburg College Press, 2007.

Smith, Willard. *Schuyler Colfax: The Changing Fortunes of a Political Idol.* Indianapolis: Indiana Historical Bureau, 1952.

Stirling, James. *Letters from the Slave States.* New York: New York Universities Press, 1969.

Sundquist, James. *Dynamics of the Party System.* Washington, DC: Brookings Institute, 1983.

Taft, Robert. *Appearance and Personality of Stephen A. Douglas.* Topeka: Kansas Historical Quarterly, 1954.

Teillard, Dorothy, ed. *Ward Hill Lamon Recollections of Abraham Lincoln.* Lincoln: University of Nebraska Press, 1994.

Temple, Wayne. *Lincoln the Rail-Splitter.* La Crosse, WI: G. Hantke at Willow Press, 1961.

———. *"The Taste Is in My Mouth a Little": Lincoln's Victuals and Potables.* Mahomet, IL: Mayhaven Publishers, 1994.

Tulis, Jeffrey. *The Rhetorical Presidency.* Princeton: Princeton University Press, 1987.

Van der Linden, Frank. *Abraham Lincoln: The Road to War.* Golden, CO: Fulcrum Publishing, 1998.

Van Deusen, Glyndon. *Thurlow Weed: Wizard of the Lobby.* Boston: Little, Brown and Co., 1947.

Villard, Henry. *Lincoln on the Eve of '61.* New York: Alfred Knopf, 1941.

Wakelyn, Jon, ed. *Southern Pamphlets on Secession: November 1860-April 1861.* Chapel Hill: University of North Carolina Press, 1996.

Warden, R. B. *Account of the Private Life and Public Services of Salmon Portland Chase.* Cincinnati: Wilstach, Baldwin, and Co., 1874.

Weed, Harriet, ed. *Thurlow Weed: Life of Thurlow Weed, including His Autobiography and a Memoir, Embellished in Portraits and Other Illustrations.* 2 vols. Boston: Houghton-Mifflin Co., 1884.

Weld, Theodore. *American Slavery as It Is.* New York: American Antislavery Society, 1839.

Welles, Gideon. *Diary of Gideon Welles.* 3 vols. Boston: Houghton-Mifflin Co., 1911.

Wells, Damon. *Stephen Douglas: The Last Years, 1857–1861.* Austin: University of Texas Press, 1971.

Whitney, Henry. *Life of Lincoln.* New York: Baker and Taylor Co., 1908.

Wilson, Edmund. *Patriotic Gore.* New York: Oxford University Press, 1962.

Wilson, Woodrow. *A History of the American People.* New York: Harper and Brothers, 1907.

Woodward, C. Vann. *The Strange Career of Jim Crow.* New York: Oxford University Press, 1974.

Zall, P. M., ed. *Abe Lincoln Laughing: Humorous Anecdotes from Original Sources, by and about Abraham Lincoln.* Berkeley: University of California Press, 1982.

Zimmerman, Charles. *The Origin and Rise of the Republican Party in Indiana, 1854–1860.* Bloomington: Department of History of Indiana University, 1917.

Newspapers

1858–1860

Albany Argus

Albany Journal

American Volunteer

Athens (OH) Messenger

Auburn (NY) Democrat

Austin State Gazette

Baltimore Republican

Boston Daily Advertiser

Boston Daily Advertiser

Boston Evening Transcript

Charleston Courier

Charleston Mercury

Chicago Daily Democrat

Chicago Journal

Chicago Press and Tribune

Chicago Times and Herald

Cincinnati Daily Commercial

Cincinnati Inquirer

Cleveland Herald

Cleveland Plain Dealer

Columbia Star

Congressional Globe

Daily Constitutional

Daily Nashville Patriot

Detroit Advertiser

Hartford Daily Courant

Hartford Evening Press

Houston Telegraph

Illinois State Journal

Illinois State Register

Kentucky Statesman

Louisville Daily Courier

Louisville Journal

Memphis Avalanche

Missouri Daily Republican

Missouri Democrat

Montgomery Mail

North American and U.S. Gazette

Nashville Banner

Nashville Union and American

National Intelligencer

New Orleans Bee

New Orleans Daily Crescent

New Orleans Delta

New York Daily Times

New York Express

New York Herald

New York Leader

New York Tribune

New York Times

Ohio State Journal

Philadelphia Daily News

Philadelphia Inquirer

Philadelphia Press

Philadelphia Public Ledger

Philadelphia Sunday Dispatch

Pittsburgh Press

Providence Post

Richmond Enquirer

Richmond Semi-Weekly Examiner

Rochester Evening Press

Sangamon Journal

Selma (AL) Reporter

Southern Argus

Southern Confederacy

Springfield (MA) Daily Republican

The Independent

The Liberator

Toledo Herald

Troy (NY) Weekly Times

Vinton Eagle

Virginia Whig

Washington Press

Washington Times

Weekly Maquoketa Excelsior

Woechentlicher National Demokrat

Endnotes

1. Lincoln speech at Springfield, Illinois, October 4, 1854, Roy Basler, ed., Marion Pratt and Lloyd Dunlap, assistant eds. *The Collected Works of Abraham Lincoln* (New Brunswick: Rutgers University Press, 1953), hereafter *CWAL, CWAL 2, etc.* 244–247, Philip Paludan, "Emancipating the Republicans: Lincoln and the Means and Ends of Slavery," in James McPherson, *"We Cannot Escape History": Lincoln and the Last, Best Hope of Earth* (Urbana: University of Illinois Press, 1995), 53.

2. Albert Shaw, *Abraham Lincoln: The Year of His Election* (New York: Review of Reviews Corporation, 1929), 65.

3. Frances Morehouse, *The Life of Jesse W. Fell* (Urbana: University of Illinois Press, 1916), 61; Letter from Henry Fell to Alice and Fanny Fell, February 10, 1909; Carl Sandburg, *The Prairie Years II* (New York: Harcourt, Brace and Co., 1926). 344.

4. Luthin, 138.

5. Halstead, 164.

6. David Donald, *Lincoln* (New York: Simon & Schuster, 1995), 239.

7. Gustave Koerner, *Memoirs of Gustave Koerner*, 1809–1896 (Cedar

Rapids: Torch Press, 1909), 61.

8. Frank van der Linden, *Abraham Lincoln: The Road to War* (Golden, CO: Fulcrum Publishing, 1998), 8; Noah Brooks, *Abraham Lincoln and the Downfall of American Slavery* (New York: G. P. Putnam's Sons, 1894), 185–189.

9. Donald, *Lincoln*, 238.

10. Harold Holzer, *Lincoln at Cooper Union: The Speech That Made Abraham Lincoln President* (New York: Simon & Schuster, 2004), 28.

11. Andrew Freeman, *Abraham Lincoln Goes to New York* (Coward-McCann, Inc., 1960), 86.

12. Basler, *CWAL, 3*: 522–550.

13. Freeman, 86.

14. Holzer, 146–147; *New York Tribune*, February 28, 1860.

15. Henry Villard, *Lincoln on the Eve of '61* (New York: Alfred Knopf, 1941), 8–9.

16. Francis Curtis, *The Republican Party: A History of Its Fifty Years of Existence and a Record of Its Measures and Leaders, 1854–1904* (New York: G. P. Putnam's Sons, 1904), 235.

17. Abraham Lincoln, "Communication to the People of Sangamon County," March 9, 1832, *CWAL, 1*: 8–9.

18. Basler, Lincoln to Richard Thomas, February 14, 1843, *CWAL, 7*: 281.

19. Jean Baker, "Lincoln's Narrative of American Exceptionalism," in McPherson, *"We Cannot Escape History": Lincoln and the Last Best Hope of Earth*, 37.

20. Michael Burlingame, *The Inner World of Abraham Lincoln* (Chicago: University of Illinois Press, 1994), 238.

21. Ibid., 238.

22. William Herndon, "Analysis of the Character of Abraham Lincoln," *Abraham Lincoln Quarterly* (December 1941), 419–411.

23. Herndon to Ward Hill Lamon, February 25, 1879, Lamon Papers, Huntington Library, San Marino, California.

24. Basler, Fragment on Stephen Douglas,: December, 1856, *CWAL*, 2: 383.

25. Basler, Lincoln to Albert Hodges, April 4, 1864, *CWAL, 7*: 281.

26. Basler, "Fragment: Last Speech of the Campaign at Springfield," October 30, 1858, *CWAL, 3*: 334.

27. William Gienapp, *Origins of the Republican Party, 1852–1856* (New York: Oxford University Press, 1987), 287.

28. Hansen, 53-57, Gienapp, *Origins of the Republican Party, 1852–1856*, 287.

29. David Brady, *Critical Elections and Congressional Policy Making* (Palo Alto, CA: Stanford University Press, 1988), 23.

30. Edmund Wilson, *Patriotic Gore* (New York: Oxford University Press, 1962), 110.

31. Lamon to Lincoln, August 17, 1860, Lamon Papers.

32. Basler, Lincoln to Leonard Swett, May 26, 2860, *CWAL, 4*: 55.

33. Don Fehrenbacher, *Prelude to Greatness: Abraham Lincoln in the 1850s* (Palo Alto, CA: Stanford University Press, 1962), 161.

34. Don Seitz, *Lincoln the Politician: How the Railsplitter and Flatboatman Played the Great American Game* (New York: Coward-McCann Inc., 1931), 58–59.

35. Gienapp, *Origins of the Republican Party*, 417.

36. Fehrenbacher, *Prelude to Greatness*, 47; Gienapp, *Origins of the Republican Party*, 344.

37. Henry Rankin, *Personal Recollections of Abraham Lincoln* (New York: G. P. Putnam's Sons, 1916), 384–385.

38. Donald, *Lincoln,* 198.

39. Basler, Abraham Lincoln to Lyman Trumbull, May 26, 1860, *CWAL,* 4: 55.

40. Burlingame, *The Inner World of Abraham Lincoln,* 268–326.

41. Richard Norton Smith, *Abraham Lincoln and the Triumph of Politics* (Gettysburg: Gettysburg College Press, 2007), 9.

42. Nathan O. Hatch, *The Democratization of American Christianity,* (New Haven: Yale University Press, 1989), 180–186.

43. Theodore Weld to Arthur Tappan, Joshua Leavitt, and Elizabeth Wright Jr., November 22, 1833, Gilbert Barnes, Ed., *The Letters of Theodore Weld, Angelina Weld, and Sarah Grimke, 1822–1844* (New York: D. Appleton and Century Co., 1934), 4 vols., 1: 120.

44. *Testimony of the Presbyterian Synod of Kentucky,* quoted in Theodore Weld, *American Slavery As It Is,* (New York: American Anti-Slavery Society, 1839), 61.

45. George Woodward to Jeremiah Black, November, 1860, Jeremiah Black Papers, Library of Congress, vol. XXXIII.

46. Dwight Dumond, *Antislavery Origins of the Civil War in the United States* (Ann Arbor: University of Michigan Press, 1939), 121.

47. Anne Rose, *Victorian America and the Civil War* (New York: Cambridge University Press, 1992), 195.

48. Basler, Circular from Whig Committee, January 31, 1840, *CWAL, 1:* 201.

49. Dean Burnham, *Presidential Ballots, 1832–1892* (Baltimore: Johns Hopkins University Press, 1955), 368–390.

50. Basler, Speech in the U.S. House of Representatives, July 17, 1848, *CWAL, 1:* 510.

51. Donald, *Lincoln,* 131.

52. Shaw, 23.

53. Jeffrey Tulis, "On Presidential Character," in Jeffrey Tulis and Joseph Bessette, Eds., *The Presidency in the Constitutional Order* (Baton Rouge: Louisiana State University Press, 1981), 301–305.

54. Rita Carey, *The First Campaigner: Stephen A. Douglas* (New York: Vantage Press, 1964), 13.

55. Emerson Fite, *The Presidential Campaign of 1860* (New York: Macmillan, 1911), 99.

56. Allen Guelzo, *Lincoln and Douglas: The Debates That Defined America* (New York: Simon & Schuster, 2008), 297.

57. Douglas' anonymous letter, February 11, 1858, Robert Johannsen, *The Letters of Stephen A. Douglas*, (Urbana, IL: University of Illinois Press, 1961), 411–412.

58. Douglas to unknown correspondent, December 6, 1857; Carey, 73.

59. Franklin Nichols, *The Disruption of American Democracy* (New York: Macmillan, 1948), 63.

60. Robert Johanssen, *Stephen A. Douglas* (New York: Oxford University Press, 1973), 349.

61. Fite, 100, 102.

62. Fite, 182–183, 102, 104.

63. Potter, 409; speech of Judah Benjamin, *Congressional Globe,* 36th Cong., first session, v. 3, 2233.

64. George Milton, *The Eve of Conflict: Stephen A. Douglas and the Needless War* (Boston: Houghton-Mifflin Co., 1934), 426.

65. Joseph Holliday, "The Critical Election of 1860," Paper for 1996 Cincinnati Civil War Round Table, 4.

66. *Cleveland Plain Dealer*, April 20, 1860.

67. Milton, 328.

68. Murat Halstead, *Three Against Lincoln: The Caucuses of 1860* (Baton Rouge: Louisiana State University Press, 1960), 8.

69. Ibid., 9.

70. August Belmont to Caroline Belmont, April 25, 1860, Belmont Papers, Library of Congress.

71. Halstead, 18.

72. Ibid., 19.

73. P. G. Auchampaugh, "The Buchanan-Douglas Feud," *Journal of the Illinois Historical Society* (April–July 1932) 145.

74. Luthin, 133.

75. Ulrich Phillips, *Correspondence of Robert Toombs, Alexander Stephens, and Howell Cobb* (Washington, DC: U.S. Government Printing Office, 1913), 468.

76. Halstead, 68–69.

77. *Official Proceedings of the Democratic National Conventions Held at Charleston and Baltimore, 1860* (Cleveland: Neun's Print, 1860), notes.

78. Michael Holt, *The Fate of Their Country: Politicians, Slavery Extension, and the Coming of the Civil War* (New York: Hill and Wang, 2004), 117–120.

79. *Official Proceedings of the Democratic National Conventions*, 55–66.

80. Halstead, 88.

81. James Buchanan in a talk to a crowd of well-wishers at the White House on June 25, 1860, in *The Works of James Buchanan* (Philadelphia: J. P. LIppincott, Co., 1908-1911), 11: 358.

82. Shaw, 16.

83. R. M. Johnston, *The Life of Alexander Stephens* (Philadelphia: J. P. Lippincott Co., 1878), 355.

84. Robert Rosen, "Democratic Debate: Another Charleston 'Fandango'?" www.Charleston news.net, accessed October 20, 2008, 2.

85. Ibid.

86. Stephen Douglas to the convention committee, June 6 and June 20, 1860, *Official Proceedings of the Democratic Conventions*, 178–179.

87. Van der Linden, 28–43.

88. Holliday, 3.

89. Howard Nash Jr., *Third Parties in American Politics* (Washington, D.C.: Public Affairs Press, 1959), 1–51.

90. *Selma (AL) Reporter*, June 28, 1860.

91. *Louisville Journal*, May 15, 1860.

92. *Louisville Journal*, May 30, 1860.

93. David Potter, *The Impending Crisis, 1848–1861* (New York: Harper & Row Publishers, 1976), 417; Halstead, 133.

94. Numerous newspapers zeroed in on the moderation and political acceptability of the two men.

95. Halstead, 133.

96. *Louisville Journal*, May 15, 1860.

97. Ibid.

98. Ibid.

99. Ibid., 139.

100. *Louisville Journal*, June 26 and 28, 1860.

101. Herndon's description in James Baker, *Abraham Lincoln: The Man and the Myth* (Fort Worth: Harcourt College Publishers, 2000), 2–3.

102. Unidentified man to William Britten, May 1860, LP.

103. Truman Bartlett and Carl Schurz, *Abraham Lincoln; Biographical Essay with an Essay on the Portraits of Lincoln* (Boston: Houghton-Mifflin Co., 1896), 14; Allen Rice, ed., *Reminiscences of Abraham Lincoln by*

Distinguished Men of His Times (New York: North American Review Publishing, 1886), 479–480.

104. Dorothy Lamon Teillard, ed., Ward Hill Lamon, *Recollections of Abraham Lincoln* (Lincoln: University of Nebraska Press, 1994), 22.

105. Mildred Berry, "Abraham Lincoln," in William Brigance, Ed., *A History and Criticism of American Public Address* (New York: McGraw-Hill, 1943–1955), 850.

106. Ibid., 829.

107. Gary Ecelbarger, *The Great Comeback: How Abraham Lincoln Beat the Odds to Win the 1860 Republican Nomination* (New York: St. Martin's Press, 2008), 140.

108. Description from *Houston Telegraph*, reprinted in the *New York Tribune*, June 12, 1860.

109. Gabor Boritt, *The Historian's Lincoln* (Chicago: University of Illinois Press, 1988), 51.

110. *Illinois State Journal,* June 3, 1856; Horace White, in William Herndon and Jesse Weik, *Life of Lincoln: The Historical and Personal Recollections of Abraham Lincoln as Originally Written by William Herndon and Jesse Weik, with Introduction and Notes by Paul Angle* (Cleveland: World Publishing, 1949), 10–22.

111. Lois Einhorn, *Abraham Lincoln, the Orator: Penetrating the Lincoln Legend* (Westport, CT: Greenwood Press, 1982), 24.

112. Rice, 9.

113. Frederick Meserve and Carl Sandburg, *The Photographs of Abraham Lincoln* (New York: Harcourt, Brace and Co., 1944), 6.

114. Bartlett and Schurz, 12.

115. Ibid., 14.

116. Baker, 24–25.

117. Jeremiah Bonham, *Fifty Years Recollection,* (Peoria, IL: Franks Publishing, 1883), 159–160.

118. P. M. Zall, ed., *Abe Lincoln Laughing: Humorous Anecdotes from Original Sources, by and about Abraham Lincoln* (Berkeley: University of California Press, 1982), 12–14.

119. Richard Norton Smith, 7.

120. Basler, Lincoln Address Before the Young Men's Lyceum of Springfield, Illinois, *CWAL 1*: 109.

121. James Putnam to Leonard Swett, July 20, 1860, LP.

122. *Athens (OH) Messenger,* September 7, 1861.

123. *Boston Daily Advertiser,* September 12, 1848.

124. Herbert Mitgang, *Abraham Lincoln: A Press Portrait* (Chicago: Quandrangle Press, 1971), 18–19.

125. Donald, *Lincoln,* 194.

126. John Nicolay and John Hay, *Abraham Lincoln: A History* (New York: Century Co., 1890), 160.

127. Curtis, 291.

128. Burlingame, 244–245.

129. Fehrenbacher, 145.

130. H. Draper Hunt, *Hannibal Hamlin of Maine* (Syracuse: Syracuse University Press, 1969), 114.

131. William Herndon, *Herndon's Lincoln: The True Story of a Great Life* (Indianapolis: Bobbs-Merrill, 1970 reprint), 190.

132. William Smith, "A Reporter with Lincoln in 1859 and 1860"; Rufus Wilson, *Intimate Memories of Lincoln* (Elmira, NY: Primavera Press, 1945), 260–274.

133. Basler, Lincoln speech in Columbus, Ohio, September 16, 1859, *CWAL, 3*: 423.

134. Basler, Lincoln speech in Peoria, Illinois, October 16, 1854, *CWAL, 2*: 247–283.

135. Basler, Abraham Lincoln in the Lincoln-Douglas Debates of 1858, *CWAL, 3*: 16.

136. Lincoln letter to the *Sangamon Journal*, June 13, 1836; Abraham Lincoln to Theodore Canisius, May 17, 1859, LP.

137. Mitgang, 46.

138. Robert Harper, *Lincoln and the Press* (New York: McGraw-Hill, 1951), 47.

139. Donald, *Lincoln,* 201.

140. James McPherson, *The Battle Cry of Freedom* (New York: Oxford University Press, 1988), 72.

141. Jay Monaghan, *The Man Who Elected Lincoln* (Indianapolis: Bobbs-Merrill Co., 1956), 159.

142. Ibid., 161.

143. Ibid., 116.

144. *New York Tribune*, October 26, 1858.

145. George Baker, ed., *The Works of William Seward* (Boston: Houghton-Mifflin, 1884), 5 vols., 4:289–302.

146. Harriet Weed, ed. *Thurlow Weed: Life of Thurlow Weed, Including His Autobiography and a Memoir, Embellished in Portraits, and Other Illustrations* (Boston: Houghton-Mifflin Co., 1884), 2 vols., 2: 423.

147. Halstead, 160; Frederick Seward, ed. *William H. Seward: An Autobiography from 1801–1834; with a Memoir of His Life; and Selections from His Letters, 1831–1846* (New York: D. Appleton Publishers, 1877), 3 vols., 1:288.

148. Marcus Ward to William Seward, May 2, 1860, William Seward Papers, University of Rochester, Princeton University.

149. Joseph Schafer, "Who Elected Lincoln?" *American Historical Review*, vol. XLVII (1941) 52–63; James Sundquist, *Dynamics of the Party System* (Washington, DC: The Brookings Institute, 1983), 44.

150. Weed to Seward, May 2, 1860, Seward Papers; Gordon Leidner, "How Lincoln Won the 1860 Republican Nomination," *Washington Times*, August 10, 1996.

151. M. L. Hull to Seward, May 8, 1860, Seward Papers.

152. Henry Stanton to Seward, May 6, 1860, Seward Papers.

153. "William Seward," Union College pamphlet, 8, Seward Papers.

154. Murat Halstead, *Cincinnati Daily Commercial*, May 18, 1860.

155. For more on Chase, see Albert Bushnell Hart's *Salmon Portland Chase, American Independent Series of Biographies* (Boston: Houghton-Mifflin, Co., 1899); J. W. Schucker's *Life and Public Services of Salmon Portland Chase* (New York: Appleton, 1874), and R. B. Warden's *Account of the Private Life and Public Services of Salmon Portland Chase* (Cincinnati: Wilstach, Baldwin, and Co., 1874).

156. John Niven, *Salmon Chase: A Biography* (New York: Oxford University Press, 1995), 220–221; Doris Kearns Goodwin, *Team of Rivals* (New York: Simon & Schuster, 2005), 243.

157. *Ohio State Journal*, September 1859, in Allan Nevins, *The Emergence of Lincoln* (New York: Charles Scribner's Sons, 1950), 36.

158. Jean Baker, *Mary Todd Lincoln* (New York: W. W. Norton Co., 1987), 158–159.

159. Bartlett and Schurz, 91.

160. Henry C. Whitney, *Life of Lincoln* (New York: Baker and Taylor Co., 1908), 286.

161. Koerner, 80.

162. Willard King, *Lincoln's Manager, David Davis* (Cambridge: Harvard University Press, 1960), 128.

163. Jesse Dubois to Lincoln, May, 1860, LP.

164. Ecelbarger, 193.

165. Larry Mansch, *Abraham Lincoln: President-Elect* (Jefferson, NC: Macfarland Co., 2005), 47; Donald, *Lincoln,* 248.

166. Luthin, 160.

167. Monaghan, 154; Ecelbarger, 147.

168. Ibid., 157.

169. Ecelbarger, 164.

170. Koerner, 83.

171. C. Vann Woodward, *The Strange Career of Jim Crow* (New York: Oxford University Press, 1974), 33–40; Richard Carwardine, *Lincoln: A Life of Purpose and Power* (New York: Alfred Knopf, 2006), 108–109.

172. Goodwin, 227.

173. Seward, 268.

174. Sandburg, 340.

175. Seward Senate speech, March 11, 1850, *Congressional Globe,* 31st Congress, 1st Session, 265.

176. Seward speech in Rochester, New York, October 25, 1858, Seward Papers.

177. Mark Delaney to Lincoln, May 16, 1860, LP.

178. Seward to Theodore Parker, July 1858, Seward Papers.

179. Greeley's letter was reprinted in the *Charleston Mercury* and numerous other Southern newspapers to undermine the Republicans.

180. Thomas Pitkin, "Western Republicans and the Tariff in 1860,"

Mississippi Valley Historical Review (December 1940) 407; Ludwell Johnson, *Division and Re-Union: America, 1848–1877* (New York: John Wiley and Sons, 1978), 63.

181. Basler, Abraham Lincoln to Richard Corwine, May 2,1860, *CWAL,* 4: 48n.

182. Abram Dittenhoefer, *How We Elected Lincoln: Personal Recollections* (Philadelphia: University of Pennsylvania Press, 2005), 28.

183. Lorman Ratner and Dwight Teeter Jr., *Fanatics and Fire-Eaters: Newspapers and the Coming of the Civil War* (Urbana: University of Illinois Press, 2003), 85.

184. William Baringer, *Lincoln's Rise to Power* (Boston: Little, Brown and Co., 1937), 93.

185. Thurlow Weed Barnes, *Memoirs of Thurlow Weed* (Boston: Houghton-Mifflin Co., 1884), 2 vols., 2: 292.

186. Halstead, 162.

187. Lincoln had said that in Hartford and New Haven, Connecticut, on March 6, 1860, and in many other places asserted that "we think slavery a great moral wrong."

188. Basler, Lincoln speech in New Haven, Connecticut, March 6, 1860, *CWAL, 4*: 23.

189. Basler, Lincoln Speech in Dayton, Ohio, September 17, 1859, *CWAL, 3*: 440.

190. Monaghan, 122.

191. Lincoln to Charles Ray, November 1858, LP; Monaghan, 124.

192. Rose, 208.

193. Herndon to Lyman Trumbull, January 27, 1861, in David Donald, *Lincoln's Herndon* (New York: Alfred Knopf, 1948), 31.

194. Luthin, 106.

195. Einhorn, 25.

196. Basler, Lincoln to Owen Lovejoy, August 11, 1855, *CWAL, 2*: 234.

197. U.S. Census figures, 1860.

198. Brady, 156.

199. William Bourne to Lincoln, September 24, 1860, LP.

200. Richard Norton Smith, *Abraham Lincoln and the Triumph of Politics* (Gettysburg: Gettysburg College, 2007), 21.

201. Wayne Temple, *Lincoln the Rail-Splitter* (La Crosse, WI: G. Hantke at the Willow Press, 1961), 16–19.

202. David Davis to Lincoln, May 15, 1860.

203. Monaghan, 163.

204. King, 136.

205. Basler, Lincoln note on the margin of the front page of the *Missouri Democrat* newspaper that he sent to his handlers in Chicago, *CWAL, 4*: 50.

206. Whitney, 289; Sandburg, 342; Monagan, 168.

207. Basler, Lincoln note, May 17, 1860, *CWAL, 4*: 50.

208. Koerner, 89.

209. Edwin Bradley, *Simon Cameron: Lincoln's Secretary of War* (Philadelphia: University of Pennsylvania Press, 1966), 150–156.

210. Ibid., 151.

211. Seward to Thurlow Weed, March 15, 1860, Seward Papers. Seward wrote, "Mr. Cameron claims all the delegates in Philadelphia but one. He says he wants to see you."

212. King, 137.

213. Some charged that state leaders such as Smith baited Davis into offering a post in return for their votes. See Nevins, 256. The story of the deals offered in Chicago always remained murky.

214. Alexander McClure, *Abraham Lincoln and Men of War-Times:*

Some Personal Recollections of War and Politics during the Lincoln Administration (Lincoln: University of Nebraska Press, 1996), 25.

215. Charles Roll, "Indiana's Part in the Nomination of Abraham Lincoln for President in 1860," *Indiana Magazine of History*, XXV (1929), 1–13.

216. Luthin, 138.

217. Halstead, 164.

218. Sam Bowles to Weed, March 5, 1860, in Barnes, *Memoirs of Thurlow Weed,* 316.

219. Barnes, 245.

220. Sandburg, 340.

221. Halstead, 164.

222. Maurice Baxter, *Orville Browning: Lincoln's Friend and Critic* (Bloomington: Indiana University Press, 1957), 102.

223. Halstead, 161; Nevins, 255.

224. Luthin, 44.

225. Melvin Hayes, *Mr. Lincoln Runs for President* (New York: Citadel Press, 1960), 36; Luthin, 56.

226. Leonard Swett to Josiah Drummond, May 27, 1860, LP; Osborn Oldroyd, *Lincoln's Campaign: Or the Political Revolution of 1860* (Chicago: Laird and Lee, 1896), 71–73.

227. Elbridge Spaulding to Seward, May 16, 1860, Seward Papers.

228. Leonard Swett to Josiah Drummond, May 27, 1860; Oldroyd, 71–73.

229. Charles Johnson, *Official Proceedings of the Republican National Conventions, 1856, 1869, 1864, and 1892* (Minneapolis: Harrison and Smith, 1892), 148–154.

230. Interview with Joe Medill, *Saturday Evening Post*, August 5, 1899; Halstead, 171; Sandburg, 345; Leidner, 3.

231. Johnson, 153; Kenneth Stampp, "The Republican National Convention of 1860," J. Jeffrey Auer, Ed., *Antislavery and Disunion, 1858–1861* (New York: Harper and Row, 1963), 209.

232. *Springfield (MA) Daily Republican*, May 22, 1860.

233. Leidner, "How Lincoln Won the 1860 Republican Nomination," *Washington Times*, August 10, 1996; Koerner, 91; Nicolay and Hay, 1:272.

234. Nevins, 260; Norman Graebner, ed., *Politics and the Crisis of 1860* (Urbana, IL: University of Illinois Press, 1961), 95; Monaghan, 172.

235. Hayes, 67; Nicolay and Hay, 1: 278.

236. Leonard Swett to Josiah Drummond, May 27, 1860; Oldroyd, 71–73.

237. Van der Linden, 53.

238. Gerald Capers, *Stephen A. Douglas: Defender of the Union* (Boston: Little, Brown Publishers, 1959), 210.

239. Ibid., 131–133.

240. Seitz, 146–147.

241. Baringer, 96; Luthin, 64; Basler, Reply of the Republican National Convention, May 18, 1860, *CWAL,* 4: 51.

242. Seitz, 178.

243. Hayes, 75.

244. *Auburn Democrat*, reprinted in the *Charleston Mercury* June 2, 1860.

245. Weed to Seward, May 20, 1860, Seward Papers.

246. Ibid.

247. Bennett to Seward, May 24, 1860, Seward Papers.

248. Hall to Seward, May 22, 1860, Seward Papers.

249. Grier to Seward, May 18, 1860, Seward Papers.

250. Smith, *Lincoln and the Triumph of Politics*, 30.

251. Simon Cameron to Seward, May 20, 1860, Seward Papers.

252. Charles Sumner to Seward, May 20, 1860, Seward Papers.

253. *Louisville Daily Courier*, May 26, 1860.

254. Ibid., 203.

255. Ibid., 202.

256. James Leach and Kentucky delegates to Caleb Cushing, June 23, 1860, *Official Proceedings of the Democratic National Conventions*, 153.

257. *Charleston Mercury*, May 5, 1860.

258. Lyman Samuel to Seward, May 12, 1860, Seward Papers.

259. Halstead, 253.

260. *Official Proceedings of the Democratic National Conventions*, 178–179, 183.

261. Luthin, 94.

262. *Louisville Journal*, May 23, 1860.

263. *Richmond Semi-Weekly Examiner*, May 18, 1860.

264. Leonard Swett to Thurlow Weed, July 4, 1860, Barnes, *Memoirs of Thurlow Weed*, 2: 298.

265. William Davis, *Jefferson Davis: The Man and the Hour* (New York: Harper Collins, 1991), 282.

266. Felicity Allen, *Jefferson Davis: Unconquerable Hero,* (Columbia: University of Missouri Press, 1999), 250.

267. Stewart Mitchell, *Horatio Seymour of New York* (Cambridge: Harvard University Press, 1938), 213.

268. David Potter, 413.

269. William Cooper, *Jefferson Davis: American* (New York: Alfred Knopf, 2000), 313.

270. *Charleston Mercury*, June 29, 1860.

271. The conversation between the New Yorker and Buchanan was reported in the *New York Commercial Advertiser* and reprinted in

the *Charleston Mercury* on July 7, 1860. Davis did not tell the story himself until he wrote his memoirs in 1882.

272. *Austin State Gazette*, April 7, 1860.

273. *New York Herald*, May 30, 1860; Holliday, 4; Ollinger Crenshaw, *The Slave States in the Presidential Election of 1860* (Gloucester, MA: Peter Smith Press, 1969), 290.

274. *Richmond Enquirer*, July 10, 1860.

275. His departure was noted in the *New York Herald* and in other newspapers in editions printed in late August and early September, 1860; Crenshaw, 304.

276. Dumont, 107.

277. Crenshaw, *The Slave States in the Presidential Election*, 61.

278. William Dodd, "The Fight for the Northwest," *American Historical Review*, vol. XVI, (July 1941), 59, *Louisville Journal,* June 27, 1860.

279. Many newspapers, North and South, put together their own tallies, *New York Tribune,* July 16, and October 4, 1860.

280. *Philadelphia Press*, July 7, 1860.

281. Crenshaw, 70, 70n.

282. Halstead, 36.

283. Crenshaw, 59-62; *New York Daily Times*, May 23, 1860.

284. Dodd, 779.

285. *Memphis Avalanche,* June 4, 1860.

286. *New Orleans Delta,* May 2, 1860.

287. *Louisville Journal,* quoted in the *Memphis Enquirer*, June 30, 1860.

288. *North American and U.S. Gazette*, September 29, 1860.

289. King, 146.

290. S. K. Stow to Amos Briggs, *Troy (NY) Weekly Times*, October 20, 1860.

291. Lincoln to Anson Henry, July 4, 1860; *CWAL* 4: 81–82.

292. Nevins, 310.

293. Bunker, 52–53.

294. David Mazmanian, *Third Parties in Presidential Elections* (Washington, DC: Brookings Institute, 1974), 46–47.

295. Carey, 12.

296. Crenshaw, 297.

297. Edgar club description from George Rives to Lincoln, August 2, 1860, LP; *Boston Evening Transcript*, October 17, 1860.

298. Sam Greer to Lincoln, September 28, 1860, LP.

299. John Fry to Lincoln, August 8, 1860, LP.

300. William Cullen Bryant to Lincoln, June 16, 1860, LP.

301. Invitation to Lincoln by H. M. Gaylord, Buffalo, N.Y., October 1, 1860, Concord (NH) Republican Wide Awakes flyer, LP.

302. Lamon, who had known Lincoln for fourteen years when he was elected, expressed this belief in his book.

303. Baringer, 98.

304. Herndon, 196n.

305. Stephen Oates, *With Malice Towards None: The Life of Abraham Lincoln* (New York: Harper & Sons, 1977), 180.

306. George Fogg to Lincoln, August 6, 1860, LP.

307. Mitgang, 181.

308. Seitz, 41, 182; Luthin, 120–121, 184.

309. Luthin, 152.

310. King, 158.

311. David Donald, *We Are Lincoln Men* (New York: Simon & Schuster, 2003), 179.

312. Alexander McClure to Lincoln, August 21, 1860, LP; Arthur

Schlesinger, Fred Isreal, and David Frent, eds., *The Election of 1860 and the Administration of Abraham Lincoln* (Philadelphia: Mason Crest Publishers, 2003), 21.

313. Elihu Washburne to Lincoln, September 10, 1860.

314. Mansch, 5; Oldroyd, 150.

315. R. J. Brown, "Abe Lincoln's Campaign Newspaper," Historybuff.com, retrieved October 18, 2008 from www.Historybuff.com; Carey, 14.

316. Alexander McClure to a mass meeting of Republicans in Philadelphia on October 15, 1860, *Philadelphia Daily News,* October 15, 1860.

317. David Wallace, of Woodly, Connecticut, to Lincoln, July 21, 1860, LP.

318. Davis Meerse, "Buchanan, Corruption, and the Election of 1860," *Civil War History*, March 1966, 118.

319. House report No. 184, 35th Congress, 2d Session.

320. Ibid.

321. Meerse, 123; Joe Klein, *President James Buchanan: A Biography* (Norwalk, Conn.: Easton Press, 1987), 338–340.

322. James Buchanan message to Congress, June 22, 1860, *Works,* 10: 399–405; Buchanan to James Gordon Bennett, *New York Herald,* June 18, 1860, *Works,* 10: 434.

323. Amos Briggs, *Troy (NY) Weekly Times,* October 20, 1860.

324. *New York Daily Tribune*, March 9 and 19, 1860; J. E. Folet to Lincoln, June 2, 1860, LP.

325. Phillip Auchampaugh, *James Buchanan and His Cabinet on the Eve of Secession* (Lancaster, PA: Lancaster Press, 1926), 95.

326. *Proceedings of the First Three Republican National Conventions of 1856, 1860 and 1864* (Minneapolis: C.W. Johnson & Co., 1893), 131–132.

327. John Sherman to William Sherman, November 26, 1860, Sherman letters.

328. *Congressional Globe,* 36th Congress, 2d Session, Appendix, 136.

329. James Grimes to Lyman Trumbull, November 13, 1860, LP.

330. August Belmont to John Forsyth, November 22, 1860, Belmont Papers.

331. *Louisville Journal,* May 22, 1860.

332. *Chicago Daily Democrat,* August 8, 1860.

333. Horace White to Lincoln, September 29, 1860, LP.

334. Lincoln to John Hill, September 29, 1860, LP.

335. A study of his letters shows that he also wrote back and forth to Republican candidates for Congress, offering encouragement and some advice. They, in return, let him know how things looked in their district for the presidential race.

336. Schuyler Colfax to Lincoln, June 25, 1860, LP.

337. Thurlow Weed to Lincoln, August 12, 1860, LP.

338. Simon Cameron to Lincoln, August 28, 1860, LP.

339. Joe Medill to Lincoln, August 30, 1860, LP.

340. John Harvey to Lincoln, September 28, 1860, LP.

341. Anonymous note to Lincoln, September 3, 1860, LP.

342. Amos Tuck to Lincoln, September 9, 1860, LP.

343. Tom Dudley to Lincoln, September 20, 1860, LP.

344. Abraham Lincoln papers.

345. Tom Tullock to Lincoln, August 18, 1860, LP.

346. Amory Holbrook to Lincoln, July 21, 1860, LP.

347. Ibid.

348. Elbridge Spaulding to Lincoln, July 21, 1860, LP.

349. Levi Powell to Lincoln, July 20, 1860, LP.

350. John Hanks to Lincoln, July 22, 1860, LP.

351. William Bourne to Lincoln, September 23, 1860, LP.

352. Sam Glover to Lincoln, September 18, 1860, LP.

353. Ed Pierce to Lincoln, July 21, 1860, LP.

354. Joe Casey to Lincoln, September 14, 1860, LP.

355. Henry Sherman to Lincoln, July 20, 1860, LP.

356. George Card to Lincoln, July 21, 1860, LP.

357. J. Scammon to Lincoln, May 29, 1860, LP.

358. R. H. Brooke to Lincoln, July 21, 1860, LP.

359. Sam Field to Lincoln, July 22, 1860, LP.

360. John Carson to Lincoln, August 19, 1860, LP.

361. John Pickell to Lincoln, September 26, 1860, LP.

362. Ben James to Lincoln, September 27, 1860; John Carson to Lincoln, July 19, 1860, LP.

363. Joe Medill to Lincoln, July 24, 1860, LP.

364. E. C. Blankenship to Lincoln, September 10, 1860, LP.

365. Morton Bradley to Lincoln, August 2, 1860, LP.

366. Oliver Parker to Lincoln, September 28, 1860, LP; A. Tyler to Lincoln, October 22, 1860, LP; J. R. Shoemaker to Lincoln, October 17, 1860, LP; R. G. Bassett to Lincoln, October 17, 1860, LP; M. J. Thomas to Lincoln, October 20, 1860, LP.

367. Peter Wyckoff to Lincoln, October 5, 1860, LP.

368. Joe Colbert to Lincoln, October 2, 1860, LP.

369. George Savidge to Lincoln, October 8, 1860, LP.

370. Hugh East to Lincoln, October 15, 1860, LP.

371. Sam Artus to Lincoln, October 16, 1860, LP.

372. L. Clapham to Lincoln, October 28, 1860, LP.

373. Zenas Robbins to Lincoln, October 18, 1860, LP.

374. William Knoer to Lincoln, October 17, 1860, LP.

375. William Knoer to Lincoln, October 1860, LP.

376. William Matthews to Lincoln, June 19, 1860, LP.

377. Libbie Bailey to Lincoln, October 29, 1860, LP.

378. George Lincoln to Lincoln, September, 1860, LP.

379. John Murr to Lincoln, June 1, 1860, LP.

380. Grace Bedell to Lincoln, October 15, 1860, LP.

381. Offices of D. L. Olmsted and Co. to Lincoln, May 29, 1860, LP.

382. William Hemstreet to Lincoln, August 10, 1860, LP.

383. Alexander McClure to Lincoln, July 18, 1860, LP.

384. James Hamilton to Lincoln, July 18, 1860, LP; George Ashmun to Lincoln, June 18, 1860, LP.

385. Taber, Hawk, and Co., managers of Richmond House, Chicago, May 29, 1860, LP.

386. Lincoln to Hannibal Hamlin, July 18, 1850, to Simeon Francis, August 4, 1860, *CWAL* 4: 84–85, 89–90; Baringer, 101.

387. Russell Errett to Lincoln, August 24, 1860, LP.

388. Abraham Lincoln speech notes for Chicago, Illinois, talk, February 28, 1857, *CWAL* 2: 390–391.

389. George Fogg to Lincoln, August 23, 1860, LP.

390. D. C. Gillespie to Lincoln, October 22, 1860, LP.

391. Lincoln to Abe Jonas, July 21, 1860, LP.

392. James Lesley to Lincoln, July 31, 1860, LP. Joe Casey, Cameron's man, often wrote Lincoln of the fine speeches Cameron delivered for him, especially one in Erie, Pennsylvania, on September 12 that attracted 25,000 people; Bradley, 154.

393. George Davis to Lincoln, August 29, 1860, LP.

394. James Churchman to Lincoln, September 12, 1860, LP.

395. Hannibal Hamlin to Lincoln, September 8, 1860, LP.

396. David Davis to Lincoln, July 1, 1860, LP.

397. Thurlow Weed to Lincoln, June, 1860, LP.

398. Henry Winter Davis to David Davis, June 10, 1860, LP.

399. Carey, 12; David Davis to Lincoln, June 7, 1860, LP.

400. Curtis, 343.

401. Certificate from the Chicago Republican Wide Awake Club, June 1, 1860; Nicolay and Hay, 2: 284; *New York Tribune,* June 2, 1860.

402. *Hartford Daily Courant,* July 27, 1860.

403. Seward, *Works,* 4: 384.

404. William Gienapp, *Essays on American Antebellum Politics, 1840–1860* (Arlington, TX: Texas A&M University Press, 1982), 76.

405. William Gillette, *Jersey Blue: Civil War Politics in New Jersey, 1854–1865* (New Brunswick, NJ: Rutgers University Press, 1995), 99.

406. Koerner, 2: 99; Gillette, 98; Oldroyd, 104–105.

407. George Copeland to Lincoln, June 18, 1860, LP.

408. Fite, 227.

409. Ibid.

410. Luthin, 160–162.

411. Republican Party letter to Lincoln, September 29, 1860, LP; Luthin, 147.

412. Carey, 16.

413. Jean Baker, *"Not Much of Me": Abraham Lincoln as a Typical American* (Fort Wayne: Louis A. Warren Lincoln Library and Museum, 1988), 4–6.

414. King, 151.

415. Ibid. 145.

416. *Chicago Press and Tribune,* June 5, 1860, LP.

417. William Fry, of the *New York Tribune,* to Lincoln, August 4, 1860, LP; *CWAL,* 4: 111.

418. Hatch, 207.

419. Norman Judd to Abraham Lincoln, June 1860, LP.

420. Lyman Trumbull to Abraham Lincoln, June 1860, LP.

421. Caleb Smith to Lincoln, August 30, 1860, LP.

422. George Sparrow to Lincoln, August 2, 1860, LP.

423. James Dwight to Seward, July 23, 1860, Seward Papers.

424. Norman Eastman to Seward, July 27, 1860, Seward Papers.

425. William Burkingham to Seward, September 29, 1860, Seward Papers.

426. Nevins, 302.

427. James Harvey to Lincoln, June 13, 1860, LP.

428. *Cleveland Plain Dealer*, August 10, 1860.

429. *Chicago Journal,* October 4, 1858.

430. *Detroit Advertiser*, August 18, 1860.

431. Schuyler Colfax to Lincoln, June 25, 1860, LP.

432. Mark Delahay to Lincoln, June 24, 1860, LP.

433. Buchanan, 87, 92–93.

434. *Southern Confederacy*, reprinted in the *New York Times,* August 7, 1860.

435. Crenshaw, 304.

436. David Potter, "Why the Republicans Rejected Both Compromise and Secession," George Knoles, ed. *The Crisis of the Union, 1860–1861* (Baton Rouge: Louisiana State University Press, 1965), 99; Edwin Morgan's letters in Temple Hollcroft, Ed., "A Congressman's Letters on the Speaker Election in the Thirty-Fourth Congress," *Mississippi Valley Historical Review*, XLIII (1956), 444–458, that focused on the Banks selection in 1854–1855.

437. *Philadelphia Press*, July 30, 1860.

438. Mary Scrugham, *The Peaceable Americans of 1860–1861* (New York:

Octagon Books, 1976, reprint of 1921 edition), 46.

439. *New York Tribune*, September 22, 1860.

440. Fite, 189.

441. James Watson Webb to Lincoln, August 3, with clipping from unidentified New York newspaper.

442. *Charleston Mercury,* October 4, 1860.

443. Don Piatt, *Memories of Men Who Saved the Union* (New York: Belford, Clarke Co., 1887), 28–30.

444. Ibid., 28.

445. Luthin, 176.

446. Ibid., 29.

447. Potter, in Knoles, 90.

448. Ibid., 432; Oates, 187.

449. Democratic statement by Joshua Henry and others, *Albany Argus*, October, 1860.

450. W. J. Cash, *The Mind of the South* (New York: Alfred Knopf, 1941), 52, 167.

451. Story recounted in *Kentucky Statesman,* October 5, 1860.

452. David Thomas, "Southern Non-Slaveholders in the Election of 1860," *Political Science Quarterly*, June 1911, 222–237.

453. Ibid., 234.

454. Potter, in Knoles, 72.

455. Ibid., 60, 62.

456. William Harris, *Lincoln's Rise to the Presidency* (Lawrence: University Press of Kansas, 2007), 228. Numerous Southern newspapers, such as the *Daily Nashville Patriot*, September 19, 1860, editorialized that not only were the Republicans a sectional party, but a minority party; *The Daily Constitutionalist* (Augusta, Georgia), November 3, 1860.

457. Ratner and Teeter, 86–91.

458. *New York Herald,* September 29, 1860; *Charleston Mercury*, August 25, 1860.

459. John Nicolay memo, November 5, 1860, Nicolay manuscripts, Library of Congress.

460. *Louisville Journal,* August 12, 1860.

461. *Columbia Star* editorial, reprinted in the *New York Times*, October 29, 1860; Oates, 187.

462. *Montgomery Mail,* October 18, 1860.

463. Henry Wise to J. H. Reagan, October 10, 1860.

464. J. D. Ashmore to James Hammond, July 10, 1860.

465. Robert Gourdin to Porcher Miles, August 20, 1860.

466. Laurence Keitt to Porcher Miles, October 3, 1860.

467. Crenshaw, 213.

468. *Charleston Mercury*, October 11, 1860.

469. *Nashville Banner,* December 18, 1860; *Virginia Whig*, reprinted in the *New York Times*, October 29, 1860.

470. *New York Herald*, in Harris, 228.

471. Curtis, 339.

472. Klein, 353.

473. George Prentice to Lincoln, October 26, 1860, LP.

474. Charles Gibson to O. H. Browning, October 28, 1860, LP.

475. W. T. Early to Lincoln, October 29, 1860, LP.

476. Broadsides, Caddo Parish, Louisiana, October 20, 1860, LP; Jon Wakelyn, ed., *Southern Pamphlets on Secession: November 1860-April 1861* (Chapel Hill: University of North Carolina Press), 1996, x–xxix.

477. *Charleston Mercury,* October 18, 1860.

478. Thomas Sweeney to Lincoln, October 20, 1860, LP.

479. George Davis to Jesse Dubois, October 20, 1860, LP.

480. Jeffrey Tulis, *The Rhetorical Presidency* (Princeton: Princeton University Press, 1987), 74–79.

481. William Cullen Bryant to Lincoln, November 1, 1860, LP.

482. Francis Blair to Lincoln, October 31, 1860, LP.

483. George Davis to Lincoln, October 30, 1860, LP.

484. George Fogg to Lincoln, October 27, 1860, LP; *New York Times*, October 25, 1860.

485. George Fogg to Lincoln, October 24, 1860, LP.

486. Letter to William Speer from Lincoln, October 23, 1860; *CWAL* 4: 130.

487. Lincoln to George Prentice, October 29, 1860, LP.

488. Russell McClintock, *Lincoln and the Decision for War: The Northern Response to Secession* (Chapel Hill: University of North Carolina Press, 2008), 26.

489. Donald, *Lincoln,* 260.

490. Henry Winter Davis to Lincoln, August 14, 1860, LP.

491. Dan Roberts to Lincoln, October 16, 1860, LP.

492. Ulysses Doubleday to Lincoln, late September, 1860, LP.

493. Abner Doubleday to Ulysses Doubleday, September 23 and 25, 1860, LP.

494. George Keith to Lincoln, July 21, 1860, LP.

495. J. W. H. Underwood to Howell Cobb, February 2, 1844.

496. Capt. George Hazzard to Lincoln, October 21, 1860, LP.

497. Gen. Winfield Scott to Lincoln, October 29, 1860, LP.

498. Paul Angle, Lincoln in the Year 1860 and as President-Elect (Springfield, IL: Lincoln Centennial Association, 1927), 47, 49, 50.

499. W. B. Orvis to Lincoln, October 5, 1860, LP.

500. Maj. Thomas Phil to Lincoln, October 16, 1860, LP.

501. F. R. Shoemaker to Lincoln, October 17, 1860, LP.

502. George Thompson to Lincoln, October 30, 1860, LP.

503. Col. David Hunter to Lincoln, October 20, 1860, LP.

504. David Potter, *Lincoln and His Party in the Secession Crisis* (Baton Rouge: Louisiana State University Press, 1942), 62–63.

505. Stories about the violence at the rally were published in numerous newspapers; George Howard to Lincoln, November 2, 1860, LP; Worthington Snethen to Lincoln, November 3, 1860, LP.

506. Potter, 343.

507. S. Spencer to Lincoln, October 29, 1860, LP.

508. Milo Holcomb to Lincoln, July 29, 1860, LP.

509. Burnham, 704.

510. Stanton Davis, *Pennsylvania Politics, 1860–1863* (Cleveland: Western Reserve University Press, 1935), 29.

511. *New York Tribune,* June 19, 1856.

512. Burnham, 241.

513. Charles Leib to Lincoln, June 6, 1860, LP.

514. *Annual Report of the American Historical Association II* (1902), 278. Salmon Chase, in Ohio, wrote Charles Sumner, in Massachusetts, that Ohioans were watering down their antislavery platforms to please the Know-Nothings in order to win their vote.

515. *American Volunteer*, November 27, 1856.

516. *Philadelphia Public Ledger*, February 28, 1856.

517. Lyman Trumbull to Lincoln, June 8, 1860, LP.

518. Morton McMichael to Lincoln, June 10, 1860, LP.

519. Thurlow Weed to Lincoln, June 10, 1860, LP.

520. Theopain Geary, *A History of Third Parties in Pennsylvania* (Washington, DC: Catholic University of America Press, 1938), 226.

521. William Reynolds to Lincoln, July 25, 1860, LP.

522. Charles Amber, ed., *Correspondence of Robert M. T. Hunter, 1826–1876* (Washington, DC: U.S. Government Printing Office, 1918), 333–334; A. Cheesebrough to Lincoln, October 22, 1860, LP.

523. Luthin, 206.

524. Alexander McClure to Lincoln, June 16, 1860, LP.

525. Thurlow Weed to Lincoln, July 11, 1860, LP.

526. Tom Dudley to David Davis, September 18, 1860, LP.

527. James Harvey to Lincoln, June 5, 1860, LP.

528. George Fogg to Lincoln, August 18, 1860, LP.

529. Thurlow Weed to Lincoln, July 27, 1860, LP.

530. David Davis to Lincoln, August 5, 1860, LP.

531. David Davis to Thurlow Weed, June, 1860, LP.

532. Simon Cameron to David Davis, September 7, 1860, LP.

533. Lincoln to Alexander McClure, August 31, 1860, LP.

534. Simon Cameron to Lincoln, August 17, 1860, LP.

535. Charles Leib to Lincoln, September 24, 1860, LP.

536. John Sanderson to Lincoln, September 8, 1860, LP.

537. Thurlow Weed to David Davis, September 25, 1860, LP.

538. John Sanderson to Lincoln, September 22, 1860, LP; *Philadelphia Inquirer*, October 3, 1860.

539. Simon Cameron to Lincoln, September 22, 1860, LP.

540. John Goodrich to Henry Dawes, June 8, 1860, LP.

541. *New York Herald*, October 16, 1860, LP.

542. David Davis to Weed, August 24, 1860, LP.

543. *Pittsburgh Press,* May 28, 1859.

544. Alexander McClure to Lincoln, August 21, 1860, LP.

545. J. E. Breerly to Lincoln, September 28, 1860, LP.

546. Alexander McClure to Lincoln, August 11, 1860, LP.

547. Lionel Crocker, "The Campaign of Stephen A. Douglas in the South, 1860," Jeffery Auer, Ed., *Antislavery and Disunion, 1857–1861* (New York: Harper & Row, 1962), 270; Potter, 437; Nevins, 296–297; Harris, 235, 239.

548. Levi Powell to Lincoln, July 20, 1860, LP.

549. *Philadelphia Sunday Dispatch*, October 21, 1860.

550. *Richmond Enquirer,* August 28, 1860.

551. Potter, 436–440.

552. Burnham, 390; Carey, 13.

553. Lincoln to Cassius Clay, July 20, 1860; *CWAL*, 4: 85.

554. Cassius Clay to Lincoln, August 12, 1869, LP.

555. Cassius Clay to Lincoln, August 6, 1860, LP.

556. Van der Linden, 70.

557. Charles Zimmerman, *The Origin and Rise of the Republican Party in Indiana, 1854–1860* (Bloomington: Department of History of Indiana University, 1917), 394.

558. Caleb Smith to Lincoln, August 30, 1860, LP.

559. John DeFrees to Weed, August 25, 1860, LP.

560. Charles Murphy, *The Political Career of Jesse D. Bright* (Indianapolis: Indiana Historical Society, 1931), 134.

561. King, 148; Richard Thompson to Lincoln, June 12, 1860, LP.

562. Ibid., 408.

563. John Usher, of Terre Haute, to Jesse Williams, September 21, 1860, LP.

564. Zimmerman, 397.

565. W. K. Edwards to Richard Thompson, June 4, 1860, LP.

566. William Sharp to Lincoln, October 20, 1860, LP.

567. Robert Diamond, ed., *Congressional Quarterly Guide to U.S. Elections* (Washington, DC: Congressional Quarterly Publishing, 1975), 604–608.

568. Caleb Smith to Lincoln, August 30, 1860, LP.

569. King, 149.

570. David Davis to Lincoln, July 24, 1860, LP.

571. Lincoln to Jonas Abraham, July 21, 1860, LP.

572. Lincoln to Samuel Haycraft, June 4, 1860; *CWAL* 4: 69–70.

573. David Davis to Lincoln, June 27, 1860, LP.

574. Burnham, 368.

575. Hansen, 84.

576. Dodd, 62.

577. Lincoln to Ward Lamon, June 11, 1858, LP.

578. Jean Folkerts and Dwight Teeter, Jr., *Voices of a Nation* (Boston: Allyn and Bacon, 1998), 179.

579. Burnham, 388.

580. Diamond, 608.

581. Edwin Morgan to Lincoln, September 17, 1860, LP.

582. David Davis to Lincoln, August 29, 1860, LP.

583. Burnham, 632.

584. *New York Herald*, June 11, 1860.

585. Francis Spinner to Lincoln, August 23, 1860, LP.

586. Elbridge Spaulding to Lincoln, September 9, 1860, LP.

587. Lyman Trumbull to Lincoln, June 8, 1860, LP.

588. Lincoln to Lyman Trumbull, June 5, 1860; *CWAL*: 4: 71–72, Thurlow Weed to Lincoln, July 11, 1860, LP.

589. Lincoln to Thurlow Weed, September 17, 1860, LP.

590. Lyman Trumbull to Lincoln, May 31, 1860, LP.

591. Nevins, 2: 272; James Russell Lowell, "The Election in November," *Atlantic,* October 1860.

592. Monaghan, 189.

593. Luthin, 203.

594. Glyndon van Deusen, *Thurlow Weed: Wizard of the Lobby* (Boston: Little, Brown and Co., 1947), 256.

595. Lyman Trumbull to Lincoln, May 30, 1860, LP.

596. Van Deusen, 235.

597. *Chicago Daily Democrat,* October 2, 1860.

598. David Davis to Lincoln, September 24, 1860, LP.

599. Baringer, 106.

600. Seward, *Works* 4: 422.

601. Ibid., 2: 452.

602. Thurlow Weed to Lincoln, August 27, 1860, LP.

603. Burnham, 632–646.

604. James Putnam to Lincoln, September 8, 1860; Elihu Washburne to Lincoln, September 4, 1860, LP.

605. Bell campaign newspapers, May 1860.

606. *Louisville Journal,* May 21, 1860.

607. Joseph Parks, John Bell of Tennesee (Baton Rouge: Louisiana State University Press, 1950), 382.

608. Erik Sheldon Lunde, diss. "The Idea of American Nationalism: A Study in Presidential Campaign Literature, 1860–1876" (University of Michigan, 1971), 28.

609. Ibid.

610. *Louisville Journal,* July 13, 1860.

611. Parks, 379.

612. *Louisville Journal,* July 13, 1860.

613. Parks, 381.

614. William Davis, *Breckinridge: Statesman, Soldier, Symbol* (Baton Rouge: Louisiana State University press, 1974), 54–56.

615. Ibid., 144–145.

616. Ibid., 209.

617. News clips in the Lincoln papers.

618. *Louisville Journal,* June 5, 1860.

619. "The Lost Speech," in *Life and Works of Abraham Lincoln*, ed. Marion Miller (New York: Centenary Edition, 1907), 9 vols., 2: 300–301.

620. Lincoln to George Robertson, August 15, 1855, LP.

621. Bloomington, Illinois, speech, in Roulhac Hamilton, "Lincoln's Election: An Immediate Menace to Slavery in the States?" *American History Review* (July 1932), 703.

622. Ibid.

623. Dwight Dumond, *The Secession Movement* (New York: Macmillan, 1931), 113.

624. *New York Herald*, September, 1860, reprinted in the *Charleston Mercury*, September 7, 1860.

625. *Charleston Mercury,* September 5, 1860.

626. Fite, 190.

627. Woodrow Wilson, *A History of the American People* (New York: Harper and Brothers, 1907), 5 vols., 4: 190.

628. Edwin Pollard, *The Life of Jefferson Davis* (Freeport, NY: Books for Library Press, 1969), 54.

629. Cited in Roulhac Hamilton, 701.

630. Samuel Halsey to Joe Halsey, August 24, 1856, Jeremiah Morton Papers, University of Virginia.

631. Ibid.

632. Davis, *Breckinridge: Statesman, Soldier, Symbol,* 230.

633. Breckinridge to E. Griswold, July 4, 1860.

634. Davis, *Breckinridge: Statesman, Soldier, Symbol,* 239.

635. Horace White to Lincoln, June 4, 1860, LP.

636. Nevins, 284.

637. *Nashville Union and American,* October 12, 1860.

638. Oates, 145.

639. David Black, *The King of Fifth Avenue: The Fortunes of August Belmont* (New York: Dial Press, 1981), 193–194.

640. Ibid.

641. Miles Taylor to Douglas, July 29, 1860.

642. August Belmont to Douglas, July 28, 1860.

643. Miles Taylor to Douglas, July 22, 1860; Black, 194.

644. *New York Herald,* July 19, 1860.

645. Douglas' Raleigh, North Carolina, speech, August 30, 1860.

646. Allen Johnson, ed., *Dictionary of American Biography* (New York: Charles Scribner's Sons, 1928–1937), 102–103.

647. *Charleston Mercury,* June 29, 1860.

648. Dumond, *The Secession Movement,* 35–91.

649. *Louisville Journal,* May 22, 1860.

650. See Milledge Bonham Jr., "New York and the Election of 1860," *New York History Magazine,* April 1934.

651. *New York Herald,* July 5, 1860.

652. Teillard, 22.

653. *New York Herald,* July 3, 1860.

654. Milton, 490.

655. Douglas to Nathaniel Paschall, July 4, 1860; Johannsen, *Letters* (Urbana: University of Illinois Press, 1961), 497.

656. Stephen Douglas to Charles Lanphier, July 5, 1860; Johannsen, *Letters*, 497–498.

657. Johannsen, *Letters*, 658.

658. *Boston Daily Advertiser*, July 18, 1860.

659. August Belmont to Douglas, July 18, 1860, Belmont Papers.

660. Carey, 69.

661. Milton, 491.

662. *New York Herald*, October 30, 1860.

663. Hayes, 132–133.

664. *Charleston Mercury,* May 31, 1860.

665. Hayes, 134.

666. *Louisville Journal,* July 1, 1860.

667. Bunker, 46–47.

668. Autobiography written for John Scripps, June, 1860; *CWAL* 4: 64.

669. *New York Herald,* July 21, 1860.

670. *New York Herald,* July 25, 1860.

671. *New York Herald,* July 1, 1860.

672. *New York Times*, August 10, 1860.

673. Hayes, 156.

674. F. O. Prince to Douglas, August 10, 1860.

675. Herschel Johnson to Alexander Stephens, July 4, 1860.

676. John Eddy to Lincoln, September 24, 1860, LP.

677. Douglas Schoen, *On the Campaign Trail* (New York: Regan Books, 2004), 8.

678. *Louisville Journal*, May 23, 1860.

679. John Rhodes, *History of the United States, from the Compromise of 1850 to the McKinley-Bryan Campaign of 1896* (Port Washington, NY: Kennikat Press, 1917), 345.

680. Damon Wells, *Stephen Douglas: The Last Years, 1857–1861* (Austin: University of Texas Press, 1971), 250–252.

681. *New York Herald*, August 27, 1860.

682. Crocker, 269.

683. Johannsen, *Douglas*, 789; *Southern Argus (Norfolk, VA)*, August 25, 1860.

684. George Hazzard to Lincoln, October 21, 1860, LP.

685. Wells, 252; *New York Times*, September 1, 1860.

686. William Porter, "Doctrine of Coercion," pamphlet of the 1860 Association.

687. *Charleston Mercury*, September 3, 1860.

688. *Richmond Enquirer*, August 31, 1860.

689. *New York Herald*, September 6, 1860.

690. *Richmond Enquirer*, September 3, 1860.

691. *New York Herald*, August 27, 1860.

692. *New York Herald*, September 1, 1860.

693. *New York Herald*, September 6, 1860.

694. Ibid.

695. Joseph H. Barrett, *Life of Abraham Lincoln* (Cincinnati: Moore, Wilstach & Baldwin, 1864), 153.

696. *Richmond Enquirer*, September 4 coverage of Yancey's speech, which was delivered on August 14.

697. Johannsen, 793.

698. *National Intelligencer*, October 5, 1860.

699. *Chicago Times and Herald*, October 9, 1860.

700. Johannsen, 795.

701. *Illinois State Journal*, October 4, 1860.

702. Robert Taft, *Appearance and Personality of Stephen A. Douglas* (Topeka:

Kansas Historical Quarterly, 1954), 17.

703. *Cleveland Herald,* September 22, 1860; *Illinois State Journal,* September 22, 1860.

704. *Illinois State Register,* October 8, 1860.

705. Johannsen, *Douglas,* 795.

706. Charles Francis Adams Sr., *Charles Francis Adams Diary* (Cambridge: Belknap Press of Harvard, 1964–1993), 8 vols., 3: 63–66.

707. George Daniels letter to his mother, October 21, 1860. Daniels was an eyewitness to Douglas' arrival in Alton.

708. Wells, 251.

709. Carey, 47–50.

710. *Weekly Maquoketa (IA) Excelsior,* October 16, 1860.

711. Carey, 14.

712. George Daniels letter, October 21, 1860.

713. Phillips, 485.

714. Crocker, 270.

715. Robert Toombs letter, in Crenshaw, 71n.

716. Van der Linden, 72.

717. Johannsen, 800.

718. Gideon Welles, *Diary of Gideon Welles,* (Boston: Houghton-Mifflin Co., 1911), 3 vols., 1: 34.

719. *Daily Illinois State Journal,* October 20, 1860.

720. *New York Times,* July 26, 1860.

721. Crenshaw, 184–185.

722. Wells, 254; Wilson, *Slave Power,* 2: 700.

723. Elbridge Spaulding to Lincoln, July 21, 1860.

724. Henry Tanner to Lincoln, October 10, 1860, LP.

725. Alexander McClure to Lincoln, October 3, 1860, LP.

726. Dittenhoefer, 29.

727. *New York Times*, October 3, 1860.

728. *Albany Journal*, October 20, 1860.

729. *Chicago Daily Democrat*, October 3, 1860.

730. *Louisville Courier*, reprinted in the *New York Times*, October 27, 1860.

731. Henry Wilson speech in Dunbar Rowland, *Jefferson Davis, Constitutionalist: His Letters, Papers, and Speeches* (Oxford, MS: Mississippi Department of Archives, 1923), 161–162.

732. *The Liberator*, May 18, 1860.

733. *Providence Post*, October 24, 1860.

734. *New Orleans Bee*, January 19, 1860.

735. Avery Craven, *The Coming of the Civil War* (Chicago: University of Chicago Press, 1957), 419.

736. Davis, 243.

737. Alexander McClure to Lincoln, August 1, 1860, LP.

738. Leonard Swett to Lincoln, July 18, 1860, on instructions, LP.

739. Starr Clark to Lincoln, August 1, 1860, LP.

740. George Davis to Lincoln, August 29, 1860, LP.

741. John Sanderson to Lincoln, September 18, 1860, LP.

742. Alexander McClure to Lincoln, September 24, 1860, LP.

743. Caleb Smith to Lincoln, August 30, 1860, LP.

744. Thurlow Weed to Lincoln, August 2, 1860, LP.

745. Burnham, 688.

746. Minden, New York, 1863 Democratic polling book, New York Historical Society.

747. Hayes, 204.

748. Carl Schurz to Lincoln, August 22, 1860, LP.

749. Oldroyd, 110–112.

750. Ibid., 85.

751. Tom Thomas to Daniel Ullman, September 8, 1860, Ullman papers, New York Historical Society.

752. Stuyvesant Institute Newsletter, November 5, 1860.

753. N. S. Hubell to Daniel Ullman, June 13, 1860, Ullman Papers.

754. Edmond Rose to Daniel Ullman, July 5, 1860; William Lampont to Ullman, July 5, 1860, Ullman Papers.

755. E. L. Pelet to Ullman, July 21, 1860; N.E. Sheldon to Ullman, July 25, 1860; J. Cealde to Ullman, October 1,1860, Ullman Papers.

756. Alexander McClure to Ullmann, August 1, 1860, Ullman Papers.

757. Ibid.

758. David Davis to Lincoln, date unknown, LP.

759. Robert Swierenga, "The Ethnic Voter and the First Lincoln Election," *Civil War History Magazine*, March, 1965, 27–47.

760. Alex McClure to Lincoln, August 18, 1860; Simon Cameron to Lincoln, August 1, 1860, LP.

761. R. W. Miles in a letter to the *National Intelligencer,* August 4, 1860.

762. *Richmond Enquirer,* August 28, 1860.

763. *Richmond Enquirer,* August 21, 1860.

764. *Charleston Mercury,* July 11, 1860.

765. *Louisville Journal,* July 3, 1860.

766. Breckinridge New York Committee letter, September 16, 1860.

767. Thurlow Weed to Lincoln, August 27, 1860, LP.

768. Anonymous letter to Lincoln, July 1860, LP.

769. John Richardson to Lincoln, July 31, 1860, LP.

770. Thurlow Weed to Lincoln, August 12, 1860, LP.

771. Syd Kidd to Lincoln, September 28, 1860, LP.

772. David Davis to Lincoln, August 14, 1860, LP.

773. Sanders editorial in unidentified New York newspaper, July 30, 1860.

774. Davis, 241.

775. *New York Times*, October 31, 1860.

776. *Charleston Courier,* October issues, reprinted in the *New York Times,* October 23, 1860.

777. *Charleston Courier,* quoted in the *New York Times,* October 24, 1860.

778. *Cincinnati Inquirer,* October 23, 1860.

779. *Charleston Mercury*, October 24, 1860.

780. *New York Times,* November 3 and 4, 1860.

781. Norman Judd to Lincoln, August 1, 1860, LP.

782. *Charleston Mercury,* September 27, 1860.

783. *Richmond Enquirer,* reprinted in the *Charleston Mercury,* October 15, 1860.

784. *New York Herald,* August 28, 1860.

785. *Charleston Mercury,* October 19, 1860.

786. Crenshaw, 151.

787. James Thompson letter, October 11, 1860, Frank Nash Papers, University of North Carolina.

788. James Harvey to Lincoln, May 27, 1860, LP.

789. Leonard Swett to Lincoln, October 1, 1860, LP.

790. John DeFrees to Lincoln, October 3, 1860, LP.

791. Anson Henry to Lincoln, October 3, 1860, LP.

792. Leonard Swett to Lincoln, October 1, 1860, LP; David Davis to Thurlow Weed, August 24, 1860, LP; King, 158.

793. James Buchanan to Lewis Coryell, September 26, 1860, *Works,* 11: 2.

794. Hunt, 125; Hannibal Hamlin to Lincoln, September 9, 1860, LP.

795. John DeFrees to Lincoln, October 1, 1860, LP.

796. Telegraph, Alexander McClure to Lincoln, October 10, 1860, LP.

797. Crenshaw, 293.

798. Blair's election news in the *Chicago Daily Democrat,* August 8, 1860; E. D. Baker to Lincoln, October 2, 1860, LP

799. Telegrams, Illinois and Mississippi Company, October 9–15, 1860, LP.

800. Carl Schurz to Lincoln, October 10, 1860; Bellamy Storer to Lincoln, October 10, 1860, LP.

801. *Baltimore Republican*, October 1860; Donald, 255.

802. James Hendrickson, *Joe Lane of Oregon: Machine Politics and the Sectional Crisis, 1849–1861* (New Haven: Yale University Press, 1967), 236.

803. Mark Delahay to Lincoln, October 10, 1860; C. T. Shaw to Lincoln, October 20, 1860, LP.

804. Schuyler Colfax to Lincoln, October 11, 1860, LP.

805. Alexander McClure to Lincoln, October 12, 1860, LP.

806. William Bascom to Lincoln, October 12, 1860, LP.

807. Carl Schurz to Lincoln, October 10, 1860, LP.

808. Ward Hill Lamon to Lincoln, October 10, 1860, LP.

809. *Washington Press*, September 21, 1860.

810. Elliot Sheppard to Lincoln, September 24, 1860, LP.

811. John Forney to Thurlow Weed, September 27, 1860, LP.

812. The poll was taken by Dean Richmond's organization and published in his Albany newspaper.

813. *Albany Argus*, October 1860.

814. Clark Wheeler to Lincoln, October 19, 1860, LP.

815. James Harvey to Lincoln, October 5, 1860, LP.

816. James Webb to Lincoln, November 5, 860, LP.

817. Clark Wheeler to Lincoln, October 19, 1860, LP.

818. *Troy (NY) Weekly Times,* October 30, 1860.

819. Seward, 2: 471; Thurlow Weed to Lincoln, October 18, 1860, LP.

820. Thurlow Weed to Lincoln, October 28, 1860, LP.

821. Francis Spinner to Lincoln, October 28, 1860, LP.

822. Pennsylvania Republican State Committee circular, October 1860, LP.

823. Philander Jones to Lincoln, May 1860, LP.

824. William Kellogg to Lincoln, May 26, 1860, LP.

825. Hiram Payne to Lincoln, May 28, 1860, LP.

826. John Harris to Lincoln, October 12, 1860; Samuel Haycraft to Lincoln, October 27, 1860; Alex McClure to Lincoln, October 15, 1860; George Foley to Lincoln, June 2, 1860; James Harvey to Lincoln, June 25, 1860; J. E. Hurlbut to Lincoln, June 27, 1860; Hughes East, to Lincoln, October 15, 1860; James Briggs to Lincoln, October 10, 1860; Joshua Giddings to Lincoln, October 12, 1860; David Davis to Lincoln, October 31, 1860, LP.

827. Republican Party State Committee circular, October 18, 1860, LP.

828. Thurlow Weed to Lincoln, November 3, 1860, LP.

829. Thurlow Weed to Lincoln, June 10, 25, 1860; Edwin Morgan to Lincoln, June 14, 1860, LP.

830. McClintock, 22.

831. Halstead, 308.

832. *New York Express*, September 18, 1860.

833. Ibid.

834. Crowd description and Douglas speech in *New York Herald*, September 18, 1860.

835. Ibid.

836. Milton, 497; *Richmond Enquirer,* November 2, 1860.

837. Mitchell, 674.

838. *New York Herald*, October 8, 1860.

839. Milton, 497, *New York Herald*, October 10, 1860.

840. *Charleston Mercury*, October 15, 1860. The speech was reprinted in dozens of newspapers, North and South.

841. *Cincinnati Press and Tribune*, October 20, 1860; George Hazzard to Lincoln, October 21, 1860, LP.

842. George Sanders to Douglas, October 18, 1860.

843. *New York Times*, October 23, 1860.

844. *Albany Journal*, October 13, 1860, reprinted in the *Hartford Evening Press*, October 15, 1860.

845. *New York Tribune*, October 22, 1860.

846. *New York Tribune*, October 18, 1860.

847. *New York Tribune*, October 22, 1860.

848. *New York Tribune*, November 3, 1860.

849. Russell Hicks to Lincoln, June 22, 1860, LP.

850. *New York Tribune*, October 9, 1860.

851. *New York Times*, October 4, 1860.

852. James Terwilliger telegram to Daniel Ullman, September 15, 1860, Ullman Papers.

853. Chardon Township, Ohio, Republican Committee Voting Instructions, LP.

854. Elliott Sheppard to Lincoln, October 15, 1860, LP.

855. David Phillips, of Illinois, October 29, 1860, LP, plus similar letters from Indiana and other states.

856. Dittenhoefer, 40.

857. Seth Gates to Lincoln, October 23, 1860, LP.

858. I. B. McKeehan to Lincoln, October 22, 1860, LP.

859. *New Orleans Daily Crescent*, October 13, 1860.

860. Luthin, 151.

861. *New York Herald*, October 31, 1860.

862. *New York Tribune*, November 2, 1860.

863. *Louisville Courier*, reprinted in the *New York Tribune*, October 18, 1860.

864. Oldroyd, 133–135.

865. Luthin, 192–194.

866. Sam Weed, "Hearing the Returns with Mr. Lincoln," in Rufus Wilson, *Intimate Memories of Abraham Lincoln* (Elmira: Primavera Press, 1945), 327.

867. McClintock, 21.

868. Burnham, various sections.

869. Thomas, 229.

870. John Wright to Lincoln, November 6, 1860, LP.

871. Henry Lucas, *The Netherlanders in America: Dutch Immigrants to the United States and Canada, 1789–1950* (Ann Arbor: University of Michigan Press, 1955), 529.

872. Burnham, 86–88.

873. Lucas, 529 and Appendix A; Burnham, 864.

874. Ibid., 318–320.

875. Burnham, 368–390.

876. Ibid., 390–411.

877. Swierenga, 27.

878. Burnham, 716.

879. Ibid., 704–720.

880. Ibid., 676–696.

881. Donald, 223.

882. *Albany Evening Journal,* November 5, 1860, LP.

883. Simon Cameron to Lincoln, November 6, 1860, LP.

884. Oldroyd, 141.

885. David Davis to George Perrin Davis, November 14, 1860, LP.

886. Henry Bowen, in *The Independent*, April 4, 1895.

887. Ibid., 632–646.

888. Donnal V. Smith, "The Influence of the Foreign-Born of the Northwest in the Election of 1860," *Mississippi Valley Historical Review*, XIX (1932): 193, 202, 204.

889. Harris, 245.

890. McPherson, 233.

891. Ibid.

892. Dittenhoefer, 42.

893. *New York Tribune* almanac, 1860.

894. Harris, 324–325.

895. Nevins, 456–458.

896. Lincoln to Thurlow Weed, December 17, 1860; *CWAL* 4: 154.

897. Bronson Murray to Ward Hill Lamon, January 9, 1861; Teillard, 311–312.

898. Buchanan's Fourth Annual Message to Congress, December 3, 1860, *Congressional Globe*, II, Appendix, 1–7.

899. Dumond, 166.

900. *Missouri Daily Republican*, January 14, 1861; Dwight Dumond, *Southern Editorials on Secession* (New York: The Century Co., 1931), 393–395.

901. Teillard, 58.

902. Donald Reynolds, *Editors Make War* (Nashville: Vanderbilt University Press, 1970), 139–160.

903. *National Intelligencer*, March 5, 1861.

904. Ibid., 458–459.

905. Abraham Lincoln's first Inaugural Address, March 4, 1860, *CWAL* 4: 262–271.

906. Teillard, 54.

Index

Also by Bruce Chadwick:

ISBN   9781402204067

ISBN   9781402206955

ISBN   9781402207532

ISBN   9781402209413

ISBN   9781402211362

HON. ABRAHAM LINCOLN, OF ILLINOIS,

FOR PRESIDENT.

HON. HANNIBAL HAMLIN, OF MAINE,

FOR VICE PRESIDENT.

PUBLISHED BY CURRIER & IVES.   Entered according to Act of Congress, in the year 1860, by Currier & Ives, in the Clerk's Office of the District Court of the Southern Dist of N.Y.   152 NASSAU St NEW YORK.

THE REPUBLICAN BANNER FOR 1860.